DOMESDAY STUDIES: The Eastern Counties

By the same author

THE DOMESDAY INQUEST AND THE MAKING OF DOMESDAY BOOK

AN INTRODUCTION TO DOMESDAY BOOK

DOMESDAY STUDIES: THE *LIBER EXONIENSIS*

DOMESDAY STUDIES

The Eastern Counties

R. WELLDON FINN, M.A.
Sometime Scholar of Peterhouse, Cambridge

ARCHON BOOKS
Hamden, Connecticut
1967

First published 1967

Made and printed in Great Britain by
William Clowes and Sons, Limited, London and Beccles

CONTENTS

Acknowledgement

We are grateful to The Clarendon Press, Oxford, for permission to include an extract from *The Making of Domesday Book* by V. H. Galbraith.

Abbreviations frequently used in the text

Blake	E. O. Blake (ed.): *Liber Eliensis*
Davis: *Kal.*	R. H. C. Davis (ed.): *The Kalendar of Abbot Samson*
Davis: *Reg.*	H. W. C. Davis (ed.): *Regesta Regum Anglo-Normannorum*, vol. i
DB	Domesday Book
FB	*The Feudal Book of Baldwin, Abbot of Bury St Edmunds*
H	N. E. S. A. Hamilton (ed.): *Inquisitio Comitatus Cantabrigiensis, subjicitur Inquisitio Eliensis*
ICC	*Inquisitio Comitatus Cantabrigiensis*
IE	*Inquisitio Eliensis*
Lib. Exon.	*Liber Exoniensis*
DBB	F. W. Maitland: *Domesday Book and Beyond*
Dom. Geog.	H. C. Darby (ed.): *The Domesday Geography of England*
EHR	*English Historical Review*
FD	D. C. Douglas: *Feudal Documents from the Abbey of Bury St Edmunds*
FE	J. H. Round: *Feudal England*
MDB	V. H. Galbraith: *The Making of Domesday Book*
Rural Eng.	R. Lennard: *Rural England: 1086–1135*
Soc. Stud.	D. C. Douglas: *Social Studies in Medieval East Anglia*
VCH	*Victoria County History*

My dear Darby,

In the last fifteen years you and I have spent a good few hundred hours, severally and jointly, wrestling with some of the problems that Domesday Book poses – from the interpretation of partly illegible figures and exotic phrases and their depiction in honest maps to the best place in which to treat some aspect of its information and the most revealing form of presentation of tabular material. So you may not be surprised when I say that the technique which lies behind 'Domesday Geography', and of Roy Versey's meticulous lists of geographical information, has had a great deal to do with the shaping and making of this book, even though little which is strictly geographical appears therein. But then you would hardly be expecting geography from

R. Welldon Finn

Professor H. C. Darby

Preface

The less familiar of the two volumes which make up Domesday Book is a lengthy and confused compilation, and its text does not readily lend itself to systematic and neatly divided commentary. Yet so much of our knowledge of eleventh-century England has been derived from it – and often from no other source – that quotations and deductions from it inevitably appear with extreme frequency in the writings of those who have made this century their special study. Accordingly, many passages which occur here will be familiar to those who are conversant with the writings of Maitland and Vinogradoff and their successors.

But these studies, though they owe a heavy debt to the work of a number of commentators upon Domesday Book, did not originate from consideration of their conclusions. Indeed, while I have re-read them all, the first draft of this book was deliberately written without reference to printed texts and commentaries. It would, however, be idle to pretend that in the light of these I, like Maitland on receiving Round's *Feudal England*, have not suppressed, corrected, and added much.

The basis of much of this study has been a scrupulous analysis, Hundred by Hundred, vill by vill, and, where relevant, by manors, of the 900 folios of the second volume of Domesday Book, commonly but so unfortunately styled 'Little Domesday'. It is indeed impossible to study Domesday Book adequately without initial analysis and subsequent synthesis, wearisome and often frustrating though this may be. This analysis has been quite independent of that constructed in connection with the *Domesday Geography of England*. It has of course been necessary at times to work also on the Domesday and related texts for neighbouring counties.

One obvious difficulty is the apparent similarity, coupled with the major differences, between the Essex text and that for

Norfolk and Suffolk, and the change from a fairly well manorialised region to one in which the 'manors' provide problems at least as provoking as those furnished by southern England or the northern sokelands. To deal with each of the shires individually would have been tiresome for the reader and would militate against a true synthesis; nevertheless, there are topics for which isolation of the Essex material has been essential.

One of the few advantages which this 'circuit' offers to the student is that two long documents with which the Domesday text can be collated and compared have survived, the *Inquisitio Eliensis* and the 'Feudal Book' of Bury St Edmunds. Where either supplements the text of Domesday Book the information has been used, but for statistical purposes the Domesday figures have been retained where differences occur.

Two of the major difficulties in giving a textual reference to this volume of Domesday Book are (*a*) the separation by the clerks of part of the information about a holding (usually it is a manor which is concerned) from the remainder by the accounts of small estates which would seem to represent components of that manor; (*b*) the considerable length of many entries, which often occupy parts of two or more folios. Here a folio reference normally refers to that on which the entry begins: the phrase quoted may thus occur on a succeeding folio. References to the Exchequer Domesday are indicated by the inclusion of the number of the relevant column, i or 2; the very few references to the folios of the *Liber Exoniensis* are italicised.

A further difficulty is that villages with identical names are to be found in more than one county; e.g. there is a Barking in both Essex and Suffolk, and a Bixley in Norfolk as well as in Suffolk. There was a Hundred of Clavering in both Essex and Norfolk. The folios quoted, however, will make it clear which county is concerned; if from 109 to 280 Norfolk; if earlier, Essex; if later, Suffolk. The provision of the name of the holding as well as the folio number for so many references might seem to be superfluous, since usually it is of no moment whether the passage refers to Exham or Wyton. But the length of some manorial accounts, and the large number of entries on many folios, could make it otherwise difficult for the reader to find the passage he requires.

The orthographic variations of personal names in the MSS. are so considerable that these have been rendered in conventional form, e.g. 'Ailid' appears here as Æthelgyth and 'Vlmar' as Wulfmær, but it has seemed over-pedantic to write Eadgyth rather than Edith or Asgeirr for Ansger, while there is small point in describing the familiar William of Warenne as 'de Varennes'. A number of the place-name identifications are based on equations later than those of the *VCH* or *The Place-Names of Essex*.

Aspects which are more than adequately treated in the *Domesday Geography of England* or other works are in consequence here touched upon only lightly; e.g. churches, the subject of a long chapter in R. Lennard's *Rural England: 1086–1185*, and the boroughs.

I have to acknowledge with gratitude the valuable criticism of H. R. Loyn, who generously gave his time to consideration of my typescript, and the contributions of all those who have debated the implications of Domesday Book with me. I have also to thank the Oxford University Press and Professor V. H. Galbraith for kind permission to reproduce quotations from his *The Making of Domesday Book* and the Cambridge University Press and Professor H. C. Darby for allowing me to reproduce three maps from *The Domesday Geography of England*, vol. i. I have also to thank University College London for appointing me to a post which facilitated these researches.

Frinton-on-Sea R. W. F.
Feast of Our Lady of Ransom, 1966

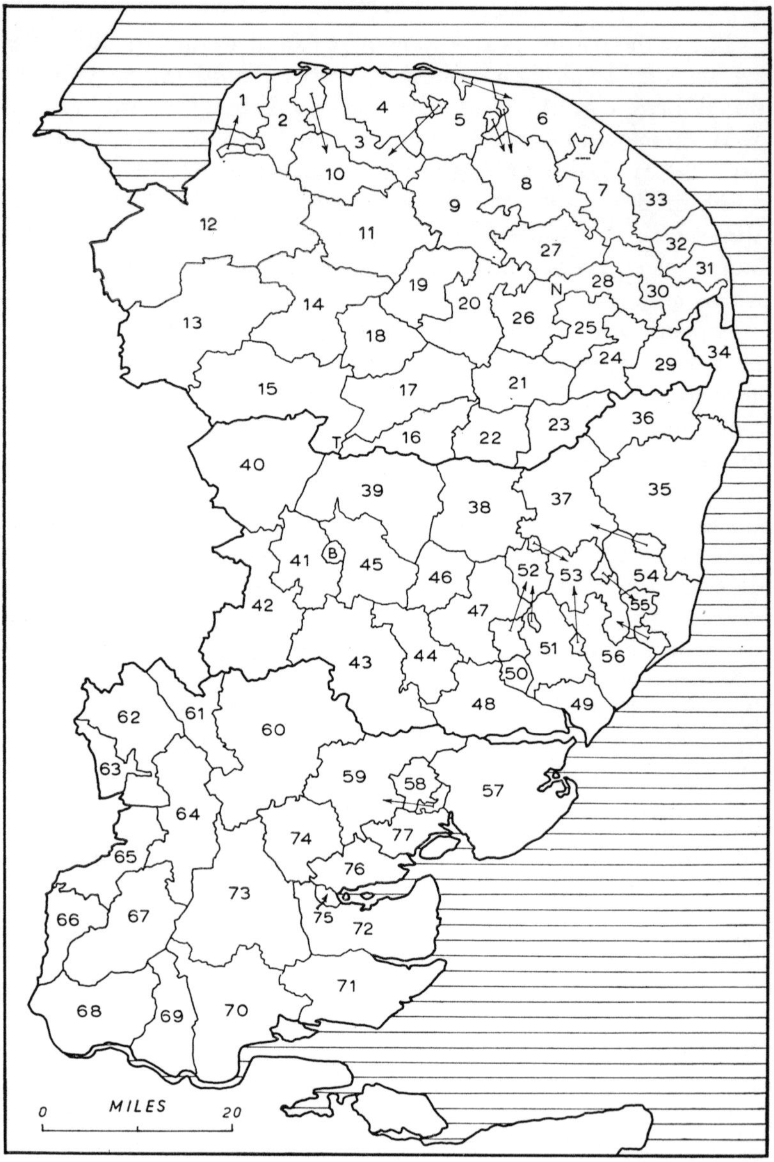

The Hundreds of the Eastern Counties

Adapted from *The Domesday Geography of England*, vol. i (ed. H. C. Darby) by kind permission of the Cambridge University Press and the author.

NORFOLK

1 Smethden
2 Docking
3 Gallow
4 North Greenhoe
5 Holt
6 North Erpingham
7 Tunstead
8 South Erpingham
9 Eynesford
10 Brothercross
11 Launditch
12 Freebridge
13 Clackclose
14 South Greenhoe
15 Grimshoe
16 Guiltcross
17 Shropham
18 Wayland
19 Midford
20 Forehoe
21 Depwade
22 Diss
23 Earsham
24 Loddon
25 Henstead
26 Humbleyard
27 Taverham
28 Blofield
29 Clavering
30 Walsham
31 East Flegg
32 West Flegg
33 Happing

SUFFOLK

34 Lothingland
35 Blything
36 Wangford
37 Hoxne
38 Hartismere
39 Blackbourn and Bradmere
40 Lackford
41 Thingoe
42 Risbridge
43 Babergh
44 Cosford
45 Thedwestrey
46 Stow
47 Bosmere
48 Samford
49 Colneis
50 Ipswich
51 Carlford
52 Claydon
53 Loes
54 Plomesgate
55 Parham
56 Wilford

ESSEX

57 Tendring
58 Colchester
59 Lexden
60 Hinckford
61 Freshwell
62 Uttlesford
63 Clavering
64 Dunmow
65 Harlow
66 Waltham
67 Ongar
68 Becontree
69 Chafford
70 Barstable
71 Rochford
72 Dengie
73 Chelmsford
74 Witham
75 Maldon
76 Thurstable
77 Winstree

N Norwich
T Thetford
B Bury St Edmunds

It is not possible to show all detached portions of Hundreds.

CHAPTER I

The Eastern Counties at the Conquest

If those whose business it was to be to conduct the Domesday Inquest in the eastern counties had foreknowledge of the difficulties which were to confront them, they can have had little enthusiasm for their task. It was to be their misfortune to have to deal with a province where the land of a number of Hundreds and villages and manors lay in more than one county, and where a true manorial system had by no means been consistently evolved. They were compelled to make use of the administrative basis of shire and Hundred, and, as the economic unit, of what they thought of as the 'manor', yet they had somehow to force their raw material into a structure governed by the fief in which it lay in 1086.

It was, too, a region peopled largely by property-owners and a peasantry whose social and economic obligations were complex and inconsistent. Men of almost every shade of rank had 'commended' themselves, sought the protection of a man greater than themselves, as it best suited them, not necessarily to one magnate but often to a variety of superiors, and indeed they might in respect of a single estate have commended themselves to more than one patron, and not invariably with equal emphasis. Again in respect of a single estate, a man might have commended himself to one lord, but a different lord had the rights or profits of jurisdiction over him. Since the devolution of English land was to depend largely on pre-Conquest ownership, the problems of inheritance must inevitably be difficult to solve. The nebulosity of conditions of land-tenure had been easy to exploit, and most of the newcomers had used them to swell their fiefs by illegitimate or highly dubious means.

The inquisitors' difficulties are ours also when we come to study the text, and our efforts at interpretation are complicated by the fact that the clerks who produced this second volume of

Domesday Book did not do their work particularly well, even when the complexity of their task is taken into account.[1] Both inquisitors and clerks could have received warning from those entrusted with the post-Conquest land settlement, who must very early have encountered all these problems, if in less detail and on broader lines.

But the Domesday Inquest was a score of years away from the early days of the Conquest. The immediate problems were pacification or suppression of the surviving English magnates and the rewarding of those who had supported the Conqueror's cause. It is to be supposed that the king and his advisers were already acquainted with the broad features of eastern England, and within it they had many friends who could fill in the details. They did not have to start under the handicap of total ignorance of their new home.

The previous earls of East Anglia, it is true, were dead; Ælfgar in 1062, and Gyrth at Hastings fight. Ælfgar's widow Ælfgifu held a little land in the east, and her sons had early made their submission.[2] There was an obvious candidate for the earldom in the person of Ralf *stalra* or 'marshal', the Breton minister of the late king, and this King William bestowed on him. Æthelmær, bishop of Elmham, like his brother Stigand, had made his peace with the new monarch; William, bishop of London and Essex, was a Norman; the heads of the two principal ecclesiastical foundations, Bury St Edmunds and Ely, would be concerned to preserve the abbey lands, and proved co-operative at first, though Ely invoked the royal wrath for her share in Hereward's revolt. Of Toli, the last Anglian sheriff, we know little, but Robert fitzWymarc, sheriff of Essex, was not English by birth, and was King William's kinsman and friend, despite the warning he had given to the king of the improbability of the invasion succeeding. William Malet, the Conqueror's intimate, who was to receive an immense East Anglian fief, was half-English by birth.

[1] I do not like having to write of the 'volumes' of Domesday Book, but it is inevitable that occasionally I have to refer to vol. i (the Exchequer text) and to vol. ii (the fair copy of Essex, Suffolk, and Norfolk material).

[2] Fol. 286b shows lands held by 'the mother of Earl Morkere' as part of *Terra Regis*. Bishop Odo of Bayeux obtained one of her manors (373b).

Many a man with an English or Anglo-Danish name was to take service with the new masters. Among the *ministri* who acquired the custody of royal estates were Godric, who seems to have acted as sheriff early in the reign, and Ælfric 'Wanz'.[1] A man who must have had considerable influence before the Conquest, Æthelwine of Thetford, and who served the newcomers afterwards, recurs in the texts. His *feudum* and the fact that he was the *antecessor* of Roger Bigot, twice sheriff of East Anglia, and had been given free men to add to his lands, are mentioned (174b, 190). He had caused a free tenant of St Benet to be outlawed (277b); he had added a Scratby free man to the rent of Ormesby (273). He had been sufficiently influential after the Conquest for one of Harold's thegns to commend himself to him (181b). His encroachments on the lands of Holme Abbey are also recorded.[2]

Some native king's reeves, who had held land and may have acted in this capacity in 1066, are to be found administering royal estates in 1086. Grimr appears among the Essex tenants-in-chief, Haghne and Ulfketel in Norfolk and Suffolk; others named as reeves in 1086 are Æthelweald, Almær, and Wulfmær.[3] Some at least of the other reeves mentioned may have functioned both before and after the Conquest, e.g. Beorhtmær, Robert Malet's reeve, Brune, reeve to Roger Bigot and apparently of Ipswich also, and Radbodo, Ralf of Beaufoy's reeve.[4]

Native reeves are indeed frequently found in 1086. We encounter Ordgar, who had succeeded Ailric as a St Edmunds reeve; Sæwulf, acting for Bishop William of Thetford; Leodmær, for whom his master Richard fitzGilbert refused to testify; and reeves of the royal manors of Thorne, Soham, and Cawston.[5] Hundred-reeves also appear, and reeves of Earl Harold; these are by no means all those recorded, but only rarely are

[1] Davis: *Regesta Regum Anglo-Normannorum*, no. 122, p. 32. Godric may again have been sheriff in 1087 (Davis: *Reg.*, no. 291, p. 76).

[2] See F. M. Stenton: 'St Benet of Holme and the Norman Conquest' (*EHR*, xxxvii, 1922, p. 233).

[3] Fols. 4b, 98; 146, 176b, 269, 280; 322b, 333, 334b, 352, 448b.

[4] Fols. 299b, 110, 337b, 229b. They may all have been deputies for their masters, who would not be permanently within the counties, and are all royal *ministri*.

[5] Fols. 371, 198b, 103, 281b, 110b, 115. Folio references out of numerical order follow the sequence of the text.

we given the names of their employers.[1] Two of the Colchester moneyers, Wulfwine and Ælfsige, were operating both before and after the Conquest.

Occasionally we get glimpses of persons otherwise virtually unknown; e.g. Ælfsige the nephew of Earl Ralf, Hardwin the brother of the earl, Godwine his connection (*avunculus*), and Ælfric Wihtgarson.[2] For 1086 we get occasional indications of the household of a nobleman. Roger Bigot had his chaplain, Ansketill (334b), and also a chamberlain, Herbert (278), and a cook, Warin (156); Earl Hugh his goldsmith (Raveningham, 279).

References to thegns are infrequent, compared with those of the record for other counties. The term appears less than a hundred times. But this does not necessarily imply that men of thegnly status were rare in the east. The same man is in different entries styled both 'thegn' and 'free man'; indeed, we are told of 'a free man who was also a thegn'.[3] The greater men of 1066, e.g. Ansger the Staller and Edric of Laxfield, are never called 'thegns'; thegns we sometimes find spoken of as being commended to a superior.[4] Where we are told whose thegns they were, we hear only of the king, the queen, the earls, and Stigand as their superiors, and nearly three-quarters of them were royal thegns: one at Rockland (203) was *teinus dominicus Regis Edwardi*. Where they are said to hold 'under' a superior, commendation is surely implied.

But the greater lay landowners in eastern England, even if they had temporarily survived the Conquest, were gone long before the Inquest took place. Some perhaps fell with Harold in battle, as did lesser men – Edric the deacon of Cavendish (449), Breme, King Edward's free man (Dagworth, 409b), an anonymous free man of Shelfhanger (275b). Some had forfeited their land; some perhaps for opposition to Norman rule,

[1] Hundred-reeves appear on fols. 120, 99; see also fols. 3, 5b, 199.

[2] Fols. 324; 281b, 338; 127b, 131, 262; 389b. Reference is probably to what fol. 129 calls 'the old earl Ralf', i.e. the *stalra*, who seems to have died about 1070, not his son the rebel.

[3] e.g. Thorir (394b), Auti, and Ketel (421); 204b. We hear also of a *francus teignus* (Goldhanger, 54b) and of a thegn holding freely (Ockendon, 57b); these, I think, have identical meanings. Fol. 254a2 records that *ipsi teini erant liberi*.

[4] A thegn of King Edward's was commended to Harold (Wenham, 377).

some for civil crimes.[1] Probably there were far more instances of outlawry, such as that of Edric the steersman of King Edward's ship, than are recorded in DB, and we are not told of those who voluntarily went overseas rather than live under Norman rule.[2]

It is difficult to determine the proportion of really large landowners at the time of the Conquest, partly because we cannot know to how many individuals a common name might refer. King Edward's eastern estates had not been especially extensive, while Earl Gyrth's do not compare with those of the Wessex earldom.[3] Edith 'the fair', 'the rich', was less well endowed here than she was farther west, but appears as Earl Alan's predecessor in all three counties. The really notable pre-Conquest figure is Edric of Laxfield, exiled in both King Edward's and King William's reigns, much of whose fief had become first William and then Robert Malet's. In Essex and Suffolk Wihtgar, also exiled after the Conquest (448), and Finnr the Dane, had possessed lands substantial enough to form the nucleus of Richard of Clare's fief.[4] Some of the great figures of Edwardian England, such as Ansger the marshal, appear, but the bulk of their estates did not lie in the three eastern counties. Neither Norfolk nor Suffolk seems to have had many men of the first rank beyond those already named, but men of the calibre of Siward of Maldon, Saxi, Ælfric 'camp', and women such as Æthelgyth, must, from the extent of their lands here and elsewhere, have possessed appreciable local, and perhaps even national influence.

Those minor men whom we find surviving the consequences of the Conquest are, however, singularly few. Of some thirty Essex representatives many were tenants of Sweyn, who like his father Robert fitzWymarc obviously had backed the newcomers' cause from the first, and had been sheriff of the county

[1] Forfeiture for theft is mentioned (Rainham, 66b).

[2] For outlawry, see fols. 24, 48, 49b, 59, 176b, 200, 274, 277b; for undescribed forfeiture, fols. 98, 350b, 382b, 383, 443b.

[3] In contrast to the accounts of other shires, *comes* is infrequently used to denote Godwine's children, thus some instances mentioning 'Harold' or 'Gyrth' may not refer to the last English royal house. But it is occasionally used, e.g. on fols. 144, 288, 444.

[4] Fewer men than might be expected are styled *dacus*, but we can find them on fols. 25, 25b, 41b.

up to 1075 at least, and perhaps at a later date also.[1] Only fifty or so English or Anglo-Danish names, other than those of royal officials and a few tenants-in-chief, occur in the East Anglia of 1086 in any but the most minor positions.[2] Several are priests, and these would perhaps have had smaller risk of losing their land. Some are described simply as *anglus* (e.g. on fols. 178, 178b). Some may indeed be minor officials who had transferred their loyalties; Stanheard (Æthelwineson on fol. 345b) appears frequently as a sub-tenant of the sheriff. Ellis thought that the father was the Æthelwine of Thetford mentioned earlier. A 'Wulfmær' (282, 446) could well be the man who had been a king's reeve before the Conquest. It is, of course, possible that a number were still holding their lands or those of their fathers under the newcomers, but are unmentioned in DB: they might often be represented among the groups and instances of unnamed free men. Besides these and the free men and women, sokemen, priests, and reeves, only the occasional smith is singled out from the lesser peasantry.[3]

It is interesting to see how influential locally some of the pre-Conquest figures who constantly recur in the folios may have been. That Thorkill ('Toki') who was William of Warenne's *antecessor*, styled both 'thegn' and 'free man', had over a score of properties in Norfolk and Suffolk, mostly classed as manors with their berewicks, to which were attached (at any rate in 1086) 18 free men and 165 sokemen, assessed at more than 39 carucates.[4] His dependants' lands would add a further 10½. He may have survived the Conquest, if *tenet prepositus et fuit Toke lib. hom.* is to be interpreted literally.[5]

In Norfolk a Haghne appears in eleven entries, who is probably the man who has also a *breve* to himself (269b), where

[1] It would be interesting to know if Ordgar, with lands in all three shires, was the former Cambridgeshire sheriff; on fol. 64b he is styled 'thegn'.

[2] We cannot say of what origins men with names such as 'Osbern' were.

[3] Fols. 314b, 334b, 339b, 435b.

[4] Quantities at Castle Acre and Heacham (160b, 163) were omitted from the text. He had held land in several other shires.

[5] Herringswell (398). But I suspect that we should read 'a free man of Thorkill's'. I doubt if the free man of Harold and of Stigand, or he whose lands went to Peter de Valognes (186b, 242b, 250, 257b, 258) is the same person or indeed a single person. But *Toka francigena* (250), Stigand's free man, may be the thegn: *francigena* is, I think, here implying 'free', not 'French'.

he is listed as a king's reeve. He is described also as a free man and as a king's thegn and commended to Stigand (130b) and as having held Heckingham (205) from the latter. His Domesday fief is small, only some three carucates or so, but before the Conquest his other manors amounted to 21¼ carucates. One had passed to Earl Hugh, and one each to Roger Bigot and to Godric the royal steward, who was administering the rest for the king. So Haghne may still have had an interest in these lands, but was farming them on the king's behalf.

Another post-Conquest reeve was Ulfketel. He too had a small post-Conquest Norfolk fief (270b), one manor of which he had not held in 1066. He occurs also in Suffolk, but his holdings can have amounted only to about 1½ carucates. Here we find him commended to Edric of Laxfield, and himself having free men commended to him (fols. 326, 333b, 335). Once he is described as the *antecessor* of William of Warenne, but William obtained only one of his Norfolk properties, and none of those in Suffolk. His Norfolk lands, of about 20 carucates, went to a variety of newcomers, but largely to Roger Bigot, listed under 'the exchange of Isaac's land', and once to the Crown. The complexities are enhanced by the Mundham in Norfolk entry (176b), where he had seized an outlawed man's estate into the king's hands. This had been asked for by Roger Bigot and granted to him, but Earl Alan claimed it as part of his Suffolk manor of Rumburgh. The Hundred had once heard Ulfketel acknowledge this a year before Earl Ralf's forfeiture, and later that Ulfketel had 'done service' in Rumburgh, but finally to Roger. Earl Alan's men were prepared to undergo the ordeal to prove their claim, quoting the fact that rent had been received by the earl. It is an excellent illustration of the complexities we shall encounter later here.

Finally, consider a lesser man or men. A king's thegn named Skúli had held Benham in Suffolk (299) for two carucates. In Norfolk we find 'Scula', 'Escule', with rather more than 14 carucates. At least half a dozen different men held these properties in 1086. We have no means of knowing how many persons are in fact represented, and of course some of the thegns and free men not named may have been the persons here discussed.

We should not, I think, necessarily interpret the addition of a place-name as evidence that a man was of some local importance. Æthelwine 'of Thetford', from his obvious influence, might have had his administrative residence in the borough, or indeed have been the royal representative therein. Siward of Maldon, with fairly extensive estates (e.g. fols. 72b–5b, 272b, 355), may have occupied a similar position. But though an Ælfric is several times styled 'of Wenham' (fols. 314, 425, 430b), this may only have been to distinguish him from numerous other Ælfrics. The lists of landholders such as Leofric 'of Hemley', to be found on fol. 314b and elsewhere, do not suggest that these had even local importance. Some may have continued to be known by their former titles even though they no longer held office. In the Oxfordshire Domesday Sweyn is styled *vicecomes*.

How many of these Englishmen and Anglo-Danes survived the Conquest we can never know, or how many may still have been the servants of the newcomers at the time of the Inquest. It is to be suspected that it was largely the upper strata of eastern society who disappeared from the scene, and that it was the small farmers, less liable to fall in conflict with the foreigner and less able to seek a new life overseas, who remained.

CHAPTER II

The Settlement

THE INITIAL TRANSFER OF ENGLISH ESTATES

At what date estates in the eastern counties passed initially to new lords is problematical. The threat of invasion from Denmark was still active in 1067, and while King William was residing at Barking in Essex after his coronation he may in consequence have done something towards removing obvious centres of disaffection. DB naturally exhibits no trace of any temporary arrangements connected therewith, unless the then numerous lordless free men to be found in 1086 near Norwich reflect a concentration of power in the hands of a royal representative. At the time of the Inquest they were the sheriff's men. Probably it was very early in the reign that the writ to Bury St Edmunds ordering the abbot to surrender the lands of those 'who stood against me in battle' was despatched.[1]

In March, 1067, the king left for Normandy, and he did not return until early December. It is possible that he had empowered his lieutenants to begin a redistribution of estates, but the *Anglo-Saxon Chronicle* states that it was after his return that he 'gave away every man's land'. On the other hand, a geld was levied early in the reign, and failure to pay may have involved forfeiture of lands. The abbot of Peterborough paid a heavy fine, in view of his predecessor's participation at Hastings, for reconciliation with King William. We hear also of a time when 'the English redeemed their lands'.[2] Inability or unwillingness to pay the sums demanded may have resulted in a transference of ownership. But, as DB shows, some who accepted the

[1] *FD*, no. 1, p. 47; Davis: *Reg.*, no. 40, p. 12, and no. VI, p. 119.

[2] Stonham (360b). Bury then obtained the estate by Ingelric's leave in mortgage for two gold marks. A somewhat similar reference is to be found under Ixworth Thorpe (367b), where the local bishop and earl are coupled with Ingelric as *barones regis*, i.e. royal legates, presumably empowered to transfer land.

Conquest did not lose all their land. One passage mentions the 'giving back' of Saxmundham (338b) by the king to Northmann the former sheriff, though in 1086 he seems to have held it of his successor, Roger Bigot.

Possibly the main initial grants were made in the early months of 1068, before the rebellions of 1068–70 limited civil activities. But whether English landholders in chief were reduced in the first few years of the occupation to the meagre quota demonstrated by DB is also problematical. Many may have been slain, suffered forfeiture, or endured voluntary or compulsory exile as a result of the first cycle of rebellions.[1] Some would have left only heiresses who for security or under virtual compulsion were to marry among the invaders. This might sometimes account for a descent of lands which otherwise seems unintelligible.

Though a date is never given for the incidents recorded, we should perhaps visualise King William both sending his *legati* to organise an official transfer of land early in the reign and also issuing writs instructing his sheriffs and *ministri* to give seizin of the estates concerned. Northmann, at some time sheriff, associated with the bishop and earl in a writ which cannot be later than 1070, gave evidence at the Inquest that the king sent him a writ ordering him to put Ralf de Savigny in possession of all the free men of whom Hubert de Port had seized Bishop Odo, which he did, being ignorant of the earlier transaction.[2] There follows a somewhat inexplicable statement that the *barones regis* 'found this in peace between Roger Bigot and Earl Hugh when they came into the shire': it was to remain so until the matter could be determined. Why Earl Hugh should be concerned is a mystery: the incident suggests the despatch of special royal envoys during the reign to consider the problems engendered by the redistribution. Of Hubert de Port's giving leave to hold land or giving seizin we hear on other occasions also, and in a similar connection of his relative Hugh de Port, sheriff of Hampshire. He seems frequently to have acted in

[1] Edric of Laxfield was exiled for the second time; see Freeman: *Norman Conquest*, v, p. 799. Wihtgar, who was active after the Conquest (Cornard, 448), forfeited his lands, and presumably went into exile (Cavendish, 448).

[2] Ashfield (377). For the writ, see *FD*, no. 3, p. 48. He must, I think, have been the Northmann fitzTancred mentioned on, e.g., fols. 348b, 350.

Bishop Odo's interests: Odo himself is once mentioned as giving orders, perhaps when he was acting as regent while the king was in Normandy.[1] Waleram, a royal officer, is also found giving livery and seizin of land (Sidestrand, 170b; Shadingfield, 412). The king's officers, however, frequently failed to act justly, and seem to have used their opportunities to enrich themselves and their friends (p. 30).

THE MANOR

The basic unit for an entry in DB, and of transference of land, was certainly the manor, even though witnesses and clerks would everywhere have found *manerium* or *mansio* difficult to define, and never more so than in East Anglia. Here manors which consisted simply of an entire vill, or of just a portion of a vill, with (so far as we can tell) no detached components, were comparatively infrequent. Some holdings in the individual vill were manors in themselves, others portions of manors whose headquarters were frequently several miles distant. The land of many a manor was not in a single Hundred; it might not even be within the single shire (p. 51).

Unfortunately the clerks inscribing East Anglia dealt with the manorial unit even less neatly than did those of other circuits. It rather looks as if, very frequently, reports were made, not for a manor as a whole, but separately for a manor and its berewicks, if any, and also for any distant component holdings. Moreover, it was not thought necessary to report or inscribe all the land of a manor consecutively; other holdings might intervene.[2]

The exact significance of the term *manerium* or *mansio* is indeed difficult to define and determine. Obviously it was deemed to be of importance to note whether a holding was or was not a manor, and indeed if it should be counted as more than one manor. The land of ten free men at Purleigh (53) had

[1] Fols. 66b, 98, 377, 450. For Odo's part in the land settlement, see also fols. 79 and 135b2, 141b2, 142ai. Odo's position is discussed in F. West: *The Justiciarship in England 1066–1232* (Cambridge, 1966). For a vivid picture of a possible means of early transfers, see R. H. C. Davis: 'The Norman Conquest' (*History*, li, 1966, pp. 282–5).

[2] This happens most frequently when the land of a manor was not all within a single Hundred. We shall later see other defects in the systems employed (p. 159).

been received by Hugh de Montfort 'as two manors', but though Fobbing (26) had in 1066 been in single ownership, Beorhtmær is said to have held it 'for one manor'. Frequently, however, this information was omitted. The formula here most commonly used is that someone held or holds an estate *pro manerio*, 'as a manor', and while in the eastern counties it is the exception for it to have been held as more than one manor, the number of occasions on which *pro i manerio*, especially in East Suffolk, is used is so great as to make it certain that the inclusion of the figure was not accidental, though its frequent omission would hardly be deliberate. It is indeed not impossible that an unformulistic entry such as that for Berden (47), which had been held by Godemann in 1066 but is 'now' held of Sweyn by Alfred 'for a manor', is intended to indicate that while it had not always been classed as a manor, now it is, especially as the pre-Conquest holder was merely of sokeman status. So may a Tendring entry (95b); Ælfric held it for 15 acres, but now Moduin (holds it) as a manor. Quite often DB does not say that a holding was or had been a manor, though the sense of the entry makes it clear that it had manorial status. Very few holdings in the Hundred of Colneis are called manors, yet it is in an area where the manors, though often very small, had been numerous; indeed, it is once said, *alii tenent in istis maneriis* (Alston, 341), but no indication is given as to which, except six, of the numerous holdings in the Hundred were manors.

THE BASIC SYSTEM OF LAND-TRANSFERENCE

There were Crown manors to which the new king would automatically succeed, noted as 'King Edward's demesne manors', but a few times their attribution is stressed. They are described as *terra regis de regno, de regione*.[1] After Edward's death, Harold Godwineson would have possessed them, and Round pointed out that some manors credited to him in DB may really have

[1] Fols. 119b, 144, 289b, 281b, 408b. Round (*FE*, p. 140) thought that *regio* was a blunder, but Maitland (*DBB*, p. 167, n. 2) considered that it might stand for 'kingship': it could imply 'the province'. It is curious that Edward could give Crown land at Sporle and Swaffham to Earl Ralf: King William took it back and included it in *Terra Regis*.

been Crown property, and not Harold's until after his election to the throne.[1] Elsewhere the Conqueror took over most of the manors of the House of Godwine, but in the east we find a number in other hands, just as some of its Herefordshire estates passed to Alfred of Marlborough. This might not be the result of royal grants, but of purchase or tenancy. Ralf de Tosny's Norfolk manors (235–6b) had been held by 'Harold'. It is, however, never stated that this was Harold *comes*. Queen Edith had enjoyed after the Conquest the power of granting her manors during her lifetime, and had transferred, for example, three in Essex and two in Suffolk to Walter the deacon (87, 426). It would be interesting to know if Earl Ælfgar's family were deprived of some of the manors said to have been his. Many were bestowed upon Queen Matilda, perhaps after her arrival in England and Earl Edwin's initial breach with the king. But that Edwin had succeeded to his father's lands is not stated in these instances.

There is no indication that the king deprived the religious houses of estates, save for the order to Bury quoted above, and that may have involved no more than the substitution of a foreign for a native tenant. Acquisition of lands properly ecclesiastical was, however, achieved by most of his barons, and both St Benet's Abbey at Holme, whose abbot, Ælfweald, had guarded the coasts against William in Harold's interests, and who fled to Denmark, and Ely, implicated in the 1070–1 revolt, could not have been as heartily supported by William as was Bury with its Norman abbot Baldwin.

William may have promised his chief followers each a definite number of English manors, perhaps in proportion to the military and naval aid they had agreed to furnish. There is in the Essex section of DB mention of Earl Eustace's 'one hundred manors', but in fact he was not in 1086 in possession of so many, and Ingelric had held some of these after the Conquest.[2]

[1] *VCH: Essex*, i, p. 336. Since Writtle (5) had furnished a ten-nights' farm, and other manors one of two nights (6, 7), this seems highly probable. There is an unusual reference (Shoebury, 44) to 'after King Edward's death', i.e. in Harold's reign.

[2] Fols. 9b, 26b. c probably stands for *centum*, 100; if it implied *cum*, the point would not arise. Eustace had 79 Essex holdings, of which 48 are called 'manors', though many not so styled were probably counted as manors.

Another phrase, on fol. 100, *in numero suorum maneriorum*, might refer to a list of holdings constructed for Inquest purposes.

The number and the assessments of an English magnate's manors must have been discoverable; certainly each sheriff, and perhaps the Treasury, would have lists of them. Thus a principle more or less satisfactory to donor and recipient would be to use these to allot to a baron the whole of the lands, wherever they might lie, of a leading Englishman. Their extent would, of course, have to be roughly commensurate with the relative proportion past and future service merited. That this principle was adopted is copiously illustrated by DB, which indeed translates the present into the past and speaks of the 'honour' of Ansger or of Finnr, or of the 'fee' of Ulfketel (fols. 412b, 393, 395b; 182b).

The previous holder was described as the newcomer's *antecessor*, though frequently the name of the predecessor is not given; a few times a baron is called the *successor* of an Englishman (fols. 138b, 139b, 240). While the greater tenants-in-chief may be found succeeding to the lands of a multiplicity of Englishmen, there is almost always one of these, or sometimes several, who stand out from the rest. Though the vicissitudes of the Conquest brought about much subsequent illegal occupation of estates, obviously William Malet should have obtained Edric of Laxfield's vast lands, Geoffrey de Manneville those of Ansger the marshal, Ralf Peverel the manors of Saxi and of Siward of Maldon, Ralf Baignard those of that wealthy woman Æthelgyth. It is plain that the estates of some men had been considered insufficient to support a baron's local dignity, and so we find him with more than one local *antecessor*, e.g. Hugh de Montfort.[1] Yet the lands of Ælfric 'camp', which were scattered over several counties, went to at least four different newcomers.

In Essex only six *antecessores* are actually given their names, and four of these occur in the account of Colchester (40b, 103b; 106–7). Norfolk and Suffolk contribute over fifty more. They are by no means all pre-Conquest landholders; Brian of Brittany is given as the predecessor of Robert of Mortain, Ingelric of Earl Eustace, Lisois de Moustières of Eudes the steward,

[1] A list of those specifically named as *antecessores*, with their successors, is given as Appendix A.

Raymond Gerold of Roger of Poitou, Eudes fitzClamahoc of Ralf of Beaufoy.[1] Some of these newcomers were dead (Eudes fitzClamahoc's death is mentioned on fol. 235b), some had forfeited their estates. Their frequent anonymity in DB rather suggests that Inquest officials and juries well knew who a baron's *antecessores* should have been.

DIFFICULTIES AFFECTING THE EXECUTION OF THE SCHEME

But the social and economic structure of Anglo-Saxon and Anglo-Danish England made it impossible to achieve an altogether satisfactory redistribution of land. The system outlined above was equitable enough so far as the larger holdings were concerned. But what principle was to be followed where a minor landholder was commended to several different men, sometimes in respect of the individual estate, and sometimes in uneven proportions, or where commendation was enjoyed by one man, but sokeright by another?[2] The newcomers would hardly wish to perpetuate such a feature, yet to change it would be to abandon an English practice, and it was their intention to preserve native traditions which did not conflict with their own interests.

DB does not invariably tell us who had the commendation or soke of the individual or of a group of men, and so sometimes we cannot tell whether a newcomer's succession was orthodox or not. It is doubtful if the royal delegates empowered to transfer estates had been given definite instructions for each situation, and DB shows the utter confusion the lack of them frequently caused (p. 133).

It furnishes, too, no great clarity as to a possible principle governing the acquisition of the lands or the services of those men who for the most part do not seem to have held manors, but are said to have been commended to some more influential landholder. Very often they seem to have gone with the land

[1] Fols. 291, 303, 279b, 139b, 138b, 229b.

[2] The free man could have free men 'under him' (which probably implies commendation), e.g. fols. 300b, 318b: sub-commendation and fractional commendation recur, e.g. fols. 307, 309, 318, 321b, 322, 333b.

of the man to whom they had been commended, and this would seem to have been the most equitable and satisfactory system to adopt.

But equally there are a very large number of entries which show men who had been commended to a pre-Conquest notable attached to the fief of a baron who was not his appointed successor. Free men and sokemen who had held under Edith the Fair had indeed become Earl Alan's; those who had been Wihtgar's were in 1086 Richard fitzGilbert's, but whether a special grant of them should have been made or not we are not told (fols. 35, 391 *et seq.*: these are orthodox successions). Yet a free man of Earl Ælfgar's and a man who had held under Siward of Maldon went to Frodo, not to the queen or to Ralf Peverel (fol. 355). Richard of Clare 'invaded' a free man at Cavendish, 'but his *antecessor* had absolutely nothing in him' (fol. 448). Sometimes these anomalies were the subject of complaints at the Inquest.

Over and over again we find in DB phrases indicating that a man was 'only commended' to the newcomer's *antecessor*, or that someone with dependants 'had only their commendation'.[1] This rather suggests that commendation by itself did not ensure good title to men's lands or services, though often enough succession to an estate seems to have rested only on the commendation-tie. Yet an instance is recorded in which Ely seized free men 'because of their commendation to the abbot'.[2]

There are, too, an enormous number of passages in which commendation is mentioned without any indication as to who had possessed it, e.g. *vi liberi homines com(mendati) lxxxv acrae* (Forncett, 189). Are we, in such instances, meant to assume that commendation had been to the man last mentioned before such an entry, or to the holder of the relevant manor? I think we must assume that it was generally agreed that by itself commendation did not imply succession; that a writ or the formal giving of livery and seizin was required also.

It is hardly to be thought that sokeright should give a better title to succession than did commendation; transference of

[1] e.g. Barton Bendish (273), Fodderstone (274). At South Hanningfield (25) two free men had held freely, and were only commended to Ely Abbey.

[2] Benham (H, p. 133; IE MS. A fol. 53ai).

superiority over land or person would not disturb the exercise of the soke. Complaint that sokeright had been lost may not imply also a claim that the possessor should have the land (e.g. at Horningtoft, 120b). Yet Ralf de Tosny claimed some free men attached to Ralf de Limésy because he had soke over them (Oxborough, 245).

Difficulty would inevitably arise where a patron was deceased or disgraced or exiled, and his dependants had been obliged to seek a new lord. They would not necessarily become the men of the nominated successor to their former protector. To some extent the solution of such a problem might depend on whether a man had the right to transfer his allegiance at will, or the power to sell or in other ways dispose of his land. After his initial outlawry, Edric of Laxfield became reconciled with King Edward, and obtained his writ and seal for his recovery of the commendation of all those free men who wished again to have him for their lord (Fordley, 310b). During his absence they had presumably been obliged to seek protection elsewhere.

Beorhtmær had been commended to the predecessor of Ralf Peverel, but could 'go with his land where he would' (Prested, 74b). Another man had since the Conquest been 'made the man' of Ralf's predecessor, 'but he did not give him his land' (Vange, 71b). Ralf obtained these manors, but can we be sure that there should not have been a special royal grant of them? Neither the free man concerned nor the Hundred-jury bore witness that someone at Manhall (62b) had 'of his own will' been made the man of Geoffrey de Manneville, though Geoffrey claimed that the king had given him 'in exchange'. Leofhild had been a dependant of Barking Abbey, and the Hundred-jury testified that she had been only the man [*sic*] of the predecessor of Geoffrey, and could not assign (*mittere*) her land to any fee but that of the abbey (Abbess Roding, 57b).[1]

Then, too, it looks as if there were numerous groups of unattached or largely independent free men and sokemen, frequent in East Anglia if not so marked in Essex. If they were not more or less closely connected with what the Inquest clerks were to think of as a 'manor', to whose lordship should they be delivered? The simplest solution would have been to consider

[1] DB includes a number of instances of post-Conquest commendation; see p. 130.

them all as the king's, and in part this principle seems to have been adopted. They could be treated as being *in manu regis*, and supervised by one of the royal *ministri*. It would be much the same thing to regard them as at the disposal of the king's sheriff, and again we find sections of DB devoted to 'Roger Bigot's free men'.[1] But the situation obviously offered opportunity for the unsanctioned acquisition of petty holdings and their inhabitants' services.

An enormous number of entries both in DB and in the second Schedule of usurpations in the *Inquisitio Eliensis* (H, pp. 178–89) demonstrate how frequently many barons had deprived Ely of her free men and sokemen. The practice must have begun early in the reign, for Lisois de Moustières, dead well before the time of the Inquest, had acknowledged Ely's right to sokemen delivered to him.[2] Perhaps it was even easier to appropriate the lands and services of peasant farmers whose legitimate descent had been in some doubt or the lord concerned someone of no particular importance. Thegnland too had been illegally acquired, and complaints to the king must have been frequent and extensive. There were moreover difficulties inherent in certain incidents occurring before the initial settlement was more than a few years old.

[1] e.g. fols. 333b, 339b. There are sections for 'the king's free men' in all three shires (99, 272b, 447). Those in Norfolk had in King Edward's day 'belonged to no *feorm*', but by 1086 had been added to a royal *firma* by Almær, who was a royal reeve. The Suffolk ones, where there was doubt as to their proper lordship, are said to be *in manu regis*. Those called *vavassores* on fol. 446 seem to correspond to the king's free men.

[2] Lakenheath and Brandon (fol. 403; H, p. 142).

CHAPTER III

After the Settlement

INCIDENTS ENGENDERING FURTHER CHANGES IN TENURE

Two further irruptions in 1069 and 1075, following any initial redistribution, and Stigand's deposition in 1070 and death in 1072, must have facilitated further wholesale transference. The date of the death of William Malet is unknown, and the slender evidence contradictory; the most likely period is 1069/71. His surrender of York and capture by the Danes would lower his credit in the king's eyes; it is suggestive that in 1086 we find a large number of his estates not in his son's hands but in those of other powerful competitors.[1] The East Anglian text contains three references to his activities; occasions when he went 'on the king's service' and 'in the marsh' (133b, 247, 332): the Chediston entry adds *ubi mortuus est.* Freeman deduced that he was slain during the invasion and rebellion in the Fenland of 1070–1, but Round disagreed.[2]

The full tale of losses from the Malet fief can never be told. In many entries it seems probable that the 'Edric' given as his *antecessor* was Edric of Laxfield, though there had been many local Edrics, including one who had been commended to his more powerful namesake (e.g. fols. 154b, 305). But there are in Norfolk and Suffolk over a score of entries which specify Edric of Laxfield as the previous holder or the possessor of the holder's

[1] Fols. 373ai, 374ai,2. Oddly enough, some passages on 374ai referring to 1086 read *et dicunt quod Willelmus Malet habere debet,* as though he were still alive. But the fact of his death is frequently mentioned, e.g. on fols. 294, 334b, 442, with varying formulae. Possibly the Yorkshire clerk was careless.

[2] Freeman: *Norman Conquest,* iv, p. 473; Round: 'The Death of William Malet' (*Academy,* 26 August, 1884). In view of William's importance, it seems curious that neither the *Anglo-Saxon Chronicle* nor the *Gesta Herewardi* mentions his death, if this occurred during the Ely campaign. Round very reasonably thought that *maresc,* marsh, might be a mistranscription of *Eurvic,* York. According to another source (Lanfranc: *Opera,* i, p. 134, ed. Giles) he died a monk of Bec.

commendation, but where the land was not in 1086 included in the Malet fief. The 1086 owners were the king, Bishop Odo, Earls Hugh and Alan, Bury St Edmunds, Roger Bigot, Hervey of Bourges, Roger de Raismes, and Humfrey *camerarius*. Many were substantial estates, and to most of these were attached free men who presumably should have passed with the manors. In a number of the entries William Malet is said to have been seized of them when he died.[1]

In some instances the difficulties of securing succession can be seen. At Hudeston (181b) the Malet *antecessor* had been associated with only one of the five free men; Roger Bigot obtained them all. At Ulverston (376b) the commendation of a priest had been as to one-sixth to the Malet predecessor, and as to the remainder to Saxi, the *antecessor* of Ralf Peverel; Bishop Odo obtained the land. A man at Livermere (363b) had been Edric of Laxfield's, but his wife was commended to St Edmund; both could sell their land. But the king gave the holding to Gernon de Peiz, who later became a monk, and then gave it back to the abbey, though only the woman's commendation and soke had been the abbot's.[2] But there are two entries which suggest that some holdings did not become Malet land for reasons unconnected with a possible deprivation of William of some of his estates. Tibenham (280) was being held by the predecessor of Walter Canud in mortgage, so perhaps the free man who had been Edric's had transferred his allegiance when Edric was exiled. This seems to be the story at Haddiscoe (182), for Edric's sokeman commended himself, after the Conquest, to 'Alwin' (probably Æthelwine of Thetford), who was seized of him 'when the king gave Roger Bigot his land' (280, 182).[3]

As a result of Sweyn of Denmark's two attacks and the support afforded them by natives, there must have been further English estates vacant, e.g. those of Earl Edwin, murdered in 1071, who was perhaps holding at least some of the lands ascribed in DB to his father Ælfgar. The elder Earl Ralf

[1] Typical examples can be found under Raveningham (130b), Hickling (148), Ingham (148), Helmingham (375b), Tuddenham (442).

[2] Hales (181b); see also Wyverstone (309, 363b).

[3] The phrase might mean 'when the king entrusted Roger with the office of sheriff', or to succeed Æthelwine as a royal officer.

probably died 1069/70, but DB gives no indication that his son did not obtain all his lands. The deposition of Stigand in April, 1070, did not necessarily deprive him of his estates, but on his death in 1072 King William would be enabled to make further extensive grants.

The last major internal revolt was that of Earl Ralf the younger and his confederates in 1075. References in DB to the consequent forfeiture of his lands and those of his Breton followers are frequent, and for all we know he may have attracted natives to his cause who would in consequence lose or quit their estates also. He does not, however, seem to have had support from the Bretons in Essex, e.g. Tihel de Helléan and Gilbert son of Saloman, who were still holding fiefs in 1086.

A distribution of the lands of Stigand and of Earl Ralf would produce obvious difficulties. Unless there was to be a successor to the earldom, Ralf's lands could hardly pass as a whole, for they would have given their owner overmuch local importance. Thus the bulk of them (over fifty entries) are to be found in the hands of the king's *ministri*, and mostly under *Terra Regis*. About another thirty were in 1086 in the possession of Earls Alan and Hugh, William of Warenne, Roger Bigot, and the bishop of Thetford, while a number of other men had rarely more than one of his holdings, possibly from royal grants for assistance in 1075. A reference to 'the division of land between the king and the earl' (150) might refer to an apportionment after the flight of Earl Ralf.

It is usually said that after the departure of Earl Ralf East Anglia had no earl.[1] But there are some grounds for doubting the accuracy of this statement. From the frequent references to sokeright being the king's and the earl's no deduction can be made, for by 1086 the king may have taken all the profits thereof, or allowed his sheriff to retain the third share. While Roger Bigot is said to have the custody of the borough of Ipswich (290), the third pennies of the borough and two Hundreds are mentioned in connection with the sum for which it was 'delivered', but this might be a reference to the elder Ralf's

[1] e.g. by Stenton: *Anglo-Saxon England*, p. 604; 'the earldom of East Anglia was suppressed', and by Douglas: *FD*, p. cxlii.

time. Again, Norwich had formerly rendered £20 to the king and the earl, and in 1086 apparently paid £70 to the king alone, but in the account of Thetford (118b) we are told of third pennies belonging *ad comitatum, in consulatu.* There may have been no earl in 1086, but Alan is said to have held Weston (147) '*because* Earl Ralf held it', and one of Alan's men was claiming a half-share in a Stratton sokeman (193) on the grounds that Earl Ralf had held him, and was prepared to submit himself to the ordeal. It is, however, certain that Alan did not obtain all Ralf's rights; equally it is said that because Ralf 'invaded' the land of nine sokemen at Horningtoft (120b), *therefore* Godric has it, while he claimed Bittering (137) as being part of Ralf's fee.

But no fewer than twenty-seven barons, besides the king, shared Stigand's Norfolk lands and interests. These represented well over 150 carucates, and were probably even more extensive than DB allows us to determine. For often the assessments are not stated, while we are not always told to whom a man was commended or if the conditions in the first of a group of entries obtained throughout it.[1] The entries are extremely mixed; some refer to large manors with extensive sokes, though frequently only his possession of the soke or commendation of the tenants is mentioned. Some he had lost during his lifetime, e.g. Flitcham (173 – second entry), and Wellingham (252b). The king had taken some of the most profitable, and other large estates had passed to Odo of Bayeux, William of Warenne, Ralf of Beaufoy, and Ralf fitzCorbucion. Few of his other successors acquired substantial gains. What principle, if any, governed transference is indeterminable: it may be that if Stigand's tenant was the *antecessor* of some baron the primary rule of post-Conquest inheritance prevailed. Haghne's manor of Heckingham (205) became Godric's. But a manor of Thorkill's went to Earl Alan, not William of Warenne, who normally obtained his lands, and Ketel's holdings to three different barons. Often a man's lands went to different successors:

[1] A certain Ketel is styled both a 'thegn' and a 'free man' of Stigand's, and he held 'under' him also (254, 264b, 243b). His other lands may thus also have been held of Stigand. No incongruity in calling a man a 'free thegn' seems to have been felt; see fol. 254a2.

Beorhtmær had possessed *plures terras*, to which Ranulf brother of Ilger mostly succeeded. But 'some part was delivered at the king's instance' (*ex parte regis*) to Ingelric and other parts to Ranulf and yet a third part to Ralf Pinel (423b).

THE ESTABLISHMENT OF LEGAL TENURE

The extensive and widespread acquisition of land or services by illegal or dubious means quite possibly began within a short time after the Conquest. Ingelric is said to have 'invaded' or 'occupied' holdings, and while we do not know how long he lived after the advent of the Normans, he was one of those entrusted with the land-settlement, and presumably made use of his opportunities for swelling his estates.[1] The first inquiry into the lands lost by Ely is dated 1071/5, and probably took place appreciably before the revolt of 1075. It failed to achieve all its objects, and a further investigation took place at Kentford in 1080.[2] In the interval between these, in 1076/7, came an inquiry into the sheriffs' misdeeds.

In the *Liber Eliensis* are preserved a number of documents which show the constant care of the administration to investigate the illegal acquisitions of the local magnates. But in considering these documents we have to remember that they do not represent the actual sequence of events: for an explanation of the story they tell we must examine the commentaries upon them.[3]

The names of those who attended the Kentford inquiry in 1080 are given: the four local abbots, three royal legates, and four sheriffs, with whom were 'their Frenchmen and Englishmen'. Though Roger (? Bigot, of Norfolk) and Robert (? Malet, of Suffolk) were absentee sheriffs, they and their fellow-officials had nine deputies present, including Hardwin d'Escalers and Guy de Raimbeaucourt from Cambridgeshire and Godric and Northmann the royal *ministri* of Norfolk and Suffolk. Also present were 'very many *milites probati* both

[1] See fols. 5, 5b, 6b, and many times in Earl Eustace's Essex *breve*, 26–34b.

[2] H, pp. xvii–xix; Blake, pp. 198, 203.

[3] Especially E. Miller: 'The Ely Land Pleas in the Reign of William I' (*EHR*, lxii, 1947, pp. 438–56).

French and English' from Essex, Hertfordshire, Huntingdonshire, and Bedfordshire'.[1]

Then we find King William's order that Ely shall have all her customary rights 'as was ordained at Kentford', also giving a list of the ecclesiastics and laymen who were present, and adding Peter de Valognes and Picot, sheriffs of Essex and Cambridgeshire in 1086, and Ivo Taillebois, Tihel de Helléan, and Hugh de Houdain, all men whom DB shows to have been concerned with local administration, the witness of Roger Bigot being mentioned also.[2]

The next eight 'chapters' continue the story. Lanfranc, Robert of Mortain, and Bishop Geoffrey of Coutances were to choose Englishmen who knew the rights in the Ely lands in King Edward's day and cause them to testify regarding them. The demesne lands, including those which it was claimed the king had bestowed on newcomers, were to be restored, and where the conquerors were holding thegnlands, they were to make the best arrangement about them that they could with the abbot, or surrender them. Another 'chapter' more or less repeats the story, and tells how the king ordered the leading barons concerned to be summoned to the plea. It is followed by his instruction that certain named men who are holding Ely estates shall restore them, then by his order that Ely shall enjoy her customary sokeright and by his forbidding the bishop of Lincoln to demand 'new customs' within the Isle of Ely. The most striking ordinance is that to Lanfranc instructing him to inspect the abbot's charters, to inquire by means of the bishops of Coutances and Winchester and others into the giving of evidence about Ely estates and its commission to writing, and to examine those who heard the plea; then quickly to let the king know the truth of the matter in writing and despatch the abbot's representative with the report. Notice is even taken of a mill at Cambridge constructed by Picot, which is to be destroyed if it interferes with the abbey mill.[3]

[1] For some reason Cambridgeshire is omitted: so are Norfolk and Suffolk, whose sheriffs also seem to have been absent. See H, p. xviii; Blake, p. 198.

[2] H, p. xviii; Blake, p. 199.

[3] H, pp. xviii–xxi; Blake, pp. 203–7.

It is possible, too, that DB reflects other occasions on which the king despatched commissions to consider unsanctioned tenure and disputes. We hear of an undated occasion on which the king *misit legatos in hanc terram* (fol. 97b – unconnected with an Ely enquiry). Bishop William of London proved by the king's orders that two Layer manors belonged to his church, and recovered Southminster (10, 10b; see also the Roding entries on 60b, 61b). This could not have been at the Domesday Inquest. Richard fitzGilbert proved his claim to St Peter's, Ipswich, in the time of Bishop Herfast (Thurlston, fol. 349b; see also an anonymous holding of Hugh de Bernières, fol. 100b).

Some of the king's writs ordering restitution or confirming decisions have survived (e.g. H, p. xix; Blake, p. 204). Two instruct local barons of the highest importance to do justice against Peter de Valognes in respect of his encroachments upon Bury lands; another records a dispute between the abbot and the local bishop (*FD*, nos 8–10, pp. 55–6).

It is obvious from DB that the Ely inquiries had resulted in partial restitution, and again writs confirming the decisions have survived.[1] On fols. 383–5b we are several times told of land which had been *derationatus* in Ely's favour, once before the bishop of Coutances, the president at the Kentford inquiry (Darmsden, 383). Several times Ely is said to have proved her right to land which had fallen into the hands of newcomers, e.g. at Horswold (363), Wingfield (385), and Soham (385). Again, Hervey de Bourges was holding of Ely at Westerfield (383b) *iussu regis*, and is also said to be *conciliatus abbati*.[2] The bishopric of Rochester, in the classic case of Isleham and Freckenham, recovered the manor through the agency of Archbishop Lanfranc by the king's orders (381). Hubert de Port adjudged land to Bishop Odo, surely before 1082, when Odo was arrested; someone deraigned fourteen free men to Earl Ralf's fee (450, 242). We even find Finnr, who probably was not active for long during the reign, associated with Ralf Taillebois in placing manors 'in the king's hand' (Belstead,

[1] H, pp. xviii–xxi; Blake, p. 204.

[2] See also Pettaugh (384), Kembrook, Walton, and Trimley (385b), Parham and Beversham (441).

418b).[1] He may have been a royal agent; his widow retained a small portion of his lands (98).

In addition to the type of entry which provides definite evidence of matters considered by the Commissioners, it is easy to find numerous passages which suggest that a claim or protest must have been made and similarly debated. Two in Essex relate to losses by Ely; both appear in the IE Schedules of 'invasions'.[2] Because Ingelric had held Orsett from the bishop of London, Earl Eustace had acquired it, 'though it was not one of his manors' (9, 26b). Creeting and Thorington (411, 412b) had not belonged to the fee or honour of Ansger, the *antecessor* of Geoffrey de Manneville, but Geoffrey was none the less holding them. Beorhtric 'Blac' had held Thorney (440b) under Wihtgar, whose lands normally passed to Richard fitzGilbert, but Hervey de Bourges held it 'by the king's gift'.

THE ACTIVITIES OF SHERIFFS AND 'MINISTRI'

It is doubtful if the volume of illegalities which DB discloses could have been attained without the frequent connivance of the sheriffs and the king's legates. Isolated passages in the text suggest that sheriffdoms frequently changed hands. There are in Essex references to 'the time of all the sheriffs', to the loss of office by Sweyn, and of its tenure by Ralf Baignard, who seems to have ceased to be sheriff by 1080; in 1086 Peter de Valognes was sheriff.[3] Roger Bigot, sheriff of Norfolk and Suffolk at the time of the Inquest, was not then in his first term of office: there is a stray reference to his acting as sheriff at an earlier date, while there follows immediately the statement that Robert Malet had also been sheriff.[4] Robert Blond had also been sheriff of Norfolk, and we are told of his activities either in this capacity or in that of a royal *minister*. He had been the *liberator* of land; he had been the king's officer, holding a *ministerium*; he had held land *in manu regis*, as sheriffs and royal agents are elsewhere frequently said to do; he had held royal land at farm,

[1] See also Bridgham (213b), Hoo (388), Westerfield (446b).

[2] Fols. 36b, 50; IE MS. C fols. 207b2, 208b2; H, pp. 204, 207.

[3] Fols. 2, 2b, 1b, 6, 6b, 7, 19b.

[4] Fol. 287b. Robert Malet had been a royal legate; see Davis: *Reg.*, no. 47, p. 13, and *FD*, no. 2, p. 47. He had held pleas at Bury St Edmunds.

added free men to a manor, and caused them to pay rent to it.[1] There are also references to the Suffolk sheriffdom of Northmann, a name which appears frequently for both 1066 and 1086. He had had a free woman's commendation and was holding Ash of Robert Malet in 1086; he is again styled 'sheriff' in a Darsham entry.[2]

We hear also of persons who, though not styled sheriff, may have acted in that capacity, and must have been royal legates. Ivo Taillebois had been the means of putting Earl Alan in possession of an Islington estate, and with his associates (*socii*) was called upon, in view of Edric's 'invasion' at Happisburgh, to warrant Earl Alan's right to it (149, 150). But these may merely imply that he had been acting as a royal agent on the occasion of a transference of the estates of the conquered. Another man said to have given livery of land is Waleram, who had certainly been the king's officer and concerned with the payments of Colchester burgesses (170b, 117b, 107b). Others had been the farmers or custodians of royal manors; Ralf Taillebois had annexed free men at Foulsham, and Ivo Taillebois had continued a practice whereby others paid rents to Earsham, a manor of which Richard Pugnant had been reeve, and this Richard too had absorbed free men into royal manors.[3] Practically all those mentioned above are found acting as sheriffs of other counties during the reign.[4] Another potential *minister* is the shadowy figure of Hugh de Houdain, for he had been responsible 'in his time' (i.e. when acting in some official capacity) for increasing the farm of the free men of Wangford Hundred (284b). Since at the time of the Inquest he was the king's prisoner (Bricett, 448b), he had probably lost any office he had held because of maladministration.[5]

Just what these frequent changes reflect is problematical.

[1] Fols. 118, 223b, 264, 268b, 110b, 277b, 276b, 243b, 124, 126b, 138, 199.

[2] Fols. 312b, 327, 334b. He is also called 'thegn' (Yoxford, 333).

[3] Fols. 114, 125b, 186, 138, 139b. Ralf Taillebois was one of those appointed to take the inventory of Ely plate and vestments in 1079 (Blake, p. 196); Ivo, and also two officials mentioned earlier, Godric and Northmann, had been present at the Kentford inquiry into Ely lands (Blake, p. 198; H, p. xviii).

[4] W. A. Morris: 'The Office of Sheriff in the Early Norman Period' (*EHR*, xxxiii, 1918, pp. 145–75).

[5] He is none the less said to 'hold' at Flowton (337b). See also *VCH: Suffolk*, i, p. 389.

Domesday Book bears repeated testimony to the illegalities practised and permitted by sheriffs.[1] Repeated protests against their wrongdoings, and the disclosures consequent upon the inquiry the king had instituted in 1076–7 into their activities, may have resulted in the dismissal of some. But, since the office of sheriff was obviously coupled with the custody or farming of groups of royal estates, discharge of it may have been an undertaking profitable enough to encourage men to pay well for the position. The *Anglo-Saxon Chronicle* accuses King William of 'giving his land for rent as dearly as he possibly could' and letting it to the highest bidder; 'nor did he reck how sinfully the reeves got it from poor men, nor how many illegalities they committed'. To huge increases in rents on royal manors DB bears ample witness (pp. 165, 174). Some may have been caused by the sheriffs' need to compensate themselves for the high price of office.

TECHNICALITIES OF TRANSFERENCE

Certainly it was held that occupation of land without royal grant or permission was illegal. Earl Ralf gave Hoveton (185b) to St Benet of Holme *concedente rege*, according to the abbot, and though there are not in our manuscript many references to the need for royal sanction for the disposal of estates, it is not infrequent in the Exchequer text.[2] But Bury had obtained a mortgage on Stoneham (360b) 'by Ingelric's leave', and King William had granted some free men at Poslingford (413b) to that abbey, and given leave for Peter de Valognes to take over land at Ixworth Thorpe (421) which had belonged to one of Queen Edith's free men.

Either consciousness of unsanctioned tenure or the requirements of inquisitors demanded that a man the legality of whose possession was dubious should give a surety. Presumably this was forfeited if the case subsequently went against him. Godwine 'Gudhen' *iterum dedit vadem* at the Inquest on account of his 'invasion', which suggests that the matter had been debated

[1] e.g. on fols. 58ai, 148b2, 181a2, 186ai, 203ai, 210b2, 217b2.

[2] See, e.g., fols. 182b2, 241bi; *Lib. Exon. 369b, 466b.*

before.[1] Hugh de Bernières held 37 acres 'from the king', but the king denied this, and 'afterwards' it was adjudged to be 'for the use of the king', so Hugh 'gave surety'.[2] In a Hevingham entry (133) Thorold, William of Warenne's man, had given surety of 5*s*. *de iustitia facienda*, for he had been adjudged to have seized the land to the king's hurt. Berenger, St Edmund's man, was 'at the king's mercy' for his 'invasion' of land at Uggeshall (449).[3] Roger Bigot stood guarantor that Wulfmær the royal reeve would act up to the surety that he had given for his 'invasion' at Somersham (448b).

Attempts to conceal an absence of authorised title to an estate were probably often made by alleging that the possessor held it 'by exchange', which was advanced as grounds for possession over one hundred times, and was done by at least a score of barons. In one instance the transfer was legitimate enough (Caister, 134; see p. 37), but never do we hear of evidence being given to warrant it, except that of the holder or his men, and rarely is it said with whom the exchange had been made.[4] There is a Norfolk section headed 'of the exchange of Isaac's land', and Roger Bigot claimed Field Dalling 'for the exchange of the land which the king gave to Isaac'.[5] It looks as if unallotted land had been taken out of the sheriff's custody, but some compensation for this loss furnished. Or did Isaac ensure the establishment of a small fief for himself by exchanging it with the king for wider estates?[6] Especially in Essex and Norfolk are we told of the exchanges of William of Warenne,

[1] Horndon-on-the-Hill (99); the judgment of the Barstaple Hundred-jury had been called for.

[2] Fol. 100b; so I interpret the wording. See also fols. 101, 103, 132b, 133, 133b, 150, 273, 273b, 278, 280, 388, 412, 446, 447, 448b, where surety was given, presumably during the Inquest proceedings.

[3] He was sick and could not attend the Inquest, but the case did not go against him by default; the land was placed in the sheriff's custody.

[4] Robert Gernons had a manor 'by exchange for land of Hugh de Montfort' (*Turchetlestuna*, 420). Once at least the Hundred-jury knew nothing of any legitimate transfer (Curling Tye Green, 69), but once the holder claimed it had been made by authority of (*per*) Hubert de Port (South Weald, 66b), whom we have seen acting as a royal legate, though in a parallel entry for the manor (16b) he says it was obtained 'by the king's gift'.

[5] Fols. 175, 176, 179.

[6] The 'exchange of Isaac's land' is referred to in Suffolk also, fol. 331. Isaac held a fief in this county (437b).

which are fifty times mentioned. They are for the exchange 'of Normandy', 'of the castle', 'of two manors of Lewes', 'of Lewes, of the land of the Saints', 'of new land': there is even a heading *De escangio Lewes*.[1] William was a considerable benefactor to the Priory of Lewes, but the reference on fol. 166b is hardly self-explanatory. Reference to 'the castle' should probably be to 'the castlery', for William held the Sussex rape of Lewes, and these exchanges seem to have been because he had lost lands which had been therein but had been transferred to the rapes of two other barons.[2]

POTENTIALITIES OF MANORIAL EXPLOITATION

Undoubtedly another of the aspects of eleventh-century East Anglia which encouraged land-usurpation was the looseness of manorial structure. It seems as if at the Conquest, and up to the time of the Domesday Inquest at least, there were large numbers of free men and sokemen whose ties with a particular manor were of the slenderest, if indeed they existed at all.

Over and over again we are told of land delivered to a new-comer to 'make up' or 'complete' a manor which had been granted to him. To make up his manor of Baylham in Bosmere Hundred Roger Bigot had received 40 acres of Buxhall in Stow Hundred, seven miles away (336). The free man who had held them had been commended to Ely, and while the abbey's deprivation of him is not recorded in IE, it seems to have protested, for the Hundred-jury said that it had never seen a writ authorising the transaction, or livery of the land given (336). A free man of Harold's with half a carucate at Gunthorpe (257b), and seventeen free men with 80 acres, had been delivered to Peter de Valognes to make up his manor of Barney (257b, 258). But a royal servant claimed 13½ of these as having been of the fief of Earl Ralf at the time of his forfeiture, and

[1] Fols. 38, 163, 164b, 157, 166b, 165b, 172.

[2] e.g. 15 of the 79 hides of Rodmell were in the rapes of Robert of Mortain and William of Braiose. See L. F. Salzman: 'The rapes of Sussex' (*Sussex Archaeol. Collns.*, lxxii, pp. 20–9, Cambridge, 1931), and *VCH: Sussex*, i, pp. 354 *et seq.* and J. F. A. Mason: 'The Rapes of Sussex and The Norman Conquest' (*Sussex Archaeol. Collns.*, cii, pp. 79–86, 1964), and *William I and the Sussex Rapes*, pp. 15–16 (Bexhill, 1966).

was prepared to undergo any form of ordeal in support of his case. The North Greenhoe Hundred-jury testified in his favour, so perhaps he did not have to do so. Land at Great Walsingham (258) had also been included in Peter's fief, but his men did not even know to make up which manor it had been delivered.

Gimingham (170b) was in 1066 a substantial 2-carucate manor. But two holdings, at Sidestrand, which itself had been a manor, and at Knapton, were delivered to complete it, making it a 4-carucate manor, the value of which had increased from 40*s.* to £4, and later to £8, probably as a result of these accessions. But in many instances the incorporations were quite small holdings; e.g. of four free men with 16 acres at Shimpling (176b) or of a free man with 20 acres at Barningham (242b) 'to make up Letheringsett'.[1]

The very numerous occasions on which we are told that something had been 'added' to a manor would seem to reflect similar activities. Almost always it is said, with varying formulae, that this was done 'in the time of King William'.[2] The Inquest, except in special circumstances, was not interested in pre-Conquest alterations in manorial structure.[3] We are, as it happens, told that at Hunstanton (136) Siward 'has once more joined this to this manor', but divorcement may have occurred after the Conquest. We are sometimes told that someone's *antecessor* had 'invaded' land (e.g. Chigwell, 90b), but the transference may still have taken place after the Conquest. The frequently-mentioned ablations from manors, including such minor features as four acres of meadow, a villein with a single acre, half a mill, or a hide of woodland, are almost all certainly post-Conquest.[4]

That the process was not an innovation is shown by the fact that Walter de Dol, exiled in 1075, made one manor out of

[1] See also fols. 170b, 171b, 173b, 206b, 233b, 245b, 246, 435b.

[2] e.g. *tempore regis Willelmi* (10), *post adventum regis Willelmi* (46), *postquam rex venit in istam patriam* (120), *in Angliam* (140), *postquam rex Willelmus conquisivit Angliam* (124b). But a Morston free man had been added to Holt (112b) 'after the death of King Edward', which might imply Harold's brief reign.

[3] It did note some changes, e.g. that Earl Harold had made Latton and Eisy into a single manor (68bi). Kelsale (330b) is an instance of the union of two manors.

[4] Witham (5), Stanway/Wormingford (5, 66), Combs (291), Wigborough (55b).

Fundenhall (153) and all the properties he added to it. Bentley had been held by Earl Gyrth, and East Bergholt by his brother Harold. Possibly they should not both have become the elder Earl Ralf's, but he had turned the manor of Bentley into a mere berewick of Bergholt (287).[1] *Additae sunt huic manerio lxxx acrae terrae pro manerio T.R.E.* (Brandeston, 431b) does not necessarily mean that the addition was made before the Conquest, but only that it was in 1066 held 'as a manor'. By its addition to a different manor it would lose its manorial status, as in the instances of the creation of berewicks. Bawsey (153b) had obviously been a manor, but had been made a berewick of Fring, though wrongly called *manerium* still by the clerk.

There are also passages which imply not so much incorporation in a manor as the imposition of the obligation of contributing to its *feorm*, where the free men had not previously belonged to any *firma*, and so, possibly, were not attached to any manor (Olden, 446).[2]

Some of the changes possibly were hardly unlawful, as where the royal reeve added 30 acres to the manor of Hatfield Broad Oak after the smith who had held them was executed for robbery (2b), or a couple of sokemen were added to the royal manor of Layer (2b).

The dispersion of the land of so many manors must have made it easy illegally to appropriate the smaller estates. Though we are not told that any change had occurred, one carucate of a single manor (339) was at Brome and one at Oakley; land at Thorpe in Ashfield (305b) lay in the manor of Bedingfield. It must always have been a temptation, where a village was divided between several holdings, for the baron with a large holding therein to assimilate the smaller properties and the services of their inhabitants. Robert Malet had five holdings at Snettisham; it must have been easy to appropriate the single demesne acre and the seven acres which Ely here seems to have lost.[3]

[1] Blo Norton was added as a berewick to Lopham by Alsige after the Conquest (178b); the lands of some sokemen had been made berewicks of Sedgeford (193b).

[2] See also Hemingstone (282, 446), and § LXIIII of the Norfolk text (272).

[3] Fols. 318, 319, 324; 318, 387; IE 69bi *bis*; H, pp. 178, 195. See also the instance where Roger Malet gave six acres when his tenant's daughter married one of Roger Bigot's men; by 1086 Roger had acquired them (Darsham, 334b).

The king may well have empowered his sheriffs and legates to organise transfers of estates and to allot holdings in which there was no clear right of succession. Possibly he and his advisers did not appreciate that East Anglia, and in lesser degree Essex, offered so many opportunities of acquiring land on grounds which did not conform with his intentions, and which could, and did, provoke trouble. Obviously it was essential to their scheme that the newly-won land should be the subject of formal transfer, not the prey of the despoiler and land-grabber.

CHAPTER IV

Aspects of the Inquest

THE ESSENTIALITY OF FORMAL TRANSFER

Nowhere, indeed, do we hear more of the giving of livery of estates, of (*de*)*liberatio*, than in the eastern counties. We find the term used of the formal transfers of land which must have been made early in the reign; to Ingelric, to Frederick the brother-in-law of William of Warenne, reputed to have been killed in the campaign in the Fenland, to the time when Stigand was yet alive, to Lisois de Moustières, the predecessor of Eudes *dapifer*, to Wihenoc, exiled for his share in the rebellion of 1075, or 'in the time of Earl Ralf' – probably the younger earl.[1]

Quite often the holder or the jury must have stated by whose gift land passed. Robert Malet obtained Burston (155), and Hugh de St Quintin Little Birch (93b), 'by the queen's gift', while Gilbert the priest claimed his land at Middleton (98) as held by reason of a gift by the queen (who might be either Edith or Matilda). Godwine Halden held Thorpe (138) 'by the gift of Earl Ralf', and three sokemen an Ormesby holding by Bishop Herfast's gift.

The number of royal officials concerned who are noted in connection with these transactions makes it certain that those so engaged were not acting simultaneously, though again we are given no clue to the time of their activities. Livery of estates had also been given by the king himself, which is probably the equivalent of the recurrent phrase *de dono regis*. Livery said to have been given by the king may really only imply that he instructed his representative to give a man seizin of his land.[2] Land added to the manor of Bowers Gifford (98) by Grimr the king's reeve 'through Robert fitzWymarc the sheriff' may not

[1] Fols. 423b, 170b, 173, 403, 231b, 164.
[2] e.g. Holt (111b), Hoo (388) – *per praeceptum regis*.

have been transferred by royal order, but we hear of Robert's son Sweyn acting as *liberator*, and certainly sheriffs frequently gave livery and seizin of land.[1] But very often the *liberator* is not named.

Land had been delivered 'for exchange'; once, unexpectedly, for Cornish land.[2] There is a reference to an estate whose holder, Wihtgar, to whose lands Richard fitzGilbert normally succeeded, had possessed the commendation of its tenants, of which Raymond Gerold had been seized and which Roger of Poitou held in 1086, but Roger de Raismes *de prima liberatione*. Unfortunately we are not told who made this formal transfer, but the Bosmere Hundred-jury testified that it had 'earlier' been delivered to Roger de Raismes (Stonham and Coddenham, 352).

We not infrequently find absence of formal livery quoted as evidence of illegal possession. Walter de Dol had been seized of the land of four men at the time of his forfeiture, and later Earl Hugh held it, but in 1086 Hugh de Montfort, *sed non tenet per liberationem, teste hundreti, et homines Hugonis detinuit* [*sic*].[3] Theodoric, the predecessor and brother of Walter the deacon, had held *Weledana* (427) 'without livery', as the Stow Hundred-jury reported.

Thus it is not surprising that at the Inquest we find landholders mentioning in support of their rights that they had received livery of the land, which must have followed receipt of the king's sealed writ ordering seizin of it to be given. They claim it *ex liberatione regis*, that they hold it *per liberationem*; they say that *liberata fuit*, name the man who delivered it to them, claim it as delivered *ad feudum antecessoris ejus*.[4] Similarly they will call on the king or his officer to warrant its livery.[5] Equally the Hundred-jury, if it had seen no writ, or the royal *legatus* or *liberator* give seizin, says so.[6] In one instance no one had

[1] For Grimr and for Robert and his son, see fols. 98, 6b *bis*.

[2] Feltwell (162), Caister (134b). The Cornish land was the Hundred-manor of Tybesta, held before the Conquest by Ralf *stalra* (121bi).

[3] Rushmere St Michael (407b). *Doai*, Douai, is an obvious mistake for Dol.

[4] Fols. 140, 294, 355, 290b, 291.

[5] e.g. fols. 60, 150, 282, 290, 310b, 439b, 446. The expressions *ad tutorem* (107b, 222, 388) or *ad defensorem* (31b, 125b) are also used.

[6] Helhoughton (172), Blofield (194b), Shipdham (277), Buxhall (336), Thorney (409b).

'deraigned' the land, and accordingly it remained 'in the king's hand'. At Barningham (279) 28 acres were *in manu regis* because no one rendered an account – ? included them in his return – of them.

THE VOLUME OF COMPLAINTS

We can only assume that illegal acquisition was widespread throughout the reign, and that the numerous complaints which must have been made to the king in consequence were one of the principal causes of the institution of the Domesday Inquest. Even cursory inspection of DB displays how frequently claims regarding land or privileges wrongfully acquired, with a wide range of formula and vocabulary and expression, appear. In Essex alone well over 300 such complaints appear in the record, and it is interesting to inspect a classification of these and similar passages suggesting, but not specifically noting, unlawful action regarding the occupation of estates.

Evidence of the shire-jury mentioned	6
Evidence of the Hundred-jury mentioned	58
Evidence of the individual mentioned	30
Mention of 'claim'	28
'Invasions', 'occupations', 'ablations', etc.	146
Additions to manors	37
Miscellaneous	10
	315

This total should, however, really be reduced by 32, since some single passages include more than one of the above categories. The gross figure for Norfolk is 255, and for Suffolk 212.

What is equally striking is that in the neighbouring counties of Middlesex and Hertfordshire the volume is so very much less. In Middlesex, so far as the record goes, the evidence of the Hundred-jury was only twice required, while but two claims are mentioned. Seven other passages alone suggest unsanctioned actions.[1]

[1] Even this is not certain; five merely refer to the placing of holdings in manors in which they did not lie in 1066 (129ai,2). For the Hundred-jury, see fols. 130a2,b2; for claims, fols. 130a2,bi.

In Hertfordshire the relevant passages may be categorised thus:

Evidence of the shire-jury mentioned	15
Evidence of the Hundred-jury mentioned	18
Evidence tendered to sheriff	1
Mention of 'claim'	8
'Invasions', 'occupations', 'ablations', etc.	7
Miscellaneous	14
	63

Sixty-three is a small number compared with the Essex figure, and should perhaps be reduced because again some passages include more than one of the above categories, while eight of the miscellaneous entries are simply concerned with attaching holdings to manors to which they did not belong in 1066.

The shire-juries of Norfolk and Suffolk are unmentioned, though it must be presumed that they were at some time in evidence at the Inquest. It may be that their opinion was sought only where the Hundred-jury could not give information, or when its members disagreed among themselves. Probably, too, the Hundred-jury would be more familiar with local land tenure and its implications than the men of rather higher status who would form the shire-jury.[1] Only one of 'the men of the shire' knew about Ailric's gift at Kelvedon to Westminster Abbey (14b). Those who could have testified were perhaps dead or overseas.

TESTIMONY AT THE INQUEST

The variety of matters on which the evidence of the Hundred-juries was sought covers the widest possible range. They testified that land should be part of a particular manor or fief. They informed the authorities whether a man had been empowered to sell his land or not, or could not withdraw himself from a specified manor or lord, or had held his land so freely that his superior merely had his commendation. They knew also who ought to have a man's soke. Some of the information

[1] In this connection it is interesting to note a comment on the Penenden Heath trial: *fecit archiepiscopus Lanfranchus alios clamores super episcopum et super Hugonem sed in hundretis debent diffiniri* (BM MS. Cott. Aug. ii. 36).

they furnished was naturally of a negative character. They had not seen, to support possession, the king's writ, or the giving of livery and seizin and a grant by a royal legate, and they could say that a man had not derived land from his predecessor.[1] They stated, too, whether land had been added to or taken away from a manor (e.g. fols. 10, 89b).

But they could also furnish less straightforward information. They estimated the value of an estate where, presumably, the holders had not done so (343).[2] They could say whether a man had cleared himself after conviction and sentence to forfeiture, and could give information about a previous sworn statement (Poringland, 278; *Wimundestuna*, 397b). They could testify to what had happened concerning disputes prior to the Inquest (Aveley, 401b).

But there were over a score of points about which they could not provide evidence, though the implication must often be that they did not know how a man had come by his land simply because he had in fact no right to it, e.g. at Great Chesterford (3b) or Lawford (25b). They did not know whether a priest had received land freely or in alms; they could give an opinion about some part of the land at Writtle (5, 2), but about the remainder 'they knew nothing'.

Quite often we are told that a claimant or witness was willing to support his statements by undergoing the ordeal. This is not mentioned in the Essex text, but occurs nearly thirty times in East Anglia; more frequently in Norfolk than in Suffolk. Those who volunteer for trial include the Midford Hundred-jury, various royal officials, Robert Farthing the man of Godric, a steward of Bury St Edmunds, the men of the vill of Cotton, the men of Earl Alan, the villeins of the manor of Bramford.[3] Twice it is a woman who is willing to subject herself (Bittering, 137; Bramerton, 277b). The form of ordeal is not normally specified, but men are said to have been willing to undergo trial by battle or ordeal in defence of their statements, and this suggests that they were men of fair social standing, as

[1] Typical examples of the above may be found on fols. 7, 54, 59, 10b, 35, 123, 194b, 277, 32, 276b, 124.

[2] This was done in Gloucestershire also (166bi); see also p. 171.

[3] Fols. 207b, 110b, 371, 275b, 285b, 276b, 393.

the names of the Hundred-jurors given in the IE suggest.[1] Trial by battle is, however, mentioned only four times; men are prepared to back their evidence *vel juditio vel* [*aut*] *bello.*[2] Trial by battle was apparently no matter for the humbler folk. But I doubt if, at Tasburgh, we should see a contrast between the Hundred which offered battle or ordeal and the Englishman for whom only *judicium* is mentioned: he might well have been entitled to use arms to establish his case.

At Barney (258) a king's sergeant volunteered to uphold his claim 'by whatever mode of trial may be adopted'; commonly the phrase is *omnibus legibus* (e.g. Mendlesham, 371). While ordeal is not specifically mentioned at Shotley (287b), the entry is an interesting one, for Roger Bigot, the sheriff, wished to prove his case by means of the men who were present *ad suas conventiones*, which may imply his formal and official giving or receiving of livery and land.[3] One feels that in an emergency he would in this instance have ordered trial by ordeal.

Evidence at the Inquest was apparently given by landholders themselves and by their officials and tenants. It is, however, possible that *ut dicit* does not imply verbal evidence given during an Inquest session, but a statement made in a feudal return or to a clerk or official when the material was being collected. Those mentioned include a variety of tenants-in-chief (though these presumably testified by means of representatives), 'the English' (the Hundred-jury?), royal and manorial reeves, a baron's 'men', and villeins from named manors.[4] The sheriff's testimony is also mentioned, and that of Bishop Odo (Badley, 393; *Bineslea*, 79), though we can hardly think that the last was proffered in person.[5]

The claims and the statements adduced in support of them, too, were only improbably a matter of verbal statement in open court, though the claimant's representatives may well have been summoned to explain on what grounds they were advancing their claim. Lists of these may have been presented

[1] See Round: *FE*, pp. 122–3.

[2] Matlask (146), Bixley (176), Tasburgh (190), Foston (213).

[3] We hear also of the *conventio Ricardi* (448); see p. 45.

[4] Representative examples may be found on fols. 98, 404b; 23; 287b, 418b; 70b, 103; 285b, 392b.

[5] The bishop was the king's prisoner.

in the form of appendixes to feudal returns listing the manors held. Again the variety of reasons offered is immense. Fanton was claimed for the king on the grounds that it had come to Westminster Abbey by means of a false writ (14). Sometimes the claim was backed by the testimony of the Hundred-jury, sometimes not; e.g. Rettendon (51); Sibyl Hedingham (87b). The claimant called on the king or his legate to warrant his legal possession; he says he obtained the land by the king's gift, or by livery or seizin, or because it was of his predecessor's fee, or by exchange.

But, as Galbraith has stressed, much of the information required by the royal Commissioners must have been in documentary form, and the statements provided in writing proved in open court.[1] Possibly there was much sorting and examination of documents before the Commissioners ever began their work. Local royal legates must have been in contact with the tenants-in-chief, telling them what would be required of them and asking questions about matters which the Inquest would surely investigate. A letter of Lanfranc, surely concerned with the Domesday Inquest, confirms this view: demesne figures so prominently in DB that the Commissioners would want to know which lands were demesne (the IE stresses whether a holding was *in dominio*, 'of the demesne land of the abbey', or not), which sub-infeudated, and which devoted to the sustenance of the monks.[2] It has been suggested that this letter was addressed to Sweyn, the former sheriff of Essex, but it has recently been pointed out that it is probable that local magnates were not included among the *legati* for a particular circuit, and that Samson, later bishop of Worcester, is indicated.[3]

THE 'INVASIONES' SECTIONS

These are a curious production. Since much of what they contain is paralleled by material in the main text which is of

[1] Galbraith: *MDB*, p. 38.

[2] F. Barlow: 'Domesday Book: A Letter of Lanfranc' (*EHR*, lxxviii, 1963, pp. 284–9).

[3] V. H. Galbraith: 'Notes on the career of Samson, bishop of Worcester' (*EHR*, lxxxii, 1967, pp. 86–101).

essentially similar character, it may be thought that they represent illegalities considered late in the Inquest proceedings, perhaps after the initial draft of the feudal *breves* had been drawn up. But there are no textual indications as to why these could not have been dealt with at the same time as those illegalities which are recorded in the main text. It is of course just possible, but on the whole unlikely, that the intention was to place the accounts of all irregularities in this section, and that the clerks making the first draft so frequently failed to omit them from the feudal *breves* that the scheme was for the most part abandoned.

It is stressed in the Essex section that they record offences *super regem*, for whoever else might suffer loss, it was unlawful to acquire or exchange land held in chief without leave of the king or of his agents. It is only infrequently that they duplicate entries to be found in the *breves*. In Essex only one passage does so, and this may be because it is part of the initial entry of the *invasiones* section, and the clerk inscribing the first draft did not appreciate that it was already recorded.[1]

The entries are grouped according to the baron concerned, though it is doubtful if they were altogether derived from feudal returns. The text of many entries is of exactly the same type as those of the *breves* and provides full statistics. We are given, though there are many omissions, the hundredal rubrics, again suggesting that the only real difference between them and the entries of the main text is one of position. Like these, too, they make mention of the evidence of the Hundred-juries and of individuals.

Formulae and vocabulary are inclined to alter at irregular intervals, suggesting that the initial work was done by several clerks and perhaps at different times. In the Essex section, most entries up to the middle of fol. 100b state that the holding is now *in manu regis*, as it properly should be where the right to possess it had not been established. Up to fol. 102 the phrase *invasit super regem* recurs. A number of times it is stated that the offender has given a pledge that he would make satisfaction if

[1] Horndon-on-the-Hill (99), *in hoc hundredo* (Barstaple, 17b). This absence of repetition is in contrast to *Terrae Occupatae* in the *Liber Exoniensis*, where almost every entry has its parallel within the feudal *breves*. It shows how differently the organisers in the various circuits treated their material.

it is shown that he had acted wrongfully; e.g. Alfred, Richard of Clare's reeve, had received the rent of a holding at Halstead (103), and *inde dedit vadem*, for this money would be the king's if judgment went against him.

One incident is twice recorded in this section, and the variations in the text suggest that each of two clerks recorded the matter independently.[1] The main differences are:

fol. 102b	*fol. 103*
This land was seized by Leodmær of Hempstead	. . . which Leodmær the reeve claimed
and held as part of the fief of Richard, and Richard does not warrant it to him (*non est sibi tutor*)	as belonging to Richard's fief, but his own men do not testify.
	And he has given pledge concerning it.

The valuation is also placed at different points in the entries. It is probably a good example of how the content and form of a Domesday entry might vary according to the clerk originally inscribing it.[2]

The Norfolk section does not specify that these *invasiones* are *super regem*, but otherwise it strongly resembles the Essex material. From the start (273b) to fol. 275, recurring at fol. 276, it seems to be stressed that the grounds on which illegal tenure is alleged is that the holder's predecessor had nothing but the commendation (sometimes, 'not even the commendation'); not until fol. 275b is an alternative reason given. Then the excuses are that the offender had acted in ignorance.[3] Again the text rarely duplicates matter in the *breves*, but the Bixley entry (176, 277b) is an exception to this general pattern.

The short Suffolk section (447b–9b) adds little to the above, but provides an occasional phrase unused elsewhere. There is

[1] This seems to be an explanation more probable than that of Round (*VCH: Essex*, i, p. 570, n. 20), who thought that the clerk was in doubt whether to assign the holding to Richard fitzGilbert or to his reeve. As the latter did not hold in chief, it is unlikely that a clerk would have considered this possibility.

[2] These entries are reminiscent of the differences between parallel entries in the Exeter Domesday and *Terrae Occupatae*; see Finn: *Domesday Studies*: *The* Liber Exoniensis, p. 67.

[3] Shelfhanger (275b), Fersfield, Diss (276b), Somerton (277b).

mention of the *conventio Ricardi* (448), which perhaps refers to the king's bestowal of Wihtgar's fief on Richard of Clare, and of a king's free man in whom Richard's predecessor 'had absolutely nothing' – neither commendation nor service, presumably. Several times we are told who gave surety for a man's offence – the sheriff for a royal reeve's 'invasion'; Thurstan fitzGuy, where a church was 'in the king's hand' after appropriation by William of Bourneville. Again there appears to be the occasional 'duplicate' entry, e.g. those for Bricett and Eye.[1] But the entry for Cornard (448) which records its geld-liability and dimensions is, most unusually, in the *invasiones* section and not in the appropriate *breve*.

[1] Fols. 405b, 448b; 319b, 449b. In the first Eye entry there is wood for three swine, in the second for 13.

CHAPTER V

The Inquest

Unless specific instructions were issued to those who were ordered to conduct the Inquest in each province and shire, the determination of their starting-point must have been a matter for intensive consideration. The obvious solution would seem to be for them to make use of those lists of local geld-liability which must everywhere have been available: without such a record the difficult task of tax-collection would have been impossible to execute satisfactorily. On what principle these were drawn up we can have only limited ideas, except that they must have existed for each Hundred or group of Hundreds, the ultimate units of imposition and of contemporary collection also. They must have indicated at least the name by which each holding was known and that of the tenant, but how, if at all, the items were grouped is indeterminable. However, in practice the inquisitors may have started without any such lists. That they *were* conducting an Inquest seems to be confirmed by the use of the phrase *priusquam haec placita fierent* (Burnham, 99b).

THE METHOD OF CONDUCTING THE INQUEST

The procedure of the Inquest, so far as this can be deduced, has been brilliantly expounded by Galbraith. He reminds us of the vast number of persons 'who must have been summoned to attend on fixed dates according to a rigid timetable', and that to whatever extent Hundred and vill, from the nature of pre-Conquest organisation, must have entered into the procedure, 'the basic unit of the enquiry . . . was the manor', so that the Commissioners 'from first to last thought in terms of owners and of manors'. The initial formality seems to have been 'to identify each estate, to fix its ownership, and thus to produce a skeleton list of manors'. The laborious and complex business of establishing the facts, and the enormous number of conflicting claims, necessitating the hearing of a multitude of witnesses, naturally implies that the Commissioners could not themselves have been concerned with the bulk of the information to be found in Domesday Book. But 'we are almost driven to think that the Commissioners must have held their sessions with some sort of draft return before them'; surely 'a vast deal of preliminary lists, copies, and valuations . . . lie behind the engrossed originals of the Survey' and 'enormous labour had already been devoted to the ordering and presentation of the material'. Even the earliest surviving draft, the Exeter Domesday, must be 'no more than a rearranged – and perhaps expanded – fair copy of still earlier written records'.

The bulk of the statistical material could not possibly have been supplied at formal sessions; there was not time for such a method of procedure. Many of the questions asked in accordance with the terms of reference 'could only be answered by the sitting tenant of each manor' or by his agents, and the information must have been provided 'partly, no doubt, in writing, partly *viva voce* . . . to the "backroom staff" of the circuit Commissioners, for it was far too bulky to be handled in court'.[1] Ultimately all the relevant information secured had to be inscribed in the form in which we find it in the surviving texts.

With Galbraith's conclusions I have long been in perfect agreement. To them I would add only two tentative suggestions. The statement of Bishop Robert of Hereford shows that there were 'two eyres of the royal commissioners to prevent or minimize collusion and fraud'.[2] Could it be that the early stages of the Inquest made plain how much land was being held by no good title, and how much conflicting testimony was available on many problems, with the result that impartial Commissioners were despatched as the result of conviction that justice could never be done by local officials who must have organised or sanctioned so many illegalities? It would be pleasant to find that the idea of the Inquest originated well before

[1] Galbraith, *MDB*, *passim*, and especially pp. 37, 81, 63, 65, 108, 115, 38, 161, 78, 82.

[2] Galbraith: *MDB*, p. 52.

Christmas, 1085, and that what was really debated at the Gloucester Council was the volume of complaints and a means of settling them satisfactorily: this would enlarge the over-short period during which the Inquest is usually presumed to have been at work. Secondly, I should like to think that the inception of the idea was the construction of a record of *Terra Regis* only, again perhaps obtained prior to the Gloucester Council, inevitably extended to include all fiefs because even this showed the extent to which the royal rights were being infringed. The *breves* for the king's lands display a large number of tenurial and other offences committed by his barons. Thirty-four of the sokemen attached to the royal manor of Witham (1b) were in 1086 in the hands of seven barons; Geoffrey de Manneville had taken away a sokeman from Hatfield Broad Oak (2); Raymond Gerold and Ingelric had deprived Stanway (4b) of half a hide and eighteen acres.[1] Twenty-five sokemen and fourteen free men were lacking from Great Massingham (109b), and Godwine, a relative of Earl Ralf's, had appropriated Quidenham (127b); these are just a few of the losses suffered by the king.

It is indeed curious that throughout DB it is attempts to harmonise statements under *Terra Regis* with parallelisms elsewhere in the text which commonly produce the maximum of difficulty, rather as though the first belongs to a date rather earlier than that of the bulk of DB, and that it is here that we sometimes find mentioned property which should be adequately recorded therein but in fact is not.[2] But no compulsive evidence in favour of either suggestion is at present available.

THE INQUISITORS' INITIAL DIFFICULTIES

Consideration of geld-lists, if something of this sort was in fact used, would at once indicate how formidable a task confronted

[1] See also a long list of losses from Lawford (6).

[2] e.g. Barrington, Exon fol. *435b* (Exchequer 94bi), unmentioned under *Terra Regis*, though royal property; Cranmore (Exon *527*), not in either Exeter or Exchequer Domesday); Pentridge (77bi), *in manu regis* but placed in the Glastonbury *breve*; the impossibility of harmonising the Devon geld accounts with *Terra Regis* for the shire; Washingborough (337bi,2), royal property but not described under *Terra Regis*. A long list of such curiosities could be given.

the inquisitors. These may of course have been constructed on a basis which showed only what the officials were to think of as a 'manor'. It is not possible to state how many manors were in existence in 1086, for many entries which must represent *maneria* were not so styled, and often it is exceptionally difficult to determine where the material relative to a manor begins or ends (see p. 161). In Essex a little over 600 entries show that each deals with a single manor, but the actual number of manors in the county must have been much greater than this.

A better idea of the task may be obtained by considering the quantity of entries and sub-entries, since an enormous number of the former describe what would seem to be the demesne and the *terra villanorum* (the latter term is indeed not actually used in these shires), and then add one or more sub-entries concerned with land added to the manor or with the holdings of individuals or groups of free men and sokemen. They are divided thus:

Essex	1,264
Suffolk	2,481
Norfolk	2,784
	6,529

These figures do not include the boroughs or the land attached to churches, nor obviously duplicated entries. No two people would ever agree on an absolutely definitive figure.

'DUPLICATE' OR 'PARALLEL' ENTRIES

It might be thought that if geld-lists were the basis there should not have appeared any duplicate entries, save perhaps those originating from inadvertent inclusion among the *invasiones* sections when these had already been inscribed within the feudal *breves*. But a holding claimed, say, by Ely, but in the possession of Robert Malet, might well appear in the return by each; alternatively a clerk may have considered it to be a wise precaution to include it in both *breves*.[1] Galbraith claims that we cannot suppose that these are 'mere accidental repetitions drawn from a single written source', and would derive a

[1] If this was the reason for dual entries, the system was not regularly followed.

second appearance from revised manorial descriptions obtained from a further meeting of the Hundred where the initial statements seemed to demand reconsideration.[1]

The quantity of 'duplicate' entries may seem to be appreciable, but appears small in relation to their potential number. Every claim, every dispute, might have produced duplicate entries.[2]

A typical example is provided by two holdings at Cringleford (150b, 189). These appear first in Earl Alan's *breve*, where they are said to be held by Roger Bigot. They are recorded also in the *breve* for the latter, and in both the pre-Conquest tenants, assessments, bordars, half-team, meadow, value, and an eighth share of the mill, are the same. Sometimes it is not absolutely plain whether two entries refer to the same man or holding or not; in both the *breves* for Robert Malet and St Edmund we find, in each case at Westhorpe (309b, 370b), seven acres worth 14*d*., the holder in 1066 of which could not sell the land. At his first appearance he is a free man who was commended to Edric, at his second merely *homo*.

In some instances, though the entries clearly refer to the same holding, there are slight differences in the details; e.g. two acres of meadow in one and five in the other (*ii* and *v* are easily confused), and a personal name incorrectly repeated in one (Bradley, 397, 447b).

In the Essex text alone there appear to be at least forty parallel passages, about a score of which refer to appropriations from the large complex royal manors. Often the lesser entry shows where the holding concerned was; e.g. two portions of the royal manor of Havering were at Leyton, and 15 acres which had been lost to St Paul's from the manor of Little Warley were at Childerditch (fols. 2b, 3, 53, 85; 10b, 92b). Were we not able to discern parallelism, we might sometimes be deceived. Those 15 acres are at their first appearance said to be held by 'Tascelin', a priest, in whom we might not recognise the 'Saisselin' who on fol. 92b appears as holding in chief, but is not there styled *presbyter*.

[1] Galbraith: *MDB*, pp. 162–5.

[2] 'Duplicate' is a somewhat misleading term, for often the details and phraseology are by no means the same; 'parallel' is perhaps more accurate.

Again we find slight textual variations, as in the instance of a hide in Writtle (5b, 26). This had been 'of Harold's fee', but in 1086 belonged to the bishop of Hereford. In the earlier entry we learn also that Harold had given it to *presbyter ejus*. Could the connection possibly arise from the fact that Leofgar, Earl Harold's Mass-priest, became bishop of Hereford, or was this priest merely commended to him or attached to the abbey at Waltham with which he was associated?[1]

LAND WITH WHICH MORE THAN ONE SHIRE WAS CONCERNED

In each of the three counties there existed the complication that land physically in one shire was administratively in another, and that some vills consisted of land in more than one county. In consequence it had to be noted that there was more land belonging to Mendham, which straddles the county boundary, than that described on fol. 379b, but that this was *inbreviata in Norfulc*. There are six entries in the Suffolk text relating to this vill, and two in the Norfolk material which make no mention of the Suffolk land.[2]

While it was common for a berewick of a manor to be in a Hundred other than that in which the *caput* was, some manors even had berewicks in neighbouring shires. Of the sixty-four holdings in the Hundred of Holt, nineteen are components of manors whose headquarters are in villages other than those in which these nineteen lie. Six belong to the manor of Holt, and nine other manors are concerned, only two of which have their headquarters in Holt Hundred. West Acre (236) in Freebridge Hundred was a berewick of Necton in South Greenhoe. Harkstead in Suffolk was a berewick of the Essex manor of Brightlingsea, but was described in the Suffolk folios (286b). Hatfield Broad Oak, also in Essex, had three berewicks in Hertfordshire, and Great Chesterford and Newport three in Cambridgeshire (2, 3b).[3] An Ardleigh holding was attached to an unnamed Suffolk manor, but was considered to be in the

[1] For comments on Essex parallel entries, see *VCH: Essex*, i, pp. 410–11.

[2] Fols. 310b, 329b, 349, 355b, 368, 379b; 195b, 210b.

[3] They are described in the relevant texts, fols. 138a2, 189b2, 190ai *bis*.

Essex Hundred of Tendring (68).[1] The formidably divided vill of Bures included holdings in both the Essex Hundreds of Lexden and Hinckford, but one part of it is said to be 'in the county of Suffolk'. Bures, straddling the Stour river, appears in the Suffolk text also.[2] Nayland appears in both the Essex and Suffolk texts, as *Eiland(a)*; the Essex portion, south of the river, was in fact the Horkesleys (47, 401b).[3]

Some vills in the neighbourhood of the county boundary appear in both the Norfolk and Suffolk texts, e.g. Mendham, mentioned above, and Rushford.[4] One of the Mildenhall holdings appears in the Norfolk Domesday (263), though Mildenhall is in the Suffolk text also (288b, 392), and the town of Thetford included land in both the East Anglian shires.[5]

The arrangements governing Diss were extraordinary. It gave its name to a Norfolk Hundred, but appears in the Suffolk text under Hartismere Hundred; moreover, Burston in the former county is said to belong 'to Diss in Suffolk' (282, 114).

But the most curious arrangement is that affecting Rumburgh. No vill or manor of that name is described in the Suffolk Domesday, though it is said to have been one of Earl Ralf's manors, but some land ascribed to the Norfolk villages of Alburgh and Mundham is said to 'belong to Rumburgh', while 60 acres in Stone Street were included in its valuation, and some land in Elmham 'belonged to the church of Rumburgh' (149b, 176b; 292b, 298). It rather looks as if the clerks, conscious of the complexities, delayed entering the vill and ultimately forgot it altogether. Or did a clerk dealing with Suffolk think that, like the other entries, it would be dealt with under Norfolk?

Some of these anomalies may have been caused by landowners transferring land (and, as we shall see, manors) from

[1] Some Essex land belonged to the Kentish manor of Chalk (9ai); perhaps that is why the Kentish sheriff was concerned with the Essex manor of Childerditch.

[2] Fols. 39b, 40b, 84b; 83, 89; 360, 392, 421b, 435b.

[3] For further remarks on all the points listed above, see *VCH: Essex*, i, pp. 338, 408.

[4] Fols. 214 *bis*, 270b; 421.

[5] Some royal land at Thetford is said to be 'beyond the water, towards Norfolk', and another part 'towards Suffolk'.

one county to another as it best suited their administrative arrangements. The Exchequer Domesday frequently notes such alterations.[1]

THE USE OF THE HUNDRED AS THE PRIMARY UNIT

That within each shire the primary unit was the Hundred is plain. With occasional lapses, for every fief the name of the Hundred was included before the account of the first holding within it. Whether feudal returns, if these were furnished (p. 61), were also drawn up by Hundreds, or whether the clerks sorted their material by checking geld-lists against feudal returns, we cannot say. A probable method of procedure would seem to be for the geld-lists to be called over in an early open-court Inquest sitting, enabling those who had complaints to make to register their protests, about which evidence would later be called. Since the holdings known by the name of a single village may appear under the rubrics of more than one Hundred, the Hundred within which a holding was liable for geld would seem to have been the determining factor.

It does not seem likely, however, that the clerks who made the first draft had any form of Hundred-return or full list of manors in a Hundred available. If they had either before them, it is improbable that they would have spelt the name of a Hundred in so many different ways. Clackclose, for example, appears as *Clachelosa*, *Claclelosa*, *Clacheslosa*, *Clakeslosa*. If they were using an account of holdings in an individual fief which also indicated the relevant Hundred, as they well may have been, it is quite conceivable that they merely copied variant spellings provided by several authors. It appears, too, that groups of Hundreds were considered together, as in the south-western shires. Perhaps it proved a convenience to have the juries for a group available simultaneously. So the highly regular order of appearance of Hundreds in any *breve* would suggest.[2]

[1] See Finn: *The Domesday Inquest*, pp. 42–4.

[2] For this order see *VCH: Essex*, i, p. 409; *VCH: Norfolk*, ii, p. 4; and P. H. Sawyer: 'The "Original Returns" and "Domesday Book"' (*EHR*, lxx, 1955, p. 182).

In contrast to the scheme adopted in the south-western counties, where frequently, in large fiefs, several clerks are found inscribing in the first draft the record of the individual Hundred, it may be that here a single clerk or pair of clerks produced it.[1] The record for some Hundreds includes certain features not found in those of others. In a few Norfolk Hundreds teams are said to be *inter homines, inter omnes*, a phrase rarely used elsewhere.[2] In South Greenhoe Hundred, but only infrequently in others, much use is made of *quando recepit, quando invenit*. The quantity of carucates is omitted far more frequently in the Hundreds of Docking, Smethden (adjacent Hundreds), and South Greenhoe than elsewhere. But an intermittent use of the verb *manere*, not really commonly used, or highly infrequent statistics for *post*, might be due to a clerk's caprice or lapses. Again, in some Norfolk Hundreds sokemen greatly outnumber the free men, whereas in others the reverse is true. Vertically through the centre of the county, for example, there is a large group of Hundreds in which sokemen are predominant; North Greenhoe has 260 sokemen against only 54 free men. On the other hand, a compact block of Hundreds in the south-east, if Walsham, where the sokemen outnumbered the free men by something like eight to one, is excepted, has a preponderance of free men over sokemen. The Hundreds may have treated ascription differently, but still the disparities suggest that between free men and sokemen the differences cannot have been marked ones.

With very occasional exceptions, often confined to royal manors, we find that every or almost every entry in some Essex Hundreds places the plough-teams before the population, while in others population precedes plough-teams. The order of appearance is quite clearly a hundredal idiosyncrasy and must in some way derive from an order of questions or of inscription of the details.

In addition to the hundredal differences, there is one especially marked feature of the shires' varying treatment of their material. Judging by the results, and their absence from

[1] See Finn: *Domesday Studies: The* Liber Exoniensis, pp. 37–9.

[2] Hundreds of North Greenhoe, Eynesford, Earsham, Henstead, and Loddon. The last three adjoin, and with Diss formed one of the Inquest's groups of Hundreds.

the IE questionnaire, no useful instruction regarding the treatment of boroughs was issued. The account of Colchester, which ends the Essex text (104–7b), with its long lists of individual house property, is quite unlike that of the East Anglian towns. The description of the Norfolk boroughs was placed after the royal lands administered by the sheriff and before those in the custody of other *ministri* (116–19); Ipswich in Suffolk comes at the end of the account of *Terra Regis* (290, 290b), but is not self-contained, for references to it and to its half-Hundred appear on twelve folios.[1]

LAND WITH WHICH MORE THAN ONE HUNDRED WAS CONCERNED

Constantly we are told of land which is ascribed to one Hundred but which for some purposes is considered as being in a different Hundred. Sometimes what we might regard as the keystone of manorial organisation, the 'hall', *halla*, *aula*, of a manor was in a Hundred other than that to which the manor was ascribed.[2] Three of the four carucates of Ingham (364) were in Bradmere Hundred; the fourth, it is said, 'lies in another Hundred'. Peasenhall was a berewick of the manor of Knoddishall in Plomesgate Hundred, but was itself in a different Hundred (338b). It is common to find some of the demesne land of a manor to be in a vill other than that in which the *caput manerii* lay.[3] The *caput manerii* of Kettleburgh (293b) is mentioned; the manor appears to have possessed at least eleven components in other villages, listed on this and the succeeding folio. Two free men were attached to Hasketon in Carlford Hundred, but 'they dwelt in another Hundred' (315b). Desning (390) was responsible for 37*d*. of geld, but not in a single Hundred. Creeting All Saints in Bosmere lay in Creeting St Peter in Stow Hundred, and was valued there, yet Creeting St Peter was valued in a Creeting 'in another Hundred' (432b, 389). Many a holding was not valued in the Hundred in which the vill which

[1] Fols. 289, 304b, 378b, 382b, 392b, 393 *bis*, 402, 410, 411b, 421b, 427, 438.

[2] e.g. Fornham St Genevieve and Woolpit (363, 362b).

[3] e.g. 24 acres of the demesne of Eye were at Thrandeston (321); one acre of 'the demesne land of the hall of Creeting' lay in Stonham (350b).

gave the property its name lay, e.g. *Thiccebrom* in Wangford Hundred (327b). A berewick was often, but not invariably, valued in the manor to which it belonged, but frequently lay in a different Hundred, e.g. East Winch (125b) in Freebridge Hundred, which was a berewick of Sporle in South Greenhoe Hundred. Had the clerks seen from Hundred-lists that such complexities existed, and inquired for each manor if any needed to be recorded, or had all the warnings been volunteered by the actual suppliers of information?

THE VILL: AN UNSUITABLE INQUEST UNIT

Villa is a term not infrequently used, but it is doubtful whether it was one considered as having a precise meaning. Bury St Edmunds is styled a 'vill' on fol. 372, and so is the borough of Ipswich (421b). The Domesday vill, as Maitland pointed out, cannot have had much in the way of organisation or corporate activity.[1] Many a village is in DB represented by more than a score of entries and sub-entries, e.g. Bredfield, Blaxhall, Bungay, and Westerfield. Coddenham, including nine concerned with church land, is dealt with in thirty-three entries.[2]

Or consider the village of Sutton. Twenty-three entries refer to it, the 12-acre manor of fol. 318 being duplicated by that of fol. 387, and those for the 9+1 free men recorded in the Ely *breve* appearing in IE (H, pp. 178 and 162). Four are said to be 'manors'; the whole village, rated at 5 carucates 46½ acres, having been shared between 74½ free men. The recorded villager population amounts only to 2½ bordars, and the total value is only £4 18*s*. With the exception of a 34-acre holding inherited by Earl Alan, and that claimed by Ely, the whole was or had been in Malet hands, for William Malet when he died was seized of the holding which in 1086 was in the hands of Hervey de Bourges.

Though such holdings are recorded under the name of a single vill, they must surely often represent distinct settlements. Each of the two principal holdings at Wyken (421, 439b) for

[1] Maitland: *DBB*, p. 12.

[2] Fols. 285, 294b, 304b, 338, 352, 375, 383, 417, 422b, 434b, 436.

example, is styled a manor, and not only had been held by different men but had descended to different lords. A church is mentioned for each of the Ashfield holdings (367, 439), and it is logical to conclude that these represent the modern Great and Little Ashfield. The separation of five of the free men at Ixworth from the other twenty-five (438b), the recording of more than one manor here, and the different name-forms (*Gisworthan*, *Icsewrda*; 438b, 439b, 440, 447), also suggest separate settlements, a suggestion enhanced by the fact that while all were in Robert Blond's hands, St Edmund had registered a claim to the soke.

The reference on a single folio (236b) to *Wretham*, *in alio Wretham*, and *in alio Wretham*, of each of which there is a separate account, suggests three distinct settlements. Distinct settlements, too, are surely indicated when we hear of villages with a common name but carefully distinguished by the clerks, e.g. *Fachenham* (367b, 420b) and *Litla Fachenham* (367b), *Waldingefelda* (360, etc.) and *altera Walingafella* (416), *Bricceia* (30) and *Parva Bricceia* (93b), *Snareshella* (277b), and *alia Snareshella* (178), *in his duabus Meltonis* (204b).

Villages in the hands of a single owner are in a minority; the quantity and character of the entries and sub-entries argue forcibly that a minority, too, consisted of a single nucleated settlement.

Frequent variations in the orthography of villar names occur. This, as with the Hundred-names, must make us think that the clerks had no document before them of ICC type, in which the name of a vill would often appear once only. Hawkedon, for example, appears as *Hauocheduna*, *Auokeduna*, and *Hauokeduna* (348b, 390b *bis*, 397); Quarles as *Haerueles* (113) and *Gueruelei* (179); Ashill as *Essalei* (232b), and *Asscelea* (268). I am inclined to think that *Saibannis* (448) stands for Cavendish, *Kanauudis*(*c*) on fols. 392b, 426, 447b, 448, and 449.

That accounts of the individual village were not being used seems to be demonstrated by the frequent separation within the single *breve* of holdings bearing its name. On fols. 306b–7 six Blaxhall holdings are recorded, but of the dozen entries on these folios they come first, fourth, fifth, eighth, tenth, and twelfth.

ADDITIONAL COMPLICATIONS: GELD-COLLECTION AND MANORIAL DIMENSIONS

There was indeed no unit which would have produced an absence of problems, or only a minimum of these. From what has been said above, we can see why the manor and not the fief or the vill inevitably became the officials' initial unit, even though in East Anglia manorial organisation was frequently imprecise. Here, too, a further problem presented itself. It would seem that there were in every East Anglian Hundred a number of centres at which the geld had to be produced, and while the constituent components are now concealed from us, there seem to have been complexities in their composition additional to the fact that they were neither composed of geographically compact districts nor invariably in harmony with manorial arrangements (p. 110).

The information listed in the preface to the IE was, on the whole, supplied in full by those responsible. This questionnaire, curiously enough, does not ask for the assessment of holdings, though this information, or the amount for which geld was paid, is regularly given in Essex and in the Exchequer Domesday. But the Norfolk and Suffolk texts do not specifically mention either.[1] The IE questionnaire, too, does not ask for the number of ploughlands, and in vol. ii this is never given. As in most of the shires in vol. i, items unmentioned in the questionnaire, e.g. saltpans and vineyards, and also the demesne livestock, appear. These, on the evidence of the Exeter Domesday, we may think were indeed returned for every circuit.

But for Norfolk and Suffolk, though not for Essex, a further piece of information was usually furnished, the dimensions of those manors for which we are also given the number of pence they had to find for every pound that the Hundred contributed to the geld. Manorial or district dimensions appear with comparative rarity in the Exchequer text, and in the record of most of the circuits, never.[2]

[1] As Galbraith says (*MDB*, p. 62), 'these particulars were already well known to the authorities from the geld accounts'.

[2] See Finn: *An Introduction to Domesday Book*, pp. 85, 115, 171.

What these dimensions represented is quite impossible to determine. They cannot in any way be harmonised either with the number of carucates recorded or the geld-liability. The problems they represent are intensified by statements such as 'it renders geld in this Hundred and is measured in another' (Burnham Westgate, 237). Could the dimensions be those of some manorial feature unmentioned, or almost so, in the two relevant counties, e.g. pasture? It is suggestive that in the shires of the Exchequer Domesday for which linear dimensions are sometimes given pasture is mentioned only half a dozen times in all.

In one entry we are told that 'the measurement of the marshland is not known' (Marham, 212b), and the Essex text shows us that in that county the pasture for sheep was in the marshes.[1] It is in the entries for this vill, too, that it is noted that the land which Hugh de Montfort holds by exchange is measured in the Ely *breve*, a phrase which occurs elsewhere also (238, 205b). Such phrases do not occur in the Suffolk text, only in that of Norfolk. A curious phrase occurs in an entry for Southwold: *haec divisio a mari usque Hernesmua* (Yarmouth, 371b). Southwold was assessed at one carucate, and is said to be of 9×5 furlongs, but this does not enable us to delimit the area concerned.

Some of the statements are extremely detailed; they say that something is one league and $4\frac{1}{2}$ feet broad (Castle Acre, 160b), or 5 furlongs long by 4 furlongs 6 perches broad (Metton, 184). In Norfolk, with a single exception, dimensions in perches are confined to eastern Hundreds, while of the eleven instances in which miles are used, nine are to be found in South Greenhoe and the other two in Freebridge, both western Hundreds. These peculiarities may again indicate the use of information from Hundred-lists or -juries, since the fiefs in which they occur are extremely varied.

Sometimes it is stated that the extent of a holding is included in the measurement of another.[2] Slightly variant forms tell us

[1] For Essex pasture, see *VCH: Essex*, i, pp. 368–74. The few references to pasture in Norfolk and Suffolk are listed in *The Domesday Geography of England*, i, pp. 131 and 184.

[2] e.g. Rippon Hall (241b), Salthouse (223b).

that Foulden (114b) is measured in William of Warenne's land, that the dimensions of Bawdeswell (147b) are separate from those of Foxley, and of holdings at Snoring and Clipston and Kettlestone (168b) are 'measured above', probably in the dimensions of Barsham; Barsham itself is said to furnish 12*d.* of geld 'in the same measurements'. East Winch (207), where in 1086 there had been only free men and sokemen in a five-holding village, is 'in the measurement of Runcton'.

Now if the clerks were dependent on information supplied for the individual fief, whether written or through the mouths of its representatives, variety in the manner of its presentation, including the treatment of the head of a manor and its components, the order in which the items of information appeared, and the amount of detail furnished, would surely occur. Such variations are common in the texts of all three counties.[1] This then may make us wonder whether the reeve, the priest, and six villeins from every village, mentioned in the preface to the IE, really appeared before the Commissioners or their subordinates except to give information on troublesome points or to swear to the truth of what had been set down in the record.[2] They may have been required merely to furnish feudal officials with statistical information and estimates of measurements.

We should expect to find less discrepancies between DB and IE and FB if written sources were used to compile these than in fact we do, though IE and FB may sometimes have been corrected to a date beyond that of the Inquest. No doubt the clerks made mistakes in taking down and inscribing the information, and omitted some of the matter supplied, or else they did not notice or trouble themselves about incomplete answers to the stock questions, or about missing information. Variations in formulae, phraseology, and order of items within the individual *breve* could have been caused by the work being done by different clerks. Equally it could be caused by provision of the information by a number of reeves. The arrangement

[1] For some shires of the Exchequer Domesday the order in which the items appear is so regular that one might think that Inquest clerks had a stock set of questions, asked in accordance with a preconceived plan. But this feature might be due, in part, to a scientific re-ordering of material by Exchequer clerks.

[2] Such an oath may have been taken at a meeting of the Hundred-court.

of the *breviate* in IE (H, pp. 168–73) suggests that a number of manors had been grouped together for administrative purposes, and each group may have been supervised by a different reeve.

POSSIBILITY OF FEUDAL RETURNS

Against the opening of a number of fiefs in all three texts there are in the margins varying contractions: *f*, *f.r.*, *n.*, *n.f.*, *n.f.r.* It was suggested by Johnson that these indicated whether a landholder had or had not made a return for his fief; *fecit retornam.*[1] When the Norfolk and Suffolk instances are examined, the probability of this being the reason for their inclusion would seem to be considerable.[2] In these shires they never appear for the more powerful magnates, e.g. the earls or Robert Malet or Hugh de Montfort, for the major religious houses of Bury St Edmunds or Ely, or, with rare exceptions, for those who were or had been royal *ministri* and reeves or sheriffs. They are absent, for example, from the fiefs of Godric and of Northmann, of Haghne the king's reeve, of Ivo Taillebois, and of Robert Blond.[3] The sole exception is the fief of Peter de Valognes, but then he was not sheriff of this county, and for his Norfolk fief appears *n* (420b, 256). One oddity is that three landholders apparently produced a return for their Suffolk lands, but not for those in Norfolk.[4]

What appears in Essex, though differing slightly from the apparent Norfolk and Suffolk basis, does not really disturb these conclusions. Fiefs XXXIV–XLI, however, have against their headings the character *m*, not used in the other two counties.[5] None was inscribed for the fiefs of those who held much land in Essex, e.g. for fiefs XX–XXV, or for Hugh de Montfort,

[1] *VCH: Norfolk*, ii, p. 2.

[2] Galbraith, however, while he 'feels sure that this is the purpose of these notes', thinks that they are '*post factum* additions, made casually and occasionally' (*MDB*, p. 82).

[3] Fols. 201b, 437b, 269b, 244b, 438b. But *f* appears against Ulfketel's heading, fol. 270b.

[4] Robert fitzCorbucion (425b, 258b), Ralf of Limésy (428, 245), and Eudes fitzSpirewic (434, 245b).

[5] Could this stand for 'a return of manors' (or just their names), *f* representing 'the whole fief'?

Geoffrey de Manneville, or Robert Gernons. Only the smaller religious houses or those who did not hold much land in Essex (e.g. Bury St Edmunds) have *f* against the headings. From fief L to the end no character appears, and the only large Essex landholder against whom *n* appears is Ralf Baignard, for whom the character appears in Norfolk also. There is a curiosity in the Norfolk *breve* of Gilbert fitzRicher (XLII, fol. 263): the word *nichil* appears, and his solitary holding has the assessment missing.

Another oddity, assuming that these characters appeared in the first draft, is that they should have been transcribed in the fair copy. Still, it may have been felt that the information might prove useful.[1]

It is of course highly possible that those men with large local fiefs, many of whom were ultimately responsible for many of the illegalities recorded, did make returns, and that no indication of this was given because it was considered to be axiomatic that they should do so. The only really substantial baron other than those mentioned above who, once the symbols begin to appear in the text, is said not to have made a return, is Ralf Baignard for his Norfolk fief (247b).

All this naturally raises a query. How, if they made no return, was information obtained about the Suffolk lands of, e.g. Walter the deacon (426) and Humfrey the chamberlain (433), or those of Tofig (? a previous sheriff) in Norfolk (264b)? It also poses the problem as to whether a return was made for the smaller fiefs against which no symbol appears.[2] It would seem reasonable to assume that returns were probably made even when no appropriate symbol appears. The fiefs for which no return seems to have been supplied are for the most part small, and it would be no very difficult matter to pick out the appropriate holdings from hundredal lists. But this further suggests that the 'return' implied by these symbols cannot be held to have included statistical information; possibly it furnished merely the names of estates and of previous holders and information about their tenurial arrangements, and perhaps assessments. The occasional use in the text of the term

[1] If transcription occurred, some may have been missed.

[2] e.g. that of Isaac in Norfolk (264). Against his Suffolk fief (437b), *f* appears.

breve might then sometimes refer, not to the Domesday record of a fief, but to a feudal return. So might the statement of Robert Malet referring to the day on which his land was *inbreviatus* (276b).

The possibility of feudal returns is enhanced by the arrangement of the lands of St Edmund. In all the western Suffolk Hundreds except Lackford the slaves are recorded after the teams, in the remainder with the villeins and bordars and before the teams. The only holdings styled manors are those which have no sub-tenants, i.e. the demesne land, and no manorial holding is said to be 'in' somewhere. It is too in the *breve* for this fief that we find the use of the unusual formula *semper arant* n *carucae* instead of the customary *tunc* y *carucae*, *modo* z.

CHAPTER VI

The Final Product: the Manuscript

The initial conception of the origin of Domesday Book for the eastern counties was altogether incorrect, and unfortunately it coloured the views of commentators for many years after its formulation. J. H. Round confidently proclaimed that it was the section of DB made first in time, on a feudal basis, from the 'original returns' which he visualised as all consisting of villar descriptions of the character of those of the ICC.[1] In his opinion the authorities, on receiving it, appreciated that a record for the remaining counties on the same lines and on the same scale would prove to be impossibly voluminous, and in dealing with these they accordingly omitted some aspects of the information supplied, and contracted the formulae, in order to reduce the returns to manageable length. He further suggested that they were, however, unwilling to have 'Little Domesday' reduced on the same system, since so much work in producing it had already been done.

This hypothesis remained unchallenged for almost half a century, but in 1942 Galbraith produced compelling reasons for its total rejection.[2] So far from being the first portion of DB to be made, it was indeed probably the last fair copy of the record of a circuit to become available to those who had the task of converting the provincial drafts into the form of the Exchequer text. Either it became available so late that work on the Exchequer text had ceased, as it may have done on the death of the Conqueror, or the complexities of East Anglian tenures may have suggested that to convert the draft to Exchequer form was an impossible or over-ambitious task.

[1] Round: *FE*, p. 141.

[2] Galbraith: 'The Making of Domesday Book' (*EHR*, lvii, 1942, pp. 161–77), and *MDB*, pp. 3–6, 30–1.

THE GATHERINGS AND THEIR ARRANGEMENT

Consideration of the text makes it obvious that 'Little Domesday' is a fair copy, and the validity of this judgment is enhanced when it is compared with the earliest surviving circuit draft, the *Liber Exoniensis*. Though the text of the eastern circuit is by no means adequately arranged, and its errors are numerous, it is a distinct improvement on what we know as the Exeter Domesday. The proportion of postscripts and *marginalia* is very much higher in the latter than in the former, strongly suggesting that it belongs to a time earlier in the work of the Inquest than that of vol. ii. Moreover, vol. ii is appreciably tidier and better arranged, as a fair copy should be, and there is less spatial subdivision of the material; the later quaternions all contain on the whole a greater number of fiefs than those of the Exeter Domesday, as though the copying clerks could at any moment have more of their material available. In addition, the accounts of many short fiefs run from one quaternion to another, whereas in the Exeter Domesday only those too long for the single gathering do so. This again suggests that here we have an improved copy of an earlier draft. Finally, there is an index for each county, to construct which apparently defeated the Exeter clerks, or else they thought that to include one for a mere draft would be premature. Possibly, however, these indexes were the last part of the work to be done, for they reproduce the often illogical order in which the fiefs appear.

Probably the consistency of the form of the gatherings and of the rulings is in itself adequate indication that vol. ii is a fair copy. The horizontal rulings are almost invariably uniform within the individual gathering; more than two-thirds of the quaternions contain 24 lines to the page. Vertical rulings, though the use of single lines greatly exceeds that of double ones, also change in form only with the gathering, and may sometimes be the mark of a change of copyist.[1] All but nine of the 57 gatherings are quaternions of eight leaves; a state of affairs very different from that of the Exeter Domesday, where

[1] For further information regarding the rulings, see *Domesday Re-Bound* (H.M.S.O.), pp. 42–3.

the gatherings are commonly of a number of pages appropriate to the length of one or more *breves*. There is good reason for the design of most of the gatherings which are not of four doubled sheets; e.g. the addition of a leaf (103) to complete the Essex *invasiones*, or the use of three sheets (275–80) at the end of the Norfolk text, where a fourth folio would have been entirely blank.[1]

Some of these irregularities may have been caused by the need to rectify copying errors. Fol. 35 is the recto of an inserted leaf; 34b and 35b may well have been written by a single hand, but it does not seem to be that of 35. The matter had to be written larger than usual to fill all the 22 lines. There is one two-leaf gathering, occurring in the middle of a *breve*. Fol. 181 displays no change of script, but 182 is in a different hand, and again is somewhat sprawling and generously spaced so as to fill the folio. Fols. 183–4 form a two-leaf prefatory section, immediately followed by a six-leaf gathering; fols. 275–80 also form a six-leaf gathering, completing the Norfolk text. The gatherings beginning on fols. 191 and 225 are each of ten leaves, and in the latter fols. 229–30 form a two-leaf insert in a different script, and with 40 lines to the page, whereas the rest of the gathering has 24.

A further indication that vol. ii is a fair copy is to be seen in the short deleted lists of fiefs which appear on fols. 9, 17, 292, and 372. Their presence was completely misinterpreted by Round.[2] They represent the fiefs to be found in the relevant gatherings of the draft from which the fair copy was made; they may also have appeared in the draft, though this seems unlikely, since they now occur only four times. They are rather an indication of what fiefs were to be inscribed in the gatherings they preface, and probably were deleted when the quaternions were collected and indexed in the order in which these now appear, since they were then of no further profit. Unless the space occupied by the relevant fiefs in the first draft was less

[1] Fol. 103 was in fact an unnecessary addition, for fol. 108 is blank. But perhaps the clerk had then no means of knowing how many folios the account of Colchester would occupy.

[2] *VCH: Essex*, i, p. 413; Round: *FE*, p. 141, n. 2; see Galbraith: *MDB*, pp. 182–3.

than that used in the fair copy, only the first set of *breves* would have gone into an eight-leaf gathering.[1] The list on fol. 372 does not agree with the *breves* which follow it; Ramsey Abbey is omitted, and it is intriguing that the account of this seems to be in a hand not that of the rest of fol. 378b, and that the opening of the Ramsey *breve* in Norfolk (215) also seems to suggest a change of clerk.

THE MAKE-UP OF THE GATHERINGS

The collection and ordering of the gatherings was, however, executed with less efficiency than was displayed by the makers of the Exchequer text. Essex is rational enough, with the ecclesiastical fiefs preceding those of the earls and greater barons, but in the East Anglian shires the *breves* for a number of lay magnates are placed before those of bishops and abbeys.

In Norfolk the *breve* of Bishop Odo immediately follows that of his half-brother the king, but Odo is not so placed in Suffolk. Then, in Norfolk, come the earls and three leading magnates, not, as in Essex and the Exchequer volume, the ecclesiastical fiefs. While Bishop William of Thetford's fief does indeed follow those of these magnates, the Church *breves* are inconsecutive; those of Godric and Hermer de Ferrières interrupt them. Suffolk, except for Odo's fief, follows the Norfolk pattern as far as fief VII; then come certain lesser barons, with the ecclesiastical *breves* coming together as XIV–XXIV. It is curious that these flaws were not corrected when collation and the indexing were done. The system could have been deliberate, though this hardly seems possible; if it was not, there must remain a suggestion that the gatherings, with the index folios still blank, had been bound in some fashion before the indexes were constructed. It has been said that the special rulings of the indexes are 'a noteworthy mark of orderly procedure', but the Norfolk list of *breves*, owing to the differences in the size of the writing in the right-hand columns, has a somewhat untidy appearance.[2] It is again curious that Norfolk should have been

[1] The other sections occupy respectively 17 folios and two lines, 21 folios, and 17 folios and five lines. But in the first draft their extents may have been different.

[2] *Domesday Re-Bound*, p. 43.

made to follow Essex in the binding when Suffolk was the county logically to come next.

THE CLERKS AND THEIR WORK

In the making of a fair copy a fresh clerk might take over at any point.[1] Equally, if the draft to be copied was complete when copying began, a number of clerks could each be given one or more quaternions to reproduce. Thus we should expect changes of handwiting to occur when a new gathering begins, or rather where we feel that they may have begun in the draft being copied. But of this there are very few signs, which may also make us think that when the fair copy was begun the draft to be copied was not yet a complete text. A change of script at the opening of a *breve* does, however, sometimes manifest itself in the Norfolk section; e.g. at fols. 153b, 157, 173, 191, 209, 235. The last five of these are the initial leaves of gatherings.

The Bury St Edmunds Suffolk *breve* (356b–70) certainly appears to display a change of clerk, possibly one whose script is not to be found earlier. Again it is suggestive that its final folio, the account of the town of Bury itself, begins a fresh gathering, at the foot of which is one of the two deleted lists of Suffolk fiefs. Obviously fol. 370 was not the first leaf of a gathering in the draft.

It is highly doubtful if the Ramsey Abbey *breve* (fol. 278b) was written by the clerk who wrote the rest of the folio or the following one. The Bury and Ely *breves*, too, have their peculiarities: the heading of each is prefaced *Suthfulc*. Though *in Suthfulc*, *Sutfulc*, *Sudfulch*, is to be be found at the end of the headings for four other *breves*, and *de Sudfulc* in that for the king's free men, its use is uncommon, and it might have been automatically copied from appearances in the draft.[2] In the Exeter Domesday, in which matter relating to each group of counties had not been separated, the name of the relevant shire naturally appeared in the cross-headings prefacing each *breve*. Just possibly, then, the Norfolk and Suffolk material was not

[1] *Domesday Re-Bound*, p. 45.

[2] Fols. 356b, 381b; 291, 304, 401, 402b.

completely separated in the draft, but the copying clerks, conscious that their texts related to the single shire (and perhaps knowing that its name would appear on each verso), normally omitted its name.

Another curiosity is on fol. 427b. Lines 16–21, which cover three entries for Carlford Hundred, are in a script smaller than that of the rest of the folio, and the horizontal ruling is ignored for ll. 16–20. It looks rather as if it was originally omitted by accident, and crammed into the space commonly and fortunately left at the close of each *breve*: obviously the fief numbered XLII, which immediately follows, was already inscribed.

Fol. 354b is also intriguing. Its five lines which conclude the *breve* of Roger Bigot may be in a script other than that of preceding folios. It ends with an unrubricated *H(undred) de Carleforda*, which is possibly an error, though we do not know if Roger had any property here which might have been omitted. But it is suggestive that fol. 346, within the same gathering, which follows, begins with the same words, as though the clerk, even though the words preface a different *breve*, could see what was coming, and did not delete the earlier example.

At fol. 334b occurs the first Suffolk instance of the prolongation of the vertical of a character, usually *f* or *s* or *d*, at the first line of a folio. It is a feature to be found in Norfolk also, and is extremely intermittent. Accordingly it may not be the mark of the individual clerk: it might derive from boredom with a monotonous task and deliberate introduction of a legitimate variation.[1] But its occurrence in Norfolk does rather suggest clerical idiosyncrasy; it makes an isolated appearance on fol. 109b, but recurs throughout the *breves* of William of Warenne (160–72b) and those from fols. 196–204.

It might be thought that the differences in the formation of the 'gallows' which frequently preface entries could serve to determine a change of writer. But often the clerk, on completing an entry, might then inscribe his own form of prefatory sign, while the entry following it might be written by a different copyist: so the Exeter Domesday text would suggest. Some of

[1] In Suffolk this seems to occur most frequently towards the end of the text. Five characters in the initial line of fol. 435, and four on 436b, were so treated.

these 'gallows' are in vol. ii most decorative, though less so than some in the Exeter Domesday.[1]

On almost every possible occasion the clerks left a space between the end of one *breve* and the beginning of the next. Obviously this was done with intent; the clerks or their superiors feared that though they were copying a text they might still be obliged to make postscriptal additions. This was a wise precaution; it is plain that an addition, referred to above, was made in a space on fol. 427b previously unfilled, the conclusion of which adjoins the opening of fief XLI. Again, fief LXVII was not begun until the third line of the ruled guides; the clerk had left what space he could after the ending of the previous fief on fol. 440, the final entry of which, filling the page and turning over the line, might indeed be postscriptal. Less space than usual was left between the fiefs towards the close of the Norfolk text, but earlier the application of the deliberate policy can be seen, e.g. beginning Bishop Odo's *breve* a few lines low on fol. 142 because 141b was completely filled; this was done also on fol. 247. There is no space on fol. 225b between fiefs XIX and XX.

THE COPYISTS' DEFICIENCIES

The mistakes made by the clerks which cursory inspection of the text displays are very few. *Marginalia* are infrequent, though they do occasionally occur, e.g. on fols. 158b, 326, 362b. In each instance it looks as if a limited amount of matter was inadvertently omitted; the postscripts are not of the type common in the Exeter Domesday, the need for many of which seems to have been the inclusion of matter probably unavailable at the time of initial inscription of a folio. Two entries for the fief of Ralf fitzHagon were indeed originally wrongly inscribed in the *breve* of Roger fitzRenard (fol. 267). These, however, were cancelled, and the matter included in its correct place on fol. 270.

The initial omissions repaired by interlineation, on the other

[1] e.g. on fols. 20b (before fief XIV), 68b (before fief XXIII) – these are the sole examples in Essex of decorative signs; for ornate initial characters, see fols. 128, l. 6, 140, l. 20, 165, l. 4, 205b, l. 12, 285b, l. 5, 291b, l. 17, 303, l. 11, 316, l. 1.

hand, are extremely numerous. So is the correction of words or figures which were seen to be mistakes. There are few signs, as there are in the Exeter Domesday, that the text was checked, but there is ample evidence of hurried and careless copying. The undeleted repetition of words and phrases is extremely marked.

Matter which is obviously postscriptal, so far as can be judged, is comparatively infrequent. When its inclusion was necessary, it was usually found possible to insert it in a partially blank line, or to interline it in whole or in part. The number of carucates was omitted on a number of occasions, and detailed study of the text discloses a number of similar lapses.

Imprecision is common. Frequently it is extremely difficult to determine just where the account of a complex manor which included holdings in several named vills ends, especially as often no indication is given whether a holding counted as a 'manor' or not. Often the final information about a manor, e.g. the dimensions and the geld it had to produce, are widely separated from the main account of it. Some entries which obviously describe the individual manor do not say that it is a manor with which they are dealing. Again, the clerk could set down that 60 acres in Bungay (301) *sunt de i manerio quod tenet rex* without specifying the manor to which they belonged. The wife of Blæcmann is described as the 'man' of Stigand (Sibton, 313), yet the commendation of females commonly appears.

Either the copying clerks or those who produced the original notes were altogether ignorant of English place- and proper names, and were totally careless about uniformity. A clerk could in small compass or even a single entry write *Masincham* and *Marsinghara* (109b, 151) for Massingham, both *Hedenaham* and *Ennaham* for Hedenham (152b), and *Thrandestuna* and *Strandestuna* for Thrandeston (310). Between fols. 310b and 316b, which all seem to be one writer's work, Laxfield appears in nine different forms, including *Lassefelda*, *Laxafella*, and *Laxefelda*.

However, even allowing for the fact that it is a fair copy, the Essex Domesday was excellently executed. Mistakes, other than orthographic ones, average only one per folio. The worst feature is the frequent omission of the names of the Hundreds, but of seventy-five instances of this, fifty-eight come between fols. 90–103b, when the work was perhaps being unduly hurried. The clerk may have thought that names were largely unnecessary in the *invasiones* section. Fourteen pieces of information had to be added as postscripts. This may sometimes not have been the clerk's fault, but caused by the late arrival of details or Inquest decisions. Obviously postscriptal work can be seen on fols. 5 (ll. 13, 18–19), 18 (l. 4), 41 (between ll. 3–4), 49 (l. 19, recording Ely's claim to Roding), 100b (after l. 22), fol. 101 (ll. 10–11). There are forty-two interlineations and sixteen corrections. Occasionally quantities were omitted, or the wrong category of livestock detailed. Sheep were recorded instead of goats at Rochford (44b); the sheep had already been noted, and *vice versa* (Totham, 54). The second entry of bordars for Springfield (75) should obviously have been slaves. Fifty bordars seem far too many for a smallish Finchingfield manor (35), and one would be a more probable quantity. So do forty for a ten-acre holding at Halstead (101b).

Changes of script might seem to be frequent, e.g. the Colchester entry on fol. 11, which might be postscriptal and fill a space originally left before the cross-head *Feudum Episcopi Lundoniensis*. It looks as if boroughs were always considered late by the Commissioners, and this passage may not have been available when the rest of the folio was written. Fol. 99 and the final seven lines of fol. 101 seem to display changes of script, but it is often impossible to determine whether consecutive passages are in different hands or not. The hand which wrote the account of Colchester (104–7b) does not seem to occur elsewhere, and this is probably late work. Some changes of script may be indicated by differences in the colour of the ink, e.g. the last two entries on fol. 25, the sentence beginning at l. 13 on fol. 25b, at the change of Hundred on fol. 26b, l. 11, and the postscript on fol. 31 at l. 14. But we can never be sure that this is not the result of discontinuous work or of substitution over an erasure, or of changes in the colour of the ink, and fading.

It is only when one reads through a text as a whole that the very large number of errors made in copying can be appreciated. In the thirty-two folios which contain the Suffolk lands of St Edmund, for example, it was found necessary on thirty occasions to interline matter originally omitted. Some of these interlineations, e.g. that on fol. 370, look as if they are additions, made by an alien hand, on checking the work. There are occasional erasures and errors through which the clerk has drawn his pen, and, as inevitably happened frequently in making a copy, words and phrases wrongly repeated, e.g. *in elemosina* (363, l. 7). There is the orthographic error of *breuita* for *beruita*, *tenet* should have been *tenent*, and *valet*, *valuit*.[1] The number of villeins at Coney Weston and of men's teams at Beccles were, among other information, omitted; the 75 carucates at Stansfield should have been acres (fols. 365, 369b, 371b). A long initial omission had to be added marginally to fol. 362b, and the cramped appearance here of ll. 18–22 almost looks as if the succeeding lines had been inscribed before these were written. At the head of fol. 370b the name of the holding was incorrectly made to precede that of the Hundred. In all there are some sixty initial errors in the *breve*, only half a dozen of which were corrected.

But the early folios of the Suffolk text are particularly well executed, and neatly inscribed. The script may change at fol. 288, which is a leaf inserted into a quaternion, at which point the record of Stigand's former lands now in the king's hands begins; if so, the original hand may return at l. 17. On the verso, with the change to Lackford Hundred, the script becomes larger, and this hand probably continues until the entry for Risbridge Hundred on fol. 289b appears. Fols. 289–90 are a double insert, and it is possible that the account of the borough of Ipswich which occupies 290, 290b, is in yet another script.[2] The hand which produced the opening folios of the text returns at fol. 291, and it also wrote the exotic account of the dispute between the bishop of Bayeux and the mother of Robert Malet (fol. 450).

It is, however, extremely difficult to determine just where a change of writer may have occurred in vol. ii. We cannot make use of variations of formulae or order of items or orthography,

[1] Fols. 363, l. 22; 365, l. 9; 357, l. 25.

[2] The width of the text on these folios is different from that of the preceding and succeeding matter.

for the clerks of the fair copy may have reproduced exactly what their predecessors of the first draft wrote down, and we have no means of knowing how the latter may have divided their work. Even though we are studying a fair copy, we do not know that the work was continuous. Indeed, it often looks as if the clerk may change when the Hundred changes, as so frequently occurs in that first draft of the Exeter Domesday. But this aspect, if inscription was not continuous, could result from the use of a different pen or ink, or the physical condition of the clerk. We should expect work done at the beginning of the day or shift to be neater than that produced under conditions of fatigue or bad light. It is not impossible, too, that this fair copy was begun as soon as sufficient of the draft text was available. This, since we know that our Exeter Domesday text was checked, might imply that not all the individual *breve* could be inscribed in a single operation, and this too would make for real or apparent changes of handwriting.[1]

Since the Exeter Domesday was not rubricated, it may be that it was not intended to decorate 'Little Domesday' until it was agreed that the surviving MS. should be its final form. Rubrication is here inextensive and rather perfunctorily executed. The name of the county was, however, added to the left-hand pages, and some indication on the facing folios of the tenant whose land they concerned, often in a highly contracted form.[2]

We do not know what material DB should contain but which was omitted by the clerks. We can but suspect, on the evidence of collation of the Exeter and Exchequer Domesdays, and of the 'satellite surveys' with the latter, that there must be a number of omissions.[3] Not infrequently the form of an entry suggests that some statistical information is missing. Collation with IE and FB, as we shall see in the chapters which follow, shows many discrepancies between the texts, and accordingly it is of importance to try to determine to what extent these had a common source. But we can use only what the material furnishes, and in

[1] For the manner in which the Exeter Domesday seems to have been constructed, see Finn: *Domesday Studies: The* Liber Exoniensis, pp. 30–47.

[2] For further details, see *Domesday Re-Bound*, pp. 45–6.

[3] Collation with, e.g. the *Domesday Monachorum*, 'Evesham A', and the Bath cartulary, displays some of these.

consequence must make statistical observations and deductions only with appreciable reservations.

VOCABULARY AND PHRASEOLOGY

Some of the formulae of vol. ii are not always easy to interpret. It is usually clear from the sense that an entry beginning *in eadem* records men and teams and other things which are not counted in the main entry. But *ex his* or *de istis*, or *de hac terra*, can present problems, but the occasional use of *de his liberis hominibus et de hac terra* shows that the details of the sub-entry are not supplementary to those of the main entry, especially where the value is said to be *in eodem pretio*, or some similar phrase; e.g. Great Ashfield (367).

There has been disagreement regarding the interpretation of the phrase *alii* (or *plures*) *tenent*, with variations. Ellis was of the opinion that it denoted other 'unrecorded agricultural tenantry', but Maitland was surely right when he expressed his belief that it implied 'not that there are in this vill other enumerated tillers of the soil, but that the vill is divided between several tenants-in-chief'.[1] Certainly in Thingoe Hundred it is never used unless someone besides St Edmund is holding in chief. Probably it was derived from the 'original returns', or a schedule of manors, where it could be seen that a vill was divided: it is suggestive that at Horringer (356b, 391b), where besides St Edmund only a sokeman of Wihtgar's had held land, *alius* is used. However, though *alius* is used at Euston (367b), there seem to be eleven free men, with two lords, also in the vill (444b). At Ingham (364) it is noted *sed rex ibi tenet*, but no Ingham holding appears under *Terra Regis*.[2]

There are, however, instances where the phrase is used and no other holding in the vill is to be found in DB. Instances include Troston and Honington (366b), Grensvill (217), Brook (210), Hardley (217b), Chedburgh (384b), Brightwell, and Kingston

[1] Ellis: *A General Introduction to Domesday Book*, ii, p. 491; Maitland: *DBB*, p. 20, n. 1; see also *VCH: Suffolk*, i, p. 359.

[2] One holding here, however, was Roger of Poitou's, and this may have been considered to be 'in the king's hand', for DB sometimes suggests that he was in temporary disfavour (p. 78).

(386). Woolpit (363b) appears only once in DB. But, as has been suggested on p. 55, those concerned may have lived in one vill but been attached to a manor in a vill of a different name. The 'hall' of Woolpit, we have just seen, was in a Hundred in which Woolpit did not lie, and there were forty free men in this berewick of St Edmund; possibly, then, the reference to others holding here is to the manor of Thurston, which may have had many components. The phrase *plures ibi participantur* (with variants), which sometimes occurs, also suggests this interpretation.[1]

Libera terra is one of the technical phrases on which the texts throw no light. It is repeatedly found in connection with the land appropriated to village and urban churches; apparently it was considered necessary to note where relevant that a church was *sine* or *absque terra*. But the phrase also occurs where it seems that the land does not belong to a church. At Foston (213) Ulfketel the man of Hermer de Ferrières claimed that the land was *libera*, though Ely said that it was the abbey's and 'lay in the church'. Ulfketel's argument seems to have been that it was available to be granted by the king. This may also be the interpretation as regards the 'free land' at Mulbarton (188), though it had been held under Roger Bigot's predecessor and Roger was in fact holding it. Again, a holding of 60 acres at Burlingham (199b) is contrasted with one with 40 which 'belong to a certain church'. But an alternative explanation could be that such land was held 'freely'; that its owner could dispose of it. For we find a sokeman of St Benet of Holme as having given a carucate of 'free land' to the abbey and still holding it of the abbey.[2] But four acres of 'free land' at Whittingham (349) seem to be contrasted with Wulfric's $1\frac{1}{2}$ carucates, and we are told nothing about the 16 acres at Henley (437b) which belong to the manor of Hemingstone and are valued there.[3] The term could possibly, like *quieta terra*, imply

[1] Kenton (326), Loudham (388b), Ringsfield (283), Willingham (407).

[2] Similar circumstances are noted at Mellis (419), where a free woman gave land to St Edmund, and Smallburgh (219b). On the other hand, the three acres at Willingham (407) could not be sold or given.

[3] Other instances of the occurrence of the term without its ascription to a church are Aldeburgh (316), Minsmer (314), Bixley (176), Hutton (20b), and Lammarsh (99b).

'geld-free', and virtually equate with *in elemosina*. In the south-west land so held does not seem to have been liable for geld.

Thrice in the Essex folios, and twice in those for Norfolk, roman figures were written in small script, below the text, at the end of five *breves*. The fiefs concerned are those of Holy Trinity, Canterbury (15), the abbey of Bury St Edmunds (20), Walter the deacon (87), Ranulf brother of Ilger (261), and Tofig (265). The figures are obviously connected with the number of hides or carucates at which the holdings were assessed, though correspondence with the Domesday text is often far from perfect. On fol. 15 they do balance, though the three final estates are totalled as seven hides instead of being recorded as two, four, and one, as in DB. In the St Edmund list Latton (2½ hides) and Alphamstone (half-hide) are given as a single figure of three hides, and there comes next a figure of *iii* unrepresented in DB; otherwise the figures agree.[1] But there are only slight likenesses on fol. 87, while the Domesday figures total 26 hides and the others 27. Those for Ranulf represent only three sub-entries in the *breve*: the 70 acres of the 7½ free men at Walcot (*lxv* at the foot of the folio), the 120 acres of the sixteen sokemen at Ridlington, and the 90 acres of four other Walcot free men. It is impossible to harmonise the statements for Tofig's lands, though the 155 acres at Swainsthorpe and the 30 at Newton Flotman correspond.

Why these additions, which from their appearance were probably inscribed later than the *breves*, appear only five times, and for such a curious selection of fiefs, is a mystery. They may, however, have been included while the Inquest was still being held, and indicate a method of summing up statistics for the purpose of producing Summaries of fiefs such as appear in IE and *Lib. Exon.*

The text of DB for every shire differs in some respects from that of any other, and many phrases and technical terms are of limited occurrence. We can never be certain about their origins, whether they derive from the individual's report for the fief or the Hundred, or from the idiosyncrasies of the clerks and a desire to vary formulistic monotony. Thus in vol.

[1] But the 36 acres at Colne are ignored, and so are the acres in the 2 hides less 15 acres of Little Waltham.

ii we occasionally find terms and phrases which are commonplace in the Exeter Domesday but rare here, e.g. *mansio* or *quod vocatur.*[1] Instead of being styled *comes*, an earl is occasionally *consul*, just as we sometimes find *consulatus* for *scira*, or *comitatus* (e.g. on fols. 20b, 14, 91). Some words, all rarely used in DB, occur but once or twice, e.g. *mercenarius* (266), *summagium* (178), *homagium* (172), *solidarius* (252), *solidati* (418), *casatus* (354), *catallus* (133). Only twice is a heriot, or a grange, mentioned (119, 445b; 290, 294). The odd phrase makes a solitary appearance: 'between the wood and the field' (294b), 'when Earl Ralf was powerful' (211b). Three times and no more is King Edward described as *rex gloriosus*, though the adjective is applied to St Edmund, king and martyr, also.[2]

Any attempt to establish the occurrences of the individual clerk is accordingly almost certain to end in frustration. The use of *viiii* for *ix* or ÷ for *est*, or the varying orthography or contraction for *carucata*, cannot be limited to one or more clerks, and the same is true of the intermittent use of *aula* or *halla*. We cannot tell whether, when we find *franci* or *franci homines*, this is a clerk's synonym for *liberi homines* or whether it was 'Frenchmen' he was recording, though we may well think that holding *libere* is the same thing as being a *liber homo.*[3]

One puzzle is presented here which recurs in DB. In Essex and Suffolk there is no hint that Roger of Poitou might have fallen into disfavour with the king, and had been deprived of his estates. But in Norfolk the heading to his *breve* reads 'the land which had belonged to Roger of Poitou' (243). The entry for his manor of Boxted (349) speaks of 'when Roger relinquished it'.[4] It is then just possible that this reflects an incident occurring after his Essex and Suffolk lands were inscribed, but before his Norfolk fief was dealt with.

[1] e.g. on fols. 99b, 415, 448b; 4b, 7, 50, 65, 67b, 119b.

[2] Fols. 415b, 416b, 425 (different fiefs, but all from Babergh Hundred); 372.

[3] Fols. 42, 43 *bis*, 44b, 70; 46, 48, 52, 35b, 38, 58.

[4] For the varying treatment of his land in DB, see Galbraith: *MDB*, pp. 187–8.

PART II

Satellite Surveys

CHAPTER VII

The Inquisitio Eliensis

The collection of documents known, though not so titled in the MS., as the *Inquisitio Eliensis*, is one of the comparatively few means we possess of checking to a limited extent the accuracy and completeness of a large portion of DB. Three copies, each apparently made late in the twelfth century, are in existence, known as MS. A (British Museum: Cotton Tiberius A.vi) and MSS. B and C (Trinity College, Cambridge: O.2.41 and O.2.1), Ellis printed MS. A, but only as far as fol. 66, in the *Additamenta* (vol. iv) section of the 'Record' edition of DB, in 1816. Sixty years later Hamilton produced a text of MS. A which gave also the variant readings of the other two MSS., together with that of the ICC, which in the original accompanies MS. A.[1]

The choice for these versions of MS. A, which Round stigmatised as 'the worst of the three transcripts', was an unfortunate one, for the best of the three texts is MS. B, not MS. C, as Round thought. Round, however, was correct in considering that A was derived from B: Hamilton wrongly thought that B was the origin of C. MS. C, however, includes matter which is now absent from A and B, if it ever was included therein.

Hamilton's is not a critical edition, and its text is sometimes inaccurate: moreover, MS. C fols. 207b2–9b2 (H, pp. 184–9) do not, as his division of the text would suggest, form a separate section.[2] However, as to give folio references for all three MSS. is inconvenient, references here will be to the pages of Hamilton's printed text, prefaced H, except where they occur in MS. C only.

[1] N. E. S. A. Hamilton (ed.): *Inquisitio Comitatus Cantabrigiensis, subjicitur Inquisitio Eliensis* (London, 1876).

[2] For further information on all the above points, see Finn: 'The *Inquisitio Eliensis* Re-considered' (*EHR*, lxxv, 1960, pp. 385–409).

THE ORIGIN OF THE 'INQUISITIO ELIENSIS'

The three MS. must have had a common ultimate origin, for the differences between the texts are in no way substantial and seem largely to be due to the individual idiosyncrasies and errors of the copying clerks. Its main source, as regards the eastern counties, can only have been a preliminary draft of what later became vol. ii of Domesday Book. One passage which indicates this is its inclusion of an account of Bergh Apton, absent from the Ely *breve* in DB vol. ii, in which the manor is credited to Godric.[1] It is plain that before the first draft of vol. ii was constructed the material on which it was based, supplied so far as the Ely *breve* was concerned largely by the abbey's officials, was substantially revised and re-ordered. The order of entries sometimes differs, while both DB and IE omit matter to be found in one or the other text.[2] Thus collation of IE with DB really tells us very little except as regards information which the Domesday clerks did not reproduce.

The ultimate source of the IE was probably not the actual documents at the disposal of the Inquest officials, unless the Ely authorities managed to recover their original material, but some form of copy thereof, which we may call Q. Certainly it was not, as Round thought, the return to the royal writ of 1086 instructing Lanfranc to inquire further into Ely's losses of lands and rights.[3] But the origin in part of the surviving IE may be slightly different. It is certainly conceivable that, as Galbraith has suggested, 'the I.E., in the form in which we know it, is a return demanded by Ranulf Flambard in 1093, when Abbot Symeon died and the possessions of the abbey were taken into the king's hands'.[4] If so, the draft made for the Domesday Inquest may well have been revised to bring it up to date, and any such revision would make collation with DB of still less moment.

[1] DB fol. 215; H, p. 136.

[2] Examples are given in my article referred to above.

[3] *FE*, pp. 133–5; H, pp. xxi, xxvii; Blake, p. 206. For the evidence which contradicts Round's theory, see E. Miller: 'The Ely Land Pleas in the Reign of William I' (*EHR*, xlii, 1947, pp. 438–56).

[4] Galbraith: *MDB*, p. 141.

THE ARRANGEMENT OF THE 'INQUISITIO ELIENSIS'

The long Cambridgeshire section of the IE is arranged solely by Hundreds; the Hertfordshire and Huntingdonshire entries are very few, but seem to be grouped on the same principle. But the material for the three shires which composed the eastern circuit is arranged differently. The demesne manors and those which Ely claimed or in which she had sub-tenants each forms a separate group, though there are occasional misplacements of entries. In Suffolk alone the demesne manors are placed in the later of the two sections for each shire. The order of entries is largely on a hundredal basis, but is not always the same as that of DB.[1]

The IE text does not reproduce everything which is to be found in DB, nor are its statistics invariably identical with those of the Inquest clerks.[2] On the other hand, it does furnish some information which is absent from DB. Thus it tells us the geld-liability and dimensions of *Apeltuna* (fol. 203, H, p. 141), which DB does not. At the end of the Norfolk section (H, pp. 136–7) it records certain churches which are unmentioned in the Ely *breve* in DB. DB sometimes gives the names of pre-Conquest tenants when IE does not, but the reverse is more frequently to be found.[3] There are occasional differences regarding the situation of holdings; e.g. DB (417b) sites 12 acres at Clopton, but the IE, doubtless correctly, places them *in Caisned* (H, p. 150), which presumably was dependent on Clopton. It tells us that its holding at Tivetshall (H, p. 136) was part of the abbey's manor of Pulham, which DB does not (215).

But the absence of frequent inexplicable discrepancies, and the close similarity of arrangement, of the order of the items, and of unusual phraseology and vocabulary, make a common ultimate origin for IE and DB certain. Striking examples of the

[1] DB wrongly has Henstead Hundred where IE gives Earsham (fol. 214b, H, p. 135).

[2] e.g. IE omits the livestock at High Easter (fol. 60; H, p. 127), and says that there were always three demesne teams at Marham where DB has four *tunc* (fol. 212b, H, p. 130). In the same entry its '40 perches' are in DB 'one furlong'. These are merely isolated examples.

[3] e.g. Leofwine 'cilt' at Wickham Market; Ælfric and Edwin at Norbury (fols. 373b, 353; H, pp. 146, 148).

last can be seen, e.g. in the Foston, Bawsey, Rixworth, and Benham entries.[1] The unexpected presence of entries recording meadow in the Schedule (irrelevantly, one would think), as in DB and IE, is equally suggestive.

THE SUMMARIES OF THE 'INQUISITIO ELIENSIS'

The inclusion in the IE of Summaries for the lands in each county, giving statistics for the demesne estates and those of the military tenants (H, pp, 121–4), certainly suggests revision or supplementation of the drafts, since they include statements as to the extent to which total manorial values had appreciated during Symeon's supremacy. This last item of information could hardly derive from a document drawn up in 1086. A similar Summary appears in the *Liber Exoniensis* for the lands of Glastonbury Abbey (fols. *173*, *527b–8*), and shows the increase in value during the rule of Abbot Thurstan. This may have originated on a similar occasion, Thurstan's exile to Caen, which occurred before 1086. Summaries of the same type are to be found elsewhere in the *Liber Exoniensis* and in the Exchequer text, but these do not seem to be of a special character.[2]

Collation of any Summary with DB displays frequent close similarities of statistics, but also occasional material differences, and the reason for the discrepancies between DB and IE might well be slight revision of Q and consequent changes in the figures between 1086 and 1093. For example, the Ely demesne manors in Essex have one hide, one demesne team, and two villeins more in the Summary than in DB.[3] The total absence of slaves from the Huntingdonshire Domesday and their inclusion in the IE Summary is not necessarily evidence of revision, for they may well have appeared in Ely's original Inquest draft material.

All that can profitably be said of the Norfolk and Suffolk

[1] DB fols. 213, 387b, 212b, 213b; H, pp. 130, 161, 137, 133. The inclusion in each text of *plures ibi tenent* (e.g. fols. 303, 386 *bis*; H, p. 160 *ter*), and the coupling of Feltwell with Thetford (fol. 136; H, p. 138), also suggest common origins.

[2] For the lands of St Petrock and of a few laymen, and on 381a2.

[3] One of these villeins may be the priest at Roding (fol. 19; H, p. 126), not separately recorded in the Summary. Miscopying probably caused the 24 slaves of DB to become 44 in the Summary.

Summaries is that the totals of the statistics from these and from the IE do not greatly differ.[1] But how to categorise the IE entries (H, pp. 130–6), whether as demesne land or held by *milites* or sokemen, is a virtually insoluble problem. The Norfolk Summary speaks of fifteen demesne manors and of nine held by *milites*; only a dozen IE entries describe the holdings as manors. In IE the demesne lands are not completely consecutive; they are interrupted by Lynn (H, p. 131) and then by Benham, which, though styled a manor, was held of the abbey by William d'Écouis, and a dozen entries where laymen hold are interrupted by six which seem to be demesne land. The biggest discrepancy is in the number of bordars, where the Summary notes 391 in all and what would seem to be the relevant IE entries only 271: the difference seems to come on the demesne manors. The statement in IE (H, p. 136) giving the value of 'all we have in Norfolk' as £100 8*s*. does not agree with the IE figures for the entries preceding it: the demesne has a total value of £107 12*s*. 6*d*. and the land of the *milites* and their sokemen of £16 2*s*. 8*d*. The Summary gives instead of these last figures £105 7*s*. 6*d*. and £12 10*s*. All we can say is that, for most categories, totalling all the entries does not display major discrepancies between IE and Summaries. For example, for Norfolk the total of teams is 124½ in IE, and 122½ in the Summary; in each 59 Suffolk slaves are recorded.

The clerk who produced these Summaries either grouped the IE entries in a fashion differing from that of the MS., and perhaps omitted some sub-entries, or was working on material which was not that of the time of DB. The figures in DB and IE differ so little that we cannot assign the source of the latter to a time greatly different from that of the Inquest.

THE 'BREVIATE' AND 'NOMINA VILLARUM'

The IE contains two further sections peculiar to itself. The first is a statistical abstract for the demesne manors (H, pp. 168–73), to which Round gave the name of the *breviate*, and which he thought was specially compiled for inclusion in the

[1] It seems reasonable to calculate on the basis of IE rather than of DB.

IE, together with the section headed in MS. B *Nomina Villarum* (H, pp. 174–5). The first gives, for what it thinks of as the demesne manors, the numbers of the demesne and of the villagers' teams, and of the villeins, bordars, and slaves. The second gives only villagers' teams.

In many ways the arrangement is quite unlike that of an Inquest product. The shires and manors appear on the whole in IE order, but not all the manors in a county come together. After every few entries, the totals for the group of those above are given, not always correctly. It looks as if the manors must have been grouped according to some common factor, perhaps administration of each group by a single reeve. The preface indeed says *et hec distinguuntur sicut prepositi tenent uniusquisque preposituram suam* (H, p. 168). Mention of *Holewelle* and *Taterugge*, places unrecorded in IE or DB, suggest either omission from Q or post-Inquest development.[1]

The number of demesne manors is slightly greater than that of the Summary, and there is not perfect coincidence between the manors said to be in demesne in the IE and the lists here, or between those of *breviate* and *Nomina Villarum*. Roding, for example, appears in neither of these lists, though it is a demesne manor in DB and IE (fol. 19, H, p. 126), but, as the texts show, already virtually lost to the abbey. Strethall, in DB and IE a berewick of the manor of Littlebury (fol. 19, H, p. 126), is here treated as a demesne manor. In 1086 Hugh de Bernières was holding this, formerly thegnland, under the abbot, and may have given up his tenancy during the following years.

The statistics are largely in accordance with those of DB and IE, though there are occasional differences which could be due either to changes or to miscopying. In some instances the Q-clerk (if the matter was in Q) wrote down the figure for *tunc*, not *modo*, and mis-totalled a group; errors which the IE clerks reproduced. The figures should be those of DB, since in the preface they are said to be *quos modo habent secundum breves regis*, e.g. both *breviate* and *Nomina Villarum* give Northwold five men's teams; these were omitted from IE (H, p. 132), but DB (213b) gives five *tunc*, three *modo*.

[1] MS. B only, fol. 268 (H, p. 175).

THE SCHEDULE OF CLAIMS

This unique section (H, pp. 175–89) can legitimately be described as a 'schedule of claims', for in the main it reproduces the material of which the IE says *has terras calumpniatur abbas de Ely secundum breves regis*; in other words, Domesday Book. It should surely be considered as a single document, for where we have a text only in MS. C, it runs straight on to the final items of A and B, and the only usurper mentioned in both, (H, pp. 175–85 and 184–9, hereinafter C1 and C2) is Roger Bigot, though it is true that property with which he was concerned appears in both parts. The entries are grouped according to landholders, not by shires, but the order of appearance is very much as it is in the IE. The section is untitled, but in the text found only in MS. C (C3) it is frequently stated that reference is to land which someone has 'taken from' or 'invaded against' the Church. There is also a reference to William of Warenne's possession of Ely estates 'after the lands of the abbey were sworn to'. Probably this refers to the Domesday Inquest, though it might relate to one of the previous inquiries into Ely's losses of land and rights.

It is a condensed set of statements; as a rule we are told only how much Ely land the usurper is holding, and where, sometimes without any detail whatever, sometimes noting whether the estate is of the demesne or thegnland or sokeland: there is no sub-classification, as in the Summaries. Typical entries are, for example,

H, p. 180 Willelmus de Escodies tenet in Nordfulc in Beneham ii carucatas thainland.

186 Hec abstulit Hugo de Monteforte – Nechtune pro manerio.

187 Hec tulit de ecclesia Eudo dapifer – in Brethenham i sochemannum.

Sometimes the total value of a group of estates is given, and quite frequently how many acres of meadow there are – why this should have been specially recorded would be difficult to determine.

The number of properties which appear more than once is appreciable. In C1 we have a long list of the holdings of Hamo de St Clair, who is unmentioned in DB or IE. In C2 these appear again, but as 'invasions' by Roger Bigot.[1] In DB they are to be found in the *breve* of Odo of Bayeux, as are Roger's Suffolk 'invasions'.[2] Perhaps Roger, as sheriff of East Anglia, had the custody of Odo's local lands after his imprisonment.

While the resemblance between these entries appearing in both C1 and C2 is considerable, there are also striking differences. The first Kenton entry in C1 is not in C2, nor is the final entry of this section of C1. Every other entry is in C2, but some of the differences are worth recording.

H, p. 182 (C1)	In Wickham the land of a free man, Leofwine *child* (for *cilt*), of 25 acres. And under the same Leofwine four free men of 7 acres.
p. 188 (C2)	Again in Wickham six free men of 32 acres, and one team.
p. 146 (IE)	In Wickham a free man, Leofwine *child*, commended to St Audrey, of 25 acres. Then one team, now one. . . .
DB, fol. 373b	In Wickham R. Bigot (has) one free man, commended to St Audrey, of 25 acres, and under him four free men (with) 7 acres. Then one team, now a half. . . . This Ralf de Savigny holds of Roger Bigot of the fee of the bishop of Bayeux.

H, p. 182 (C1)	And in Charsfield the land of Leofric and Ælfwold of 7 acres, and in the same vill the land of eight sokemen, of 3 carucates of land.
188 (C2)	Further, in Charsfield, eight free men; 3 carucates of land. In the same, 7 carucates [*sic*].

[1] H, pp. 182–3, 188. Had Roger been instructed to grant or lease them to Hamo after 1082 or 1086?

[2] H, p. 188, fols. 373–7. Sihtric, who appears in C2 (H, p. 181) does not appear in the relevant DB or IE entries; fols. 383b, 385b; H, pp. 156, 158.

152 (IE) In the same vill (Charsfield) Leofric and Ælfwold, two sokemen, who could not sell their land; 7 acres; and in the same vill three free men semi-commended to St Audrey, and five men commended to St Audrey; 3 carucates of land. This Roger Bigot holds of the bishop of Bayeux.

DB fol. 373b In Charsfield Roger Bigot holds fourteen free men; one carucate of land, and Ralf de Savigny holds of him, and 13 acres. Three and a half were commended to St Audrey and Edric of Laxfield . . . the others were commended only to the abbot. In the same, two sokemen of S. Audrey; 7 acres.

If Q had survived, perhaps we could trace what produced these textual differences.

The very numerous parallel entries in DB and IE, and in the Schedule, together with the differences of information they manifest, are intriguing. Their presence in DB is accountable, for information about the holdings concerned may have been supplied by both *de facto* and *de jure* holder, and this might produce statistical or other differences. Thus about a dozen properties claimed by Ely appear in DB both in the Ely *breve* and that of Robert Malet, e.g. the entry for Sutton (fols. 318, 387; H, pp. 162, 178).

One of the most curious features is the appearance in DB of a holding in a *breve* which is not that of the landholder to whom it is credited in the Schedule. Nine of those the Schedule ascribes to Hervey de Bourges are in his Domesday *breve*, but the early ones are in that of Ely Abbey, presumably because Hervey appears to have come to an agreement with the abbot about his tenure of them.[1]

Sometimes a source of contention occurs twice in the Schedule. The bishop of Evreux had obtained a holding at Loudham; in DB it is recorded in the account of his fief, and naturally, as Ely claimed it, it is in the IE, but in the Schedule

[1] DB fols. 441–3b, 383–8b; H, pp. 179–80.

it is not only among the bishop's invasions but in those of Roger Bigot also.[1] Perhaps the presence of so many duplications in material relating to Roger Bigot is because he, as sheriff, had authorised or acquiesced in these illegalities.

It is possible that the Schedules conceal changes in tenancy or leases of which DB also tells us nothing. There is a writ of King William's ordering Richard fitzGilbert to surrender Broxted to Ely.[2] The IE does not mention Richard in connection with this manor; it is Eudes fitzHerbert who has deprived the abbey of some of its land (H, p. 128), but DB (fol. 50) says that 'Richard' is holding it of Eudes. Either text could be in error, or Richard, conscious of his invasion and anxious to avoid trouble, sold it to Eudes and then leased it.

Some DB passages which we should certainly expect to find in the Schedule are not therein. A 22½-acre holding at Horswold is twice recorded in DB, in the Ely *breve* and in that of Roger d'Auberville.[3] But it is not in the Schedule, perhaps because while Roger seems to have acquired it illegally, he was in 1086 holding it of the abbot by order of the bishop of Coutances, who must have found in favour of Ely's claim at one of the pleas over which he presided.

The abbey, with the Hundred-jury's testimony to support it, laid claim to Fambridge, which was being held of the king by Reginald the crossbowman (fol. 97b, H, p. 128), but it is unmentioned in the Schedule. So is Hugh of Beurda's Livermere manor and also about a score of entries in DB and the main IE text which we might expect to find therein.[4]

Equally the Schedule includes passages which we should expect to find in DB and IE but do not. Many of these refer to properties in the hands of Roger Bigot; thrice the holdings of three free men seem to be missing from Earl Alan's *breve*.[5] In

[1] Fol. 388b; H, pp. 146, 189. IE and Schedule are more informative than DB; they tell us that these 20 acres were actually at Wickham, a few miles from Loudham.

[2] Davis: *Reg.*, no. 155, p. 43.

[3] Fols. 383, 404b.

[4] e.g. Chillesford, Wetheringsett (fols. 296b, 384b; H, pp. 148, 166).

[5] Debach, Charsfield, and Sharpstone: only the first of these is in the IE (H, pp. 148, 185).

eight entries and sub-entries in the *breve* of Earl Hugh (fols. 298b, 299, 302b) there is mention in some that Ely had the commendation of some of the T.R.E. tenants, and in all that she had the soke.[1] None of these appears in the IE or in the Schedule. For this there might be two reasons: (*a*) soke by itself conferred no right to tenure of the land in chief, (*b*) in five of the instances Ely is said to have only half the soke, the earl having the remainder, though she had all the soke of a free man at Winston.

There are not a few entries which suggest that they might well have appeared in IE or Schedule, e.g. that for Ringshall (336b), where the named free men had been commended to Ely, though the soke was the king's and the earl's. *Tusemera* (418) was of Ely's demesne, held by Saxo *pro suis solidatis*; in 1086 Ralf of Savigny held it of Ralf Peverel, but it is unmentioned in IE or Schedule. Yet an almost similar circumstance, at Charsfield (fol. 343b), is in both IE and Schedules (H, pp. 152; 183, 188). It may be that the abbey did not trouble itself about these mostly unimportant properties, that they were for some reason often omitted from IE and Schedules, or that recovery had been effected, though ignored in DB. It is of course possible that DB, IE main text, and Schedule do not all refer to exactly the same moment in time, but clerical lapses in such work are only to be expected.

The Schedule occasionally combines material kept distinct in DB and IE, e.g. it converts two free men with 10 acres and a free woman with 60 into three free men with 70 acres. Similar treatment was accorded the free men at *Potesfort* which immediately follows this passage.[2]

In the early part of the Schedule of claims the total value of a baron's illegal acquisitions is often given; it is significant that the totals as a rule come very close to those of DB and IE. The thirty holdings of Hervey de Bourges in the Schedule are said to be worth £12 14*s*. The value of one is omitted from DB and IE, and there the total is 10*s*. 8*d*. less, or the highly probable figure of eight *orae* at 16*d*. each.

[1] e.g. the *Manuuic*, Framsden, and Helmingham entries.

[2] Rendlesham (fol. 443b; H, pp. 148, 180): DB has a small error here.

THE 'PLACITUM' OF 1071–5

MS. C (IE fols. 210b–3b; H, pp. 192–5) is the only one to include a 'schedule' of Ely grievances (C3) which seem to have been the subject, at least in part, of the plea held some time between 1071 and 1075.[1] When the original of this schedule was drawn up, we cannot say, but it must have been at a date well anterior to the Domesday Inquest, for it speaks of men who were dead well before this began, e.g. Lisois de Moustières. The copy we now possess must have been compiled or edited at a date later than February, 1072, for it refers to the death of Stigand (C3 fol. 213a; H, p. 195).

Sometimes its text is in perfect correspondence with IE, DB, and C1 and C2, which suggests that in the intervening years Ely failed to recover the lands she then claimed. C3 (fol. 211a; H, p. 193) says that Lisois holds 2 hides 30 acres of the demesne of Rattlesden; C2 (fol. 208b2; H, p. 187) naturally credits Eudes *dapifer* with them, and IE and DB (fols. 19, 51; H, p. 126) agree with C2.

Occasionally it looks as if, during the period, some usurpers had enlarged their previous possessions at Ely's expense. A *miles* called Wihenoc is said to have half the demesne vill called Oxwick; in the IE Rainald fitzIvo holds it of the abbot, where previously he had held it of the king (DB fol. 214; H, p. 134). Wihenoc, a Breton, is frequently said to have 'invaded' lands, and presumably shared Earl Ralf's fall, after which Rainald fitzIvo obtained his lands; in DB we find him in possession of Caldecote (231b) 'because Wihenoc occupied it'.

C3 (fol. 212a; H, p. 194) says that Abbot Baldwin has fifteen sokemen and Robert of Mortain 'six men of soke' at Drinkstone. IE and DB (H, p. 142; DB fol. 291), however, mention an Ely free man here with one carucate of whom St Edmund had the soke, and C2 (H, p. 189; DB fol. 209b) gives Robert one carucate.

C3 does not seem to have been carefully prepared. Under the Norfolk heading is an entry for Brandon (fol. 213a; H, p. 195), but the reference to the six sokemen of Lisois shows that this

[1] For a brief discussion of this, see Round: *FE*, pp. 459–61; 'Ely and her despoilers'.

should have been included in the Suffolk section: here and at Lakenheath (DB fol. 403; H, p. 142) Eudes, his successor in 1086, had six Ely sokemen. Suffolk entries precede those for Norfolk, but after the final entry for the latter county we go back to Suffolk for a final string of notes beginning with the manor of Chedburgh (fol. 213a; H, p. 195). The Norfolk entries, too, begin with an entry for the vill of *Uuefsted* (fol. 212b; H, p. 194), which is apparently unmentioned in IE or DB in such a form.[1]

What C3 does give us is unique mention of the customary services due from the sokemen on certain manors (e.g. Southbourne: fol. 211a; H, p. 193), and of the appropriation by a number of barons of the sokeright Ely should have in her 5½ Hundreds, to which one of King William's writs refers (Davis: *Reg.*, no. 157, p. 43 – see also fol. 213a; H, p. 195), Godric the steward's tenure of Bergh Apton, and the king's tenure of Methwold and Croxton, 'which are rightfully demesne vills of the monastery of Ely'.

Apart from the occupation by others of Ely demesne land, the main concern of C3 seems to be with the loss of the services in a large number of villages, and with the loss of sokeright over the inhabitants of villages within the 5½ Hundreds of Ely.

The monotony of this type of entry is occasionally broken by mention of other grievances, e.g. Ralf de Savigny's appropriation of the woodland and crops and meadows at Wetheringsett (DB fol. 384b; H, p. 166), where he has one of the manor's four carucates, and, finally, a note of a villager (*rusticus*) who absconded with nineteen sheep, five swine, and three *animalia* (fol. 213b; H, p. 195). One wonders how he managed to conduct this cavalcade and escape detection! Or does the passage merely imply that he was 'bound to the soil' of Bergh Apton, and should not have become Godric's dependant when this vill passed into his hands?

THE RECOVERY OF ELY LANDS

But documents of the period other than the IE show that Ely's ceaseless complaints and litigation had not been without effect.

[1] It does not seem to be Whepstead or Wherstead, but might be Westfield (145b).

Lisois de Moustières had acknowledged the abbey's right to a holding partly in Lakenheath and partly in Brandon; however, Lisois had retained it, and his successor Eudes fitzHerbert still held it in 1086.[1] A writ of King William's, probably of 1082, orders Hugh de Montfort to surrender Barham. This manor is not mentioned in the Schedule relating to the 1071–5 plea, but Ely recovered it, for in both DB and IE she is said to be holding it in demesne.[2] Another writ, similarly dated, states that the abbot is to have his forfeited house in Norwich. Neither DB nor IE records its temporary loss, so presumably it was restored well before 1086.[3]

Yet another writ requires those who have possessed themselves of the abbey thegnlands and sokelands to return them if they cannot establish a right to them, or to make what arrangements with the abbot regarding them they can.[4] Some land, as DB and IE record, had been recovered at the plea at which the bishop of Coutances was present.[5] It may have been as a result of this same plea that we find a number of passages noting that while the lay usurper had previously held *de rege*, in chief, or even *de dono regis*, in 1086, if he still held the estate, he did so 'under' or 'of' or 'by respite of' the abbot.[6] Westerfield had been returned to Ely 'by order of the king', while in respect of a Blaxhall holding William d'Émalleville; Robert Malet's tenant, had 'come to an agreement with the abbot'.[7] A dependant of the abbey of Bury St Edmunds had at least acknowledged that he 'owed service to the Saint', who must be Audrey, not Edmund.[8]

[1] Fol. 403; H, pp. 142, 187.

[2] Davis: *Reg.*, no. 156, p. 43; DB fol. 383b; H, p. 159.

[3] Davis: *Reg.*, no. 153, p. 42; IE fol. 117; H, pp. xix–xx, 135.

[4] Davis: *Reg.*, no. 155, p. 43; H, p. xviii.

[5] e.g. fols. 214b, 383 *bis*, 404b; H, pp. 135, 157 *bis*, 158.

[6] e.g. Norton, Saham, Wingfield, Trimley, and Kembrook; fols. 214, 385 *bis*; H, pp. 133, 156 *bis*, 158, 159.

[7] DB fols. 383b, 307; H, pp. 159, 179.

[8] Rattlesden, DB fol. 381b; H, pp. 153–4. This is an interesting entry, for he had held the estate 'so long as the abbey shall be in the king's hand' (*dum abbatia esset in manu regis*). This can hardly refer to a vacancy prior to that occasioned by the death of Abbot Theodwine, and thus, though Symeon was appointed abbot in 1081, it looks as if he was not consecrated until 1086 or slightly before, which is rather what the documents of the *Liber Eliensis* addressed to Lanfranc suggest.

EVALUATION OF THE 'INQUISITIO ELIENSIS'

We cannot with certainty say that the IE furnishes us with material altogether supplementary to that of DB, for, as we have seen, it may have been edited and slightly improved and altered a few years after the Inquest was over. Nor can we be sure that when its statistics disagree slightly with those of DB they must be more accurate because they are presumably purely of Ely provenance. But occasional passages in its text do provide us with information additional to that of DB, and the Schedule enables us to see, without laboriously searching both texts, what a vast amount of time must have been devoted at the Inquest and earlier to considering Ely's numerous grievances.

CHAPTER VIII

The Feudal Book of Baldwin, Abbot of Bury St Edmunds

Cartularies of Bury St Edmunds make frequent reference to the 'Black Book', and fortunately this twelfth-century compilation, which includes the 'Feudal Book', has survived. It has been edited by Professor D. C. Douglas.[1] The MS. includes 102 royal charters and writs covering the period 1066–1189 and 130 charters of the Bury abbots for the same period, but here we shall principally be dealing with those sections (fols. 124–43b) which have a direct relationship with DB.

These sections are three in number, and consist of

(*a*) a text highly similar to, and largely in the same order as, the entries for the Abbey fief in DB for Norfolk and Suffolk (fols. 124–31b);[2]
(*b*) the relevant matter rearranged, not by Hundreds as in DB, but according to the sub-tenant concerned (fols. 132–4b);
(*c*) Lists of peasant tenants, with the amount of their taxable holdings and the sums payable to the abbey (fols. 135–43b); incomplete and ending abruptly.

Douglas gave the dating limits for the execution of the work as 7 September, 1087 and 4 January, 1098.[3]

For all their close resemblance to DB, §§(*a*) and (*b*) certainly were not derived therefrom. They include matter which is not to be found in DB, and in particular the circumstances under

[1] Cambridge University Library MS. MM.iv.19. Here references to the folios of the Feudal Book will be prefaced FB, and to the pages of Douglas's edition and commentary (*Feudal Documents from the Abbey of Bury St Edmunds*: Oxford, 1932) *FD*.

[2] There are two Essex entries (in §*b*), but none for the other counties in which the abbey held land. This suggests that the author(s) of FB were working from documents whose arrangement coincided with that of the circuits and sub-circuits of the Inquest.

[3] *FD*, pp. xlviii–xlvix. But Lennard: *Rural England*, p. 359, suggests March, 1119, as the terminal date, and that FB may not have been compiled either by or for Abbot Baldwin.

which certain manors were transferred to the abbey by Beorhtwulf Leofmærson (fols. 124b, 125b, 126b). Douglas's conclusion was that §(*a*) represents 'a survey independent of the completed Domesday and which embodies the results of an enquiry completed after the Domesday Inquest'.[1]

The possibility of the construction by the greater ecclesiastical houses of private surveys of their lands in connection with the Domesday Inquest has long been apparent. The decision to hold that Inquest may indeed well have been their inspiration. The Glastonbury *breves* in both the Somerset Domesdays are so unlike the general run of the texts that we can only think that they were in part derived from a survey supplementary to or independent of the requirements of the royal Commissioners. It may be that the source of the Feudal Book was a survey intended to be not only of private value but also in a sense the abbey's official 'return' to the *legati regis*. If so, it was probably much fuller than the document surviving in the Feudal Book. Some portions the Inquest clerks would consider to be immaterial to their purpose, and would thus omit. They, with their task so urgent, had no room for that long description of Beorhtwulf's gifts which occupies an entire half-folio of the Feudal Book. But the bulk of the contents of §(*a*) is to be found in DB, and it is reasonable to suppose that something very like the text of FB was the source of the relevant Domesday text.

§(a) THE DEMESNE MANORS

This section describes itself as an account of St Edmund's demesne manors and of the lands of his tenants which they held at the time that King William caused the 'description of the whole of England' to be made and also on the day of his death. This phrase suggests that we need not expect the information exactly to correspond with that of DB; in an interval from early 1086 to late 1087 there may well have been changes.

The Norfolk section exactly follows the structure of DB. Towards its close it develops a tendency to omission and inaccuracy; it includes neither the Heckingham nor the second

[1] *FD*, p. lxvii. The evidence for the impossibility of derivation from DB is set out on pp. l–lvii.

Hales entry on DB fol. 212b, and ignores the relevant matter in the *invasiones* section on fols. 274, 275b. Throughout slaves are consistently omitted, and there are over a score of other material omissions, notably of the existence of sub-tenants, and of the villagers in the holdings of free men and sokemen. But it corresponds so closely with the information of DB that we can only presume a common source.[1]

In part the Suffolk material bears no close resemblance to that of DB. While within each Hundred the villages appear very largely in the Domesday order, the section opens with those Hundreds which were peculiarly St Edmund's. But the omissions are considerable. Somerton and Melling in Babergh Hundred are missing, and the five villages in Bosmere, Claydon, Plomesgate, and Wilford, as are one in Carlford and two in Loes Hundreds. Hacheston, in DB under Loes Hundred, is here placed in that of Carlford. The discrepancies with the Domesday figures are far more frequent than in the Norfolk section, and the number of omissions greater; in thirty instances the bordars on the free men's and sokemen's holdings do not appear.

The Domesday *breve*, though outwardly ill-arranged, is in a sense more logical than the structure of FB. The former has six holdings in Hartismere Hundred (360b–1) separated from those at Stoke Ash and Wyverstone (370), which are immediately followed by thirty-three which are noted marginally as being 'of the fee of St Edmund' (370–1); these last, presumably, are minor holdings which had been added since the Conquest to the abbey lands. FB omits Wyverstone and nineteen of these thirty-three. In all they are of only 180 (?geld) acres, and were perhaps ignored because of their insignificance or because the abbey had not acquired them when the prototype of FB was constructed. There are, too, disagreements with DB in the statistics for six of these.

§(b) THE LANDS OF THE 'FEUDATI HOMINES'

The second section describes itself as an account of the lands of the *feudati homines*, which, it points out, had also been included

[1] Any changes in demesne manors between 1086 and 1087 must, as we might expect, have been very slight.

in §(*a*). In this there is, quite reasonably, no division by counties.

In a few respects the Norfolk passages supplement both DB and §(*a*). They include three bordars at Shottisham, and the fact that Goscelin had a tenancy at Broom. There appear to be occasional omissions and statistical differences from the Domesday text and §(*a*), one of which is spectacular. Fifty-seven sokemen holding 2 carucates 45 acres are recorded for Kirby Cane (DB 212, FB 123b), where the other documents have three free men with 3 carucates. Occasionally the arrangement is peculiar: the Snarehill tenancy is combined with that for Livermere in Suffolk (DB 209b, FB 133b), and a single entry (fol. 132b) made for three holdings at Semer, Shimpling, and Gissing (DB 211, 211b), with the details of which it does not correspond. It does not include Morningthorpe, held there by Robert de Vals, or the lands at Morningthorpe and Fritton held by 'R', or Frodo's tenancy of part of Hales (DB 212, 212b). Here again the differences can hardly be attributed to changes between 1086 and 1087.

The Suffolk entries do not include all the sub-tenancies recorded in DB.[1] They include the slaves, which §(*a*) did not, and frequently disagree with the statements of DB. At Rede (133b) Berard is said to have one carucate and one free man of 20 acres; in DB (358) he has seven free men of half a carucate and 50 acres. In FB (133) Peter the brother of Burgheard has one carucate and three bordars in Horningworth and Westley, but in DB (358b) Horningworth is not mentioned, and yet he has two carucates and five bordars. Study of the complete figures suggests either that we are dealing with two different points in time, or with two originals drawn up in very different fashion.

The only two relevant entries for Essex are included, though the Essex demesne manors were omitted from §(*a*).[2]

§(c) THE LIST OF PEASANT HOLDINGS AND RENTS

This does not describe itself, and is limited to 31 vills in three Suffolk Hundreds. It consists of long lists of peasants' names

[1] e.g. those at Henstead (358), Mickfield (360b), and Livermere (363b).

[2] *Bredingeho* (Bennington in Witham) and Channels in Little Waltham in Chelmsford Hundred; DB 19b, 20; FB 134b, 132b.

together with the extent of their holdings and sums of money, presumably representing individual liability to the geld or to the rents due to St Edmund.

In these Douglas saw the actual Domesday peasantry. He stressed 'the probability that it is the free men and sokemen of the Survey who are here mentioned by name', and that 'they prove conclusively that in this section of the Feudal Book we are dealing with the names, estates, and rents of the Domesday free men and sokemen'. But, again, Lennard is of the opinion that the peasants of these lists are in fact the successors of those recorded in DB, though he agrees that the 'acres', while probably representing fiscal assessments, 'may not have differed much from agrarian reality'.[1]

Douglas has given five illustrations of reasonably close correspondence between their totals and the comprehensive statements about the holdings of free men and sokemen in DB: these come from the first five villages in the section.[2] But for many villages there is no correspondence whatever. At Welnetham, for example, DB fol. 363 records 41 free men of 6 carucates of land; FB fol. 139 ten of 2 carucates 70 acres. Again, at Hinderclay, DB fol. 364b has seven sokemen of 40 acres against the eleven persons with 51 acres of FB fol. 142. Some of the discrepancies are very large indeed, and probably we are intended to omit, in reckoning the Domesday quantities, the sub-tenancies.

It is curious, too, that seven of the villages represented do not appear in the St Edmund's Domesday *breve*. Possibly Layham (DB 368b), though not there styled a manor, included holdings at Cosford, Huntfield, and Littlechurch appearing on FB fols. 142b, 143. On the other hand, if their FB statistics are added to those of Cosford, we produce a gigantic discrepancy; FB 67 persons and unenumerated *socii* with 6 carucates 16 acres against DB 26 free men having 2 carucates.

It must then be highly doubtful if these are throughout lists of Domesday peasantry, or else the originals were far from identical. Possibly they belong to a rather later date; if so,

[1] *FD*, pp. lviii–lvix; Lennard: *Rural Eng.*, p. 359; see also Davis: *Kal.*, p. xxxviii, n. 4.

[2] *FD*, p. lx.

there must have been appreciable changes in the Bury lands in the dozen or thirty-odd years (reckoning by the alternative terminal dates) since the Inquest.

Thus we cannot learn a great deal about DB from collation of its text with that of FB. Though FB often furnishes a useful check on the former's statements, it is of less service to us than is the IE. What would be of extraordinary interest would be to know to what extent DB and FB had a common original, and why their authors produced such frequently varying results.

PART III

Administration, Society, and the Economy

CHAPTER IX

Assessments and the Geld

Throughout DB our dealings with assessments are fraught with difficulties and frustrations, but never more so than in Norfolk and Suffolk. Here we have a system which by 1086 was unique in England, though we may see discarded traces of it in the 'hides' and 'hundreds' of the Danelaw.[1] For the East Anglian Domesday records, at or towards the account of many holdings, most of which are said to be manors, that the villages concerned have to find so many pence, often including fractions of the penny, to the king's geld, 'when the Hundred pays 20*s*.'. Each Domesday Hundred was composed of a number of 'leets', and we are told how many of these two of the Norfolk Hundreds contained.[2] The quantities of pence are often so strange, and so frequently a quantity recurs within a Hundred, that it would be a natural deduction that the quantities attributed to many vills and holdings represent division of an integral number of pence, and that they could be used to determine the composition of the leets. For example, Thedwestrey Hundred seems to have consisted of six leets, each furnishing 40*d*. or almost that sum. One of these leets would seem to have been made up of Pakenham (13½*d*.), Tostock (10½*d*.), and Thurston (16*d*.)[3]

THE EAST ANGLIAN LEET

The *VCH* for both Norfolk and Suffolk gives tables of Hundreds showing the sums due from each geld-collection centre and tentative combinations of these sums which might represent the structure of the leets.[4] But later work has demonstrated that for some Bury Hundreds the leets were not so composed, and

[1] See Round: *FE*, pp. 73, 78, 80–6.
[2] South Greenhoe (14 leets) and Clackclose (10); fols. 119b, 212b.
[3] Fols. 361b, 363b, 362b.
[4] *VCH: Norfolk*, ii, pp. 204–11; *VCH: Suffolk*, i, pp. 412–16.

accordingly all the proposed combinations must be regarded with reserve.

Two authors have subsequently discussed the leets and the Domesday Hundreds, and it is convenient to treat their work separately. The leet, according to Douglas, 'was no mere artificial division'; probably the leets represent 'the small Hundreds current at the time of initial assessment'.[1] He has shown from a Bury St Edmunds survey of 1045–65 that there were at that time small Hundreds, certainly not the same in extent as the Hundreds we find in DB, comparable to the small Danish 'Hundred' of twelve carucates, divided into 'manlots'.[2] Further, he has suggested that they may be identified with the 'hides' in documents of that date, which must be pre-Danish. These 'hides' he visualises as being 'broken up by the Danes, introducing the 15-acre bovate, which on the basis of the eight-ox team produces the 120-acre geld carucate'.[3] The leets presumably were subsequently combined into large Hundreds, those of DB, and not necessarily on any obvious principle or according to one based on a possible earlier division of the province by Hundreds and hides.[4]

If the leets represent early small Hundreds, we shall not be surprised to find, when we come to consider the Hundreds of DB (p. 115), that they do not seem to be based on a duodecimal or decimal number of hides, and of course we cannot be sure that the leets of a Domesday Hundred are always those of an earlier day.[5]

[1] D. C. Douglas: *Social Studies in Medieval East Anglia*, pp. 56, 58. Elsewhere, however, he states that the leets were perhaps 'folk-divisions which probably took their origins from the Scandinavian invasions' (*FD*, p. 166).

[2] D. C. Douglas: 'Fragments of an Anglo-Saxon Survey from Bury St Edmunds' (*EHR*, xliii, 1928, pp. 128–43).

[3] But R. H. C. Davis has pointed out that 'there is no trace of the Danish "manlot" or twelve-acre unit' in the Bury Hundreds, and in East Anglia this occurs only in north-west Norfolk (Davis: *Kal.*, p. xliii, n. 7).

[4] Does this explain what might be a unique mention of the hide in DB for East Anglia? In IE MS. C2 (fol. 208b; H, p. 187) Richard fitzGilbert is said to have *1 h et xxiiii acrae* of the demesne at Hitcham. In IE (H, p. 156) this is given as 122 acres, and in DB (fol. 385) as 120 acres, with 'iii' interlined. A blank before the figure in DB may suggest a clerk's puzzlement at his original, and possibly to someone an East Anglian 'hide' was 100 acres.

[5] B. A. Lees (*VCH: Suffolk*, i, pp. 363, 365) thinks that they may originally have been concerned not only with taxation but with the administration of justice and perhaps with military service.

In addition to the leets, we twice hear in DB of 'the ferting of Elmham' (fols. 369, 379). In the Kalendar of Abbot Samson of Bury, which is only a little less than a century younger than DB, we are told that the ferding is what in other Hundreds are called leets, and that in Babergh Hundred there are fifteen of them, which would give a Hundred of 180 carucates. We might then suspect that Babergh was really a 'Hundred-and-a-half', though it is classed as a double Hundred in the Feudal Book. The Kalendar tells us also the number of leets and of vills, and the proportion of the leet represented by each vill, in five of the Bury Hundreds. We would expect, then, the leet to be the 'fourth part' of some administrative division, and Round showed how such 'quarters' persisted even in DB.[1] In Thedwestrey and Blackbourn Hundreds the leets are in the Kalendar styled also *villae integrae*, and it may well have been that frequently a large undivided vill of itself formed a leet. Sometimes we find vills brigaded together as a geld-reception centre (e.g. Wimbotsham and Stow, fol. 206) and for the record of dimensions; it is intriguing that quite often, when there are several holdings in a vill, geld-liability and dimensions are recorded in an entry other than that for the most important.

A later theory of their evolution is that of R. H. C. Davis.[2] The district was probably very early composed of a number of 'miniature shires'; it may be that Bury's 8½ and Ely's 5½ Hundreds represent two of these. Each of them, or subdivisions thereof, would have the duty of furnishing a *feorm*, in the form of food supplies or food-rents, to the king. The *feorm* was later commuted for money payments, and the right to receive these, or the sums from a sub-district, could be bestowed by the king on bishopric or abbey or ealdorman.

About the time of the reigns of Æthelstan or Edmund the 'shires' were partitioned for fiscal purposes, the units being the Hundreds and the leets. The character of the taxation imposed may not have been solely that of gelds, the provision of the commuted food-rents may also have entered into the matter. The larger vills, styled *villae integrae*, probably of themselves

[1] Round: *FE*, p. 101; Douglas: *FD*, p. 167; Davis: *Kal.*, pp. xxix–xxx.

[2] R. H. C. Davis (ed.): *The Kalendar of Abbot Samson* (Royal Historical Society, 1954).

formed leets, but it looks as if most leets were composed of several villages. Neither the Hundreds nor the leets were necessarily compact geographical units, as the map and dissection of the intermingled Hundreds of Bradmere and Blackbourn in Davis's edition of the Kalendar demonstrate. Tenure at the time of the institution of the system may have governed groupings, and also a desire to produce equitable assessments.[1] In the Kalendar the proportion contributed by a vill to a leet is always a proper fraction, which is by no means true of the geld-liabilities of DB; e.g. one of the Thedwestrey leets was divided into four equal quarters or 'ferdings', but in DB Great Livermere is responsible for 12*d.*, Ampton for 7*d.*, Timworth for 14*d.*, and Fornham St Genevieve for 8*d.* (362b, 363, 363b *bis*). But in the Kalendar the leets of three of the five Hundreds covered have to produce exactly or almost exactly the same number of pence in every £ of geld-liability.[2]

THE GELD

'Geld' is the word normally used when the individual contribution of a manor is mentioned. But occasionally, as in other shires, 'scot' is substituted.[3] Once we encounter a term familiar from other circuits; *ad defendum* (Debenham, 305b).

But the geld, save for the sums which had to be produced at a large number of collection-centres, is rarely mentioned in the Norfolk and Suffolk texts. Never, indeed, as we so frequently are with the hides of Essex, are we told precisely that a manor should

[1] It is fair to say, as Davis points out (pp. xxviii–xxix), that all the Domesday holdings of Robert Blond and Peter de Valognes in the double Hundred of Bradmere and Blackbourn lie in the former Hundred, while Blackbourn was practically all St Edmund's. The distribution of the estates of earlier landholders may have governed the composition of Hundred and leet. In Blackbourn Hundred West Stow and South Norton formed a leet, but ten miles lie between the villages, and the land of five other leets intervenes.

[2] Cosford half-Hundred is one of the two exceptions; it totals 117¼*d.* instead of the 120*d.* it should, and the contributions of the leets vary from 12*d.* to 20*d.* Babergh is highly irregular, but the accounts are for a date a little later than that for Thingoe, Thedwestrey, and Bradmere and Blackbourn.

[3] Fols. 119b, 173, 235; on fol. 290 we have *scottabat ad geltum*, and we hear of the 'scot of the city' (Colchester, 107). 'Scot' occurs also in the south-eastern circuit (12b2, 49b2).

geld for a certain number of carucates. Indeed, some have doubted whether the carucates and acres mentioned have anything to do with assessment, but rather may represent the ploughlands of other shires.

But the strong probability is that these *are* fiscal carucates and acres.[1] Nowhere in England, with land going out of occupation and cultivation, with colonisation and reclamation of the waste, with the changing composition of shires and Hundreds and manors, should we expect to find in 1086 many Hundreds and half-Hundreds with 100 or 50 hides or 120 and 60 carucates, or, for many manors, a decimal, duodecimal, or even integral number of hides and carucates, from whatever system they may have developed. But even in Norfolk and Suffolk, where manorialisation was only partial, and with its loosely-attached land of free men and sokemen, it seems that we can see frequent traces of the original system.

But we are formidably handicapped in our examination by our ignorance, which is rarely corrected by DB, of the actual composition of the manors, past and present; in other words, which entries and sub-entries are relevant to the individual quantity of geld due. Where geld is not mentioned in the account of a large holding, often styled a manor, we have no means of knowing at what centre it may have gelded, or what proportion of that centre's quota it had to contribute. Complication is further induced by our not knowing whether the lands of the free men or sokemen were always part of the manor or vill with which they might seem to be associated or not. We do not know whether the land which is said to be 'free', *libera terra*, normally associated with the village churches, was liable for geld.[2] The lands ascribed to churches in Lackford Hundred, which we are about to examine, would add close on four carucates, assuming that the 15 acres mentioned in every Elveden entry refer to a single church with 15 acres, not four with 60 in all. In the south-western circuit the land attached to churches,

[1] This, too, is Douglas's opinion, though he seems to have been in some doubt as to whether there were 100 or 120 acres to the carucate: 'if, as is probable, the East Anglian hundred is the long hundred of 120 carucates' (*Soc. Stud.*, p. 55; see also p. 214); 'in East Anglia the carucate will normally contain 100 and not 120 acres' (*Soc. Stud.*, p. 57).

[2] For *libera terra*, see p. 76.

usually said to be *in elemosina*, seems to have been almost entirely exempt from the geld.

Lackford Hundred displays some of the complications we find in almost every East Anglian Hundred. The village of Lackford is not within it, but is rubricated as being in Thingoe Hundred, though one would expect that when the Hundreds and leets and vills were assessed it would have been within the Hundred to which it gave its name.[1] Great Livermere is for all the three entries for this vill rubricated as within Lackford, but geographically it is in Blackbourn, and seven miles from the nearest vill in Lackford, while in the Kalendar it is in Thedwestrey Hundred. Mildenhall, geographically in Suffolk, appears in the Norfolk text also, ascribed to Clackclose Hundred, but there the number of its carucates is not given, and nothing is said about geld-liability.

Of the seventeen vills which form the Suffolk Hundred of Lackford, for which there are nearly fifty entries and sub-entries, ten vills have an integral number of carucates. Of the seven vills where, in thirteen instances, acres are mentioned, the quantities are 80 (once), 60 (six times), 40 (once), 30 (three times), and 20 (once), which suggests an equation of 120 acres to the carucate. There are also two odd quantities of acres: 8 at Freckenham (381), which have been 'invaded' and added to the manor, and may represent a quota subsequent to the original assessment, and 29 at Livermere (382), which suggests a 30-acre holding which has somehow lost one of its acres.

In East Anglia instances of 100 acres, and its multiples and sub-multiples, appear with some frequency. This quantity is to be found a score of times in Norfolk, and 200 acres, not 1 carucate 80 acres, are occasionally recorded.[2] But I can find only about fifty quantities of 25, 50, 75, 150 acres, and duodecimal figures, 90, 72, 60, 48, 30, 15, 7½, overwhelmingly outnumber them. In Suffolk occurrences are slightly more numerous; 100 acres appear over thirty times. If we can trust

[1] Recent excavation has shown a pagan settlement on the opposite side of the river on which Lackford stands, facing the medieval village. Thus Lackford may not have been within the modern Thingoe when earlier administrative districts were constructed. Wangford gave its name to a Hundred, but in DB (414b) the vill is recorded as in Blythburgh Hundred.

[2] e.g. Hindolveston, Wood Norton (192b), Witton (200b).

LACKFORD HUNDRED

Acres converted at 120 to the carucate. Folio references in italics indicate holdings classed as manors; *Cocleswordа* and Icklingham were berewicks, and probably there were manors at the four vills where DB indicates none. s.t. = *sine terra.*

	geld (*d.*)	car.	ac.	churches car.	churches ac.	fols.
Santon Downham	20	6	60	—	20	*359*, 383
Brandon	20	5	—	—	30	*381b*, 403
Wangford	6	3	—	—	15	*358b*, 393
Lakenheath }	20 (Lakenheath and Undley)	6	—	—	60	*382*, 392, 403
Undley }		1	—	—	s.t.	382
Livermere	4	3	9	—	—	359, 382, *408*
Elveden	20	9	—	—	15	*303*, *358b*, *391b*, 398
Eriswell	10	6	—	—	60	*402b*
Cocleswordа†	7	8	—	—	60	402b
Mildenhall	11¼	12	90	—	40	263, 288b, 392
Icklingham	11¼	11	30	—	24	288b, *416*, *434*
Barton Mills	20	6	30	—	—	391b, 392, 435b
Worlington	20	6	—	—	s.t.	355
Freckenham	20	10	8	—	20	*381*
Herringswell	20	6	100	—	30	*358b*, 392, 398
Tuddenham	20	6	—	—	30	355, 392, *403*
Cavenham	20	5	60	—	60	391b, 403
	249½	112	27	3	109	
Lackford would add	20	5	8	—	20	*357*

† The Rev. J. T. Munday has established that this was in the southern half of his parish of Eriswell, now 'Chamberlain's' (*Proc. Suff. Inst. of Archaeology*, xxx, 2, 1965, p. 205).

the IE, there were 120 acres to the carucate; Glemham is of 180 acres in DB, but in the IE is of 1½ carucates (fol. 430; H, p. 153). The 60 acres at Hitcham of DB and IE (fol. 385; H, p. 156) are a half-carucate in the Schedule (fol. 69a2; H, p. 178). Yet often 120 or 360 acres are mentioned when we should expect one or three carucates (fols. 320, 337, 412b, 420, 420b, 433b, 441; 399). We have also '2½ carucates and 60 acres' (Downham, 359).

From the table on page 111, it will be seen that the sum for the Hundred lies between 100 and 120 carucates, that the details suggest a duodecimal basis of assessment, and that the assessments of the vills could be combined in varying ways to give duodecimal divisions. This, indeed, we find wherever we examine the details of East Anglian Hundreds.

PROBLEMS INDUCED BY THE MS.

Lackford seems to be one of the simpler East Anglian Hundreds, but as soon as we investigate its figures, we encounter complications. The only vill within it for which no geld-liability is mentioned is Undley (382), but this is said to geld in Lakenheath. The Hundred's total geld-liability is close to the 240 pence which make £1; perhaps one or more small estates had been absorbed into the Hundred since the initial distribution of liability. The total of carucates for the vills suggests that if the initial assessment had been 100 carucates, the Hundred had been slightly enlarged; or, if of 120, had lost a little of its land.

We are entitled to expect that vills contributing equal numbers of pence to a Hundred-geld of £1 should have identical quantities of carucates. We find nothing of the sort. Elveden and Worlington each has to find 20*d.* in the £, but the vills have 9 and 6 carucates respectively. Ten vills in all each contribute 20*d.*, but only three have the same number of carucates.[1]

[1] Worlington, Tuddenham, and Lakenheath – and a holding in the latter belonged in part to Brandon. The dimensions given for these three are 10 × 8 furlongs, 1 league × 6 furlongs, and 1 league × half a league.

A further problem at once presents itself. Suppose Lackford was reckoned as of 100 carucates; then it should produce £30 if the geld was 6*s*. on the carucate, as it had recently been on the hide in the south-west. Then each acre, if there were 120 acres to the carucate, must furnish the ugly fraction of 3/5*d*., or the still uglier one of 18/25*d*. if there were 100. How, without frequent approximations, could the amount of geld due from holdings with undecimal or duodecimal quantities of acres be calculated? The figures argue desperate local jugglings to secure both equitable contribution from taxpayers and satisfaction of the collectors of the tax. Perhaps if geld accounts for the area had survived we could determine how matters were adjusted; as it is, we cannot formulate a satisfactory theory.

In Norfolk North Greenhoe Hundred is not alone in presenting totally inexplicable figures. The total geld-liability is only one penny short of £1, and its vills appear to have assessments totalling 94 carucates 101 acres. But the three vills which each has to contribute 6*d*. in the £ have total assessments of 4 car. 57 ac., 1½ car., and 2 car. 80 ac.[1] Little Walsingham has to find three times that sum, but is assessed at only 2 car. 14 ac.[2] Cockthorpe and Great Snoring presumably contributed to the geld of other vills, since none is mentioned in the entries for them.

The problem of the relationship between geld-liability and quantity of carucates in DB is simplified if it is argued that there is not necessarily any connection, on the basis of the Domesday villar units, between them. As a general rule, geld-liability is ascribed to only one of several holdings in a divided vill. Thus it may be that the geld of some or all of the other holdings in the vill had to be produced at a different centre of collection. The value of four of the holdings in Lackford Hundred was included in that of Desning in Risbridge Hundred, and Cavenham was a berewick of that manor, though its geld seems to have belonged to Lackford Hundred.[3]

[1] Egmere, Quarles, and Barney. Their dimensions are given as ½ × ½ league, 4 × 4 furlongs, and ½ × ½ league. B. A. Lees's calculation of the 'potential carucates' of a vill seems to be based on the equation 144 square furlongs = 12 carucates, which gives the vills quantities of carucates often far different from the number attributed to them in DB.

[2] Its dimensions too are ½ × ½ league.

[3] Fols. 392 *quater*; 403.

While it would often not be impossible to suggest how the holdings were grouped, with appropriate quantities of carucates, to produce the sums allotted to the collecting centres, the information at our disposal is much too slender to make this a profitable occupation.

If this hypothesis is correct, it might be supposed that the idea that 'the vills were so distributed among the leets that a fair proportion of taxation fell upon each vill at the time when the assessment was made' is open to debate.[1] It seems highly improbable that the vill did not enter into the original scheme of apportionment of assessment, but the Domesday figures certainly would not suggest that it did. The alternative view must be that 'we seem then to be driven to the conclusion either that the East Anglian carucates are not geld carucates, or that beneficial carucation and the errors in the construction of Little Domesday have destroyed all traces of the data which determined the assessment'.[2] It remains to consider what the text of DB, and what has been stated earlier here, have to tell us about these possibilities.

Some of the rateable values may at first sight seem to be extremely odd. We find, for example, 4 car. 1 ac., 204 ac., 203½ ac., 91½ ac. (fols. 249, 110, 422b, 329b). The last two were in the hands of thirty-five and three free men respectively, and must result from the combination of a number of small holdings. Some may represent the addition of small men's land to manors originally rated at an even number of carucates.

It looks, too, as if we can see past division of a holding in what must have been rational proportions. What had perhaps once been a 3-carucate holding at Elmham (380) is in 1086 found as three of 2 car. 20 ac., 66 ac., and 34 ac. At *Manuuic* (298b, 305b *bis*) there were holdings of 13½, 27, and 13½ acres, and at Chediston (332) three of 13 acres and one of 26: this last might derive from the division of 40 acres. Three times at least in Norfolk we find mention of 33 acres, suggesting division of 100 acres by three. The figure appears twice for Barton Turf (219b), with 11 acres at Bramerton (175, 185b), and with both 11 and 22 at Gissing (155, 211, 211b).

[1] *VCH: Norfolk*, ii, p. 6.
[2] *VCH: Norfolk*, ii, p. 8.

SHIRE- AND HUNDREDAL ASSESSMENTS

Of a vill, or a manor, contributing to the geld of more than one Hundred there is a solitary suggestion. Desning (390), a manor in Risbridge Hundred which had components in Lackford also, is said to have to produce 37*d.* of geld in the £ 'in two Hundreds'. If this was common practice, we can have no idea how much of the geld from a collection-centre went to the Hundred in which it lay, and the number of East Anglian manors and of vills the land of which was not all in one Hundred is very large.

We receive no direct indications of beneficial assessment, save for the monks of St Edmund's privilege of receiving 60*d.* out of every £ contributed by the Hundred (fol. 372). But we cannot be sure that it had not been applied to liabilities, but that record of past reductions was not thought to be appropriate to the text of DB. When, however, we find Hundreds and half-Hundreds whose total assessments are in the neighbourhood of 100 and 50, or 120 and 60 carucates, we may legitimately doubt whether earlier reduction can have occurred.

A few entries may suggest post-Conquest beneficial assessment, but their implication is uncertain. At Burgh (400b) William de Warenne had a manor of 1 car. 20 ac., and 50 acres of free men's land: 'the whole of this William received for one carucate of land'. He had also a carucate and a half at Larling (164), 'but it was delivered to him for one carucate'. But there may have been changes here in manorial composition of which we are told nothing. A free man held a Brundall manor (268b) for one carucate; in 1086 Gilbert the crossbowman held it for two. When a Bixley holding (176) with 1½ carucates was 'received for 1½ carucates', we seem to encounter mere verbiage.

Occasional and frustrating attempts to establish the total assessments of Norfolk and Suffolk have been made, and to see what relationship they might bear to their contributions to taxation at other dates.[1] Norfolk appears to have had 33 named Hundreds in the eleventh century, plus the boroughs of Norwich and Thetford, each of which is styled a 'Hundred' in DB (234b, 118b), and Suffolk 24. With no allowance for reductions

[1] e.g. that of Maitland: *DBB*, pp. 7, 400.

of assessment, and with an arbitrary figure of 100 carucates to the Hundred, we should then expect them to produce, from a 2*s*. geld on the carucate, about £330 or £350 and £240 respectively. In 1150 their total geld is given in the Pipe Roll as just over £330 and £235. These figures may seem to harmonise unexpectedly well, until we remember that if the Hundred was supposed to be of 120 carucates the two shires should have produced figures well in excess of those in the Pipe Roll, such as £408 or £432 and £288. But then in 1150 there may have been exemptions, as in Pipe Rolls of other dates, of which we now know nothing.

It would perhaps be possible to calculate potentialities as follows. Domesday Suffolk has 24 named 'Hundreds'. Allowing for the double Hundred of Babergh (which has nothing like 200 or 240 carucates), the Hundred-and-a-half of Samford, and the half-Hundreds of Parham, Lothingland, and Ipswich, we still have 24 if we treat Blackbourn and Bradmere, intermingled in DB, as two. As in Essex, there is no consistency in the Domesday descriptions; e.g. Cosford is a 'Hundred' on fol. 288, a 'half-Hundred' on fol. 291b, and Babergh is not classed as a double Hundred on fol. 304, though it is on fol. 288b.

An explanation of the apparently mysterious statistics for Babergh Hundred has been furnished by R. H. C. Davis. Bury St Edmunds paid geld, not to the king, but *ad victum monachorum* (fol. 372), and the geld should have been of 60*d*. in the £. So was that of Sudbury, which had been taken out of Babergh and put in Thingoe Hundred to compensate for the loss of the geld of Bury St Edmunds, in which Hundred the abbey lay. Thus Babergh had been a double Hundred, but in 1086 was nearer being a 'Hundred-and-a-half'. The fact that Bury's immunity dates to at least the year 1021, and perhaps earlier, shows that the fiscal Hundred-system of East Anglia was no new thing.[1]

From B. A. Lees's tables, we arrive at a total of 2,772 Domesday carucates, which comes not too far from our higher Pipe Roll figure.[2] This gives an average of $115\frac{1}{2}$ carucates to the Hundred, which is close to the 120 we should expect. It is true that very few Domesday Hundreds have, in these tables, a

[1] For much useful and interesting information on the topic, see Davis: *Kal.*
[2] *VCH: Suffolk*, i, pp. 410–16.

number of carucates anywhere near 120 or the appropriate fraction, but then we are arguing that the composition of the Hundreds of Domesday is not that of the initial assessment, though their names may have been the same. The average hundredal geld-liability is $2\frac{3}{4}$*d.* less than 22*s.*, and if this is 10% in excess of the 20*s.* which seems to be the Domesday unit, we still can suggest that between the date of original assessment and 1086 it is probable that more land had been newly settled than had gone out of cultivation. This would surely be true if, as has been suggested earlier, much of the land of free men and sokemen represents assessments additional to an assessment of villages in integral numbers of carucates and proper fractions thereof.

Norfolk, on the above principle, has 34 Hundreds, though nothing like 3,400 carucates in DB, where there are only 33 Hundreds named. The total geld-liability in Johnson's tables is a little under £32, at £1 a Hundred, where on a basis of 33 or 34 Hundreds we may feel we should find a higher figure, and it might reasonably be suggested that Norfolk suffered more than Suffolk did in 1075 and before, so that relatively more land may have gone out of cultivation.[1]

From this point we might argue thus. Between the time of the initial assessment and 1086 the number, and perhaps the names, of the East Anglian Hundreds into which earlier leets or small 'Hundreds' were combined may not have altered. If so, we can expect to find in Suffolk in 1086 about 2,760–2,800 carucates, allowing for 23 or 24 Hundreds initially of 120 carucates each. According to B. A. Lees, there were 2,772, and DB certainly omits some assessments. A similar calculation would give 3,960–4,200 carucates for Norfolk, but DB will give us only some 60% of this quantity. But some Norfolk Hundreds are small or thinly populated, and may not have been assessed at a full 120 carucates. It is suggested that the reason why few Hundreds have in DB even an approximation to the appropriate number of carucates is appreciable changes in the composition of many Hundreds, as happened in many other shires. Such changes would not normally alter the county totals of carucates, though these would alter as new settlements created additional assessments and some land went out of occupation, and where a

[1] *VCH: Norfolk*, ii, pp. 204–11.

holding was transferred from one county to another.[1] We must remember that we have no idea in what manner leets may have been amalgamated to form later Hundreds, and the leets in a Domesday Hundred may have been combined very differently in earlier days.

The geld-liability of few East Anglian Hundreds adds up to the 20*s.* which obviously the units should produce. Henstead's total is 23*s.* 7*d.*, Clavering's only 15*s.* 8*d.* For some Hundreds, e.g. Launditch, the figures for some leets are clearly missing; the sum of its liability is only 16*s.* 8½*d.* Some Norfolk Hundreds-and-a-half and half-Hundreds seem to give sums suggesting that sometimes they are in proportion, 30*s.* and 10*s.*: Forehoe returns 29*s.* 5¼*d.*, Earsham 10*s.* 2*d.* In Suffolk, however, the double Hundred of Babergh gives only 33*s.* 1¼*d.*, but it has been said above that Babergh looks as if it might have been a Hundred-and-a-half once Sudbury had been detached. The suggestion here is again that a certain amount of liability has been transferred from one Hundred to another as the composition of a Hundred altered, while new settlements and deserted holdings have added their quotas to disturbance of neat round figures.

If the above hypotheses have any validity, we can cease to trouble ourselves about East Anglian hundredal and villar carucatage and geld-liability, for the mysterious Domesday figures, to produce intelligible results, would have to be fitted into a system of organisation and distribution which had long since been substantially altered, and of which DB yields us few traces.

ESSEX ASSESSMENTS

Attempts have also been made to establish the total hidage of Essex at the time of the Inquest. The first would allot 2,650 hides to the shire; the second 2,725, plus 80 for the borough of Colchester.[2] The basis of calculation of each of these estimates

[1] See p. 52.

[2] J. Brownbill: 'The Tribal Hidage' (*EHR*, xxvii, 1912, pp. 625–48); G. Rickword: 'The Kingdom of the East Saxons and the Tribal Hidage' and 'The East Saxon Kingdom' (*Trans. Essex Arch. Soc.*, New Series, 1911, xi, pp. 246–65, xii, pp. 38–50).

was criticised by Round.[1] Brownbill's reduction by 40% of the number of hides credited to the East Saxon kingdom in the Tribal Hidage has no textual authority, but is that which brings the total of hides roughly in correspondence with that of DB for the shires concerned. Rickword assumed the prior existence of seventy Essex Hundreds, each of 40 hides, for which again there is no textual evidence, to produce approximations to which he selected arbitrary combinations of the Domesday holdings. In 1150 Essex paid geld for 2,364 hides, a total smaller than the above figures.

We can indeed now have but unsatisfactory conceptions of the total assessment of Essex either at the time of its imposition or in 1086. Probably the initial quota had been of so many hundred hides, but we cannot assume that there were simultaneously as many Hundreds as there were hundred hides: there may have been double Hundreds, half-Hundreds, and Hundreds-and-a-half, as in Northamptonshire.[2] Some of the Essex Hundreds of 1086 look as if they might fall into one or other of these categories, but we have no reason to suppose that their composition was identical or even akin to that of the moment of initial assessment. Indeed, Round was of the opinion that 'the boundaries of the Essex Hundreds are suggestive of their late formation'.[3] We have ample evidence that the composition of Hundreds was liable to fluctuate.[4] Seven Essex Domesday 'Hundreds' are in the text styled 'half-hundreds', though some of these are called 'Hundreds' also, and none, except Clavering, seems to have a hidage very close to 50 hides.[5] There may well have been double Hundreds, and even 'two-and-a-half Hundreds', for in 1086 Tendring seems to have had over 200 hides and Uttlesford nearly 250. But we cannot now recapture the original allotment of hides.

Summing the Hundred-totals, with the frequent inclusion of acres in assessments, has been done on the assumption that in Essex 120 acres made a hide. What positive evidence we have

[1] J. H. Round: 'The Domesday Hidation of Essex' (*EHR*, xxix, 1914, pp. 477–9).

[2] See Maitland: *DBB*, p. 458.

[3] *VCH: Essex*, i, p. 407.

[4] See Finn: *The Domesday Inquest*, pp. 41–5.

[5] e.g. Waltham seems to have had about 70 hides in 1086.

certainly suggests it; for example, half a virgate is equated with fifteen acres.[1] Moreover, the numbers of acres which represent a proper fraction of a 120-acre hide – 15, 20, 30, 45, 75, 90 – occur so frequently as to make the use of this equation fully justifiable.

Probably the break-down of the hidage by villages and manors, and perhaps by Hundreds, had been on a decimal basis, for the number of holdings with a decimal quantity of hides is considerable. Clacton (11) was assessed at 20 hides, Brightlingsea (6) at 10, Wrabness (20) at 5, Michaelstow (70b) at 2½. It is noticeable that the majority of the villages and manors which had received a decimal quantity of hides are Crown manors or belonged to the earls or to religious houses, where stable conditions were most likely to persist. But most of the assessments can only suggest either a now-concealed apportionment of a decimal figure among several separated holdings, or changes in manorial composition. When we see that one Henham holding is rated at 13½ hides less 10 acres, and another at half a hide and 10 acres (71, 101), we cannot but suspect former changes in the composition of the holdings. While quantities which include 37½ or 22½ acres suggest equal division of 75 and 45 acres, no obvious reason for 52 or 16 acres presents itself.[2] Manorial assessments such as 2 hides 31 acres, or 11½ hides 13 acres, present a problem insoluble unless combination with other holdings to give decimal quantities seems reasonable.[3] But perhaps we can see possibilities at Henny, where the assessments of the six holdings include 20½, 18, 10½, and minus 4 acres, and the vill totals 7 hides 90 acres and might combine with one of several neighbouring assessments of 2 hides 30 acres.[4] But, as elsewhere, by the eleventh century any decimal basis had often become formidably distorted; sometimes by alteration of the composition

[1] Waltham (15b): see also *VCH: Essex*, i, p. 334. In the borough of Colchester holdings of 5, 10, 15, and 20 acres are frequent.

[2] Dickley (67b), Maplestead (24), Stansted (88), Tilbury-by-Clare (82b). Quantities of 37 and 38 acres, which are fairly frequent, e.g. Finchingfield (29, 39b), 'of the king's soke of Lawford' (40b), Weeley (51), may well derive from a 75-acre assessment, roughly divided in half.

[3] Baddow (70), Wigborough (18).

[4] Fols. 74, 84, 87b, 99b, 101, 101b; Pentlow, Borley (61b, 91b).

of manors, both before and after the Conquest, and sometimes by the development of new settlements and the desertion of small uneconomic estates.[1]

Except for the assessments of the individual holdings, we are told little of the geld in Essex. An estate held by a royal servant is said not to pay geld, and earlier another rendered neither customary service nor dues nor the king's geld.[2] It is possible that we have three oblique references to the levy to which the geld accounts of the south-western circuit refer. Geld was never paid by a South Weald manor; nor was the last geld paid (66b). Two holdings are said to have been 'concealed' – a statement we find also in the south-west, where it seems to originate from a check-up by means of the Inquest revelations – and surety had been given for this breach of good faith.[3]

[1] When free men have been 'added' to a manor, it is almost always noted that this had been done 'in the time of King William'. Many of these holdings have such undecimal quantities of acres that some may derive from realistic assessments laid on newly-cultivated land; e.g. the 8½ acres of the two free men added to Sternfield (297).

[2] Steeple (4b), Bardfield (41b).

[3] Bollington, Farnham (101).

CHAPTER X

Middle-class Society

References to thegns and to free men, to commendation, to sokeright and to sokemen, to the power of disposal of land and services or the reverse, to largely undefined obligations and privileges of various kinds, meet us at every turn of Domesday Book, vol. ii. The shires this covers are not, of course, alone in this, for such references are frequent throughout Danelaw territory and the neighbouring counties also, but it happens that much of the most valuable and suggestive information that we possess about the above is derived from the accounts of them. The problems here presented have been considered, and the information they provide expounded, by many men, though unanimity of opinion regarding the implications of the terse technical terms and phrases of DB is so far lacking.

Cursory study of DB vol. ii, and indeed of much of the relevant portions of vol. i, might easily inspire deductions such as the following:

(i) the thegn had a higher social and economic standing than the *liber homo*, and the free man than the sokeman;
(ii) generally speaking, the free man could sell his land and transfer his allegiance and services; the sokeman could not;
(iii) both had duties, beyond those all men of their status owed to the Crown or to the royal representative, to their superior to discharge, but those incumbent on the free man were lighter than those of the sokeman.

In substance such deductions may well have a large element of truth in them, but none is entirely valid.

For neither DB nor other document of the period defines the terms in question. Indeed, the more we study them, the more we are inclined to feel that for the most part they are incapable of strict definition. It would not be difficult, indeed, to find exceptions to any definition that we might construct. 'Commendation', we quickly discover, is an elastic term; the precise implications of sokeright cannot be stated with simplicity; and what shades of meaning *consuetudo* or *servitium* may have seem to be infinite.

Successive commentators have occupied themselves with attempting to define just what is implied by the terms 'commendation' and 'sokeright' and whether the lord's rights were over the land or the man concerned, or over both. Where a man is said to have the power to sell his land, and presumably take up residence elsewhere, did his commendation remain with the lord, or was it transferable? Where a man could 'go to what lord he pleased', did he by so doing have to quit his former lord's land? Where sokeright had been granted, was this applicable to the land, or the man, or both? What, where a man left his lord, or sold his land, happened when commendation and/or sokeright had been shared between two magnates? One thing is certain: DB may give us hints as to how these problems were regarded in the eleventh century, but never a neat and unchallengeable solution to them.[1] We can only examine what DB and allied documents have to tell us, and then form our own judgments.

It is doubtful whether the suppliers of information, the Hundred-juries, or the clerks, could have stated what to them differentiated free man from sokeman. To them the terms must have implied very much the same thing, but perhaps they did not think that normally what they styled a sokeman could commend himself, though probably it would be untrue to say that no sokeman had liberty of commendation.[2] A sokeman of Edric of Laxfield commended himself to Æthelwine of Thetford after the Conquest (Haddiscoe, 182).

[1] For the arguments, see Maitland: *Domesday Book and Beyond*, pp. 66–107; Ballard: *The Domesday Inquest*, pp. 82, 112–15; Vinogradoff: *English Society in the Eleventh Century*, pp. 120–30, 346–7, 431–46; L. F. Salzman in *VCH: Cambridgeshire*, i, p. 348; C. Stephenson: 'Commendation and Related Problems in Domesday' (*EHR*, lix, 1944, 289–310); B. Dodwell: 'East Anglian Commendation' (*EHR*, lxiii, 1948, 289–306).

[2] The text of the Bury St Edmunds *breve* for Suffolk does rather suggest that the abbey's sokemen were commended to the Saint, but the wording may be a peculiarity of the Bury return.

Certainly the statistics of the Norfolk text cannot represent the facts, for in that shire we find a large majority of free men over sokemen in some Hundreds, and vice versa. In Clackclose, for example, over 500 free men are said to have held land in 1066, but less than 100 sokemen. In Walsham, by way of contrast, there had been nearly 300 sokemen, but less than 40 free men. That Lincolnshire should have had only sokemen, and no free men, seems absurd, though this is what DB implies.[1] In any case, Domesday phraseology does not imply sharp lines of demarcation between one social grade and another; as Stenton has said, 'a group of Domesday *villani* included men whom . . . Domesday itself would have described in other districts as radknights'.[2] This fact needs to be remembered when the potential services of free men and sokemen are being considered.

THEGNS AND FREE MEN

'Thegn' and *liber homo* certainly seem also to be elastic terms. Ketel, we have seen, (p. 24) was a thegn, though styled also a 'free man', and we hear of 'a free man who was also a thegn' ('in the two Meltons', 204b). Round stressed 'the rashness of concluding that the *liber homo* was a smaller man than the thegn', instancing Leofwine *cilt*.[3] The free men on the individual holding obviously were not necessarily of equal standing; e.g. one of the six free men of East Tuddenham had four bordars, but no dependants are recorded for the other five. The free man could indeed have free men under him: a clear indication of degrees of local, and perhaps national, importance. At Mettingham (300b) Ælfric had eight free men *sub se*, though they seem to have been commended to Wulfsige, who had Ælfric's commendation, and one of the two free men at Sutton (318) commended to Edric had five free men under him. It may be mere chance that sometimes, at least, the clerk did not call 'thegns' what in fact he styled free men; commonly, when a

[1] For the modern county of Nottinghamshire, Darby's figures are 1,704 sokemen, 3 free men (*The Domesday Geography of England*, iv, p. 501).
[2] Stenton: *Anglo-Saxon England*, p. 471.
[3] *VCH: Essex*, i, p. 352; see also p. 210.

man's name is given, instead of being just *liber homo*, he proves from another entry to be a thegn.

We hear occasionally of *franci homines*, and, in most instances, the text suggests that *liberi homines* would have been an exact alternative.[1] They surely cannot be Frenchmen, for one of two 'occupied' by Lisois had been outlawed; some were rendering 'all custom' to the manor; and some were *in firma regis*. We read, too, of a *francus teignus*, of a thegn holding 'freely', of three men of whom one was a thegn and the other two *liberi homines*.[2]

We find *liberi homines* with extensive individual holdings – four carucates at Great Bircham (222b), 405 acres at West Acre (236). Even a man described as 'a half free man' – owing service or commended to two lords – had held a pre-Conquest manor (Sutton, 318), and so had fourteen free men at Bawdsey (354), though the manor was rated at only 62 acres. Equally it is common for free men to have been 'in demesne' in 1086 (e.g. fols. 309, 325), as though they had been brought into the structure of a manor with attendant loss of personal freedom.

But the holdings of some of the pre-Conquest free men were of such little importance that they must have been greatly in need of a patron. At Oakley (310) two free men had no more than half a (geld-) acre, while there were quarter-acre holdings at Olden (446) and Hoo (317b). Amounts of a single geld-acre are common, and quite frequently, where a group of tenants is specified, the smaller holdings can only have been rated at fractions of a geld-acre.[3] Their holders may have been free, but they can have been of no local importance, and many a sokeman could point to equal prosperity. At Stokerland (324) two free men had 30 acres, half a team, a half-acre of meadow, and were valued at 5*s*.; a sokeman also with 30 acres had a whole team and two acres of meadow, and was worth 8*s*. The sokeman at Sloley (219b) had a whole carucate and 2½ teams, with 12 villeins and 8 bordars, six acres of meadow, and wood

[1] e.g. Cratfield (415), Mundon (49b), Dunwich (311b), Steeple (4b).

[2] Goldhanger (54, 54b), South Ockendon (57b): see also Avon Dassett (239b2), and *Ellatone* (249b2).

[3] e.g. at East Winch (280), an unmanorialised village. Maitland (*DBB*, pp. 64–5) quoted the instances of groups of Dorset thegns who possessed little land and few plough-teams; the seven at Poorton (80bi) had only one team, and apparently no villeins, bordars, or slaves.

for 120 swine, said to be worth £2. Indeed, 'to be free did not mean to be prosperous'.[1]

FREE MEN AND SOKEMEN

Sometimes the free man seems to be differentiated from the sokeman; at Roudham (164b) there were two free men holding a carucate of land, 'and three sokemen and five bordars'. At Smallburgh (187) there were three free men 'with 12 bordars and three sokemen', but this need not be taken to imply that the sokemen were subordinate to the free men. But quite often differentiation does not seem to be implied, though perhaps this is merely the result of clerical imprecision. The land of the free men added to the manor of Fobbing (26) is described as 'of the sokemen' three lines lower down. Two of the five sokemen at Belchamp Otton (28b) were free men when Ingelric added them to the manor after the Conquest. Domesday Book, vol. i, often shows us the sokeman as a free man; e.g. of four Stanford sokemen (212b2) three were free, but the other could not sell his land. We find here, too, sokemen with manors and 'halls' (e.g. at Wandsworth, 35b2, or at Dursley, 132b2, where the land could be sold), but also 'without halls or lords' (e.g. on fol. 11ai). It is curious that at Runham (134b) there should be both 11½ free men and 11½ sokemen; it looks as if one of these was thought of as being both free man and sokeman.

Those whom DB calls sokemen the IE sometimes styled free men, and vice versa; e.g. a sokeman at Lynn (H, p. 131) is a free man in DB (fol. 276), and the same is true of some inhabitants of Outwell (H, p. 138; DB fol. 136). The free men 'who lay in the manor of Feltwell' (DB 213b) are sokemen in IE (H, p. 132), and within the IE Schedules the same men can be found described as free men or sokemen.[2] Since the free man was in someone's soke, the clerks might well call him a free man in one passage and a sokeman in another, and this may explain how, as we shall see, a sokeman apparently could have the power to sell his land.

[1] H. R. Loyn: *Anglo-Saxon England and the Norman Conquest*, p. 343.

[2] e.g. Charsfield (H, pp. 182, 188) and Winston (H, pp. 146, 182, 188; DB fol. 377).

Of sixteen free men at Carleton (121), nine are said to have been Stigand's sokemen; of six Deopham free men (227) it was said that three of them were Stigand's sokemen. To rewrite the first phrase as 'of nine of these Stigand had the soke' would hardly be doing the original an injustice.

Often a priest is styled also a free man (e.g. at Uggeshall, 299b, or Burgh, 315b), but one priest at least, Edwin, is called also a sokeman (Norbury, 353). There is a passage (Haddiscoe, 182) which suggests that a free man might be dependent upon a sokeman, but this is open to doubt. Here a sokeman of Edric of Laxfield had 30 acres, and there were four free men *sub illo*, but the reference is probably to Edric, not to his sokeman. But a sokeman could have other sokemen under him; two sokemen with half a carucate had *sub eis* seven sokemen with 20 acres (Hemblington, 139).

The Inquest, though in East Anglia it does not describe holdings as being 'soke of the manor', recognised the existence of sokeland; there are said to be 1½ plough-teams *super socam*, 'upon the soke', of Thurning (131b). That sokemen were responsible for the production of the geld due from their land seems to be indicated by the East Dereham and Thorpe in Shipdham entry (214): 'and upon all the sokemen of these two manors' is charged 15*d.* (of geld).

But we receive also occasional notification that a sokeman was not necessarily a totally unimportant person. It is not uncommon to find in East Anglia, if not in Essex, a sokeman who is said to have held his land as a manor in 1066, though it is doubtful whether it would have retained manorial status in 1086. One at Denton (390) had held a manor rated at two carucates, and the two at Wortham (361) had held their land for two manors. The fact that the name of a sokeman is given in DB (e.g. Wulfweard at Fishley, fol. 129) may not imply that he was a person of importance, but it does differentiate him from the ordinary villager.[1]

A sokeman at Writtle (5) 'could go with his land where he would'; others at Theydon Gernon and Abbess Roding (50b)

[1] For instances of named sokemen, see, e.g., fols. 295b, 315b, 318b, 321, 371, 371b, 383b, 388, 390b, 418b, 442. Incidentally, a 'sokeman' could be female (fol. 325b).

could sell their land, and the latter even possessed a slave. There are plenty of East Anglian examples of sokemen with power to sell. Though it is common for no villeins or bordars to be recorded for the holdings of sokemen (presumably they and their families worked the land without regular assistance), equally a fair number speak of bordars, often said to be *sub eis*. On the substantial holding of 2 hides less 15 acres of a sokeman belonging to the manor of Beaumont (77b) there had been two villeins, two bordars, and a slave, though by 1086 these five had been reduced to three bordars. But still the sokeman had a demesne team, though his 'men' no longer possessed the team which had ploughed their land, wood for fifty swine and two acres of meadow, and the value of the holding, or rather perhaps its rent, was in 1086 doubled from the former 20*s*. A Castle Rising sokeman (142b) is said to have had twenty-six bordars on his 60 acres, and if this seems improbable, one at Roydon on the same folio had twenty-five and two slaves. Many a free man had very much less than this, nor could he show the mill and saltpans recorded for these sokemen's holdings. Six Snettisham sokemen (142) had two carucates, ten villeins, six bordars, and a slave, together with ten acres of meadow, a half-share in a mill, and a fishery (see also a Brampton sokeman, fol. 414b). These men, it is true, were connected with royal manors, and so may well have been more favourably situated and consequently more prosperous than many of their fellows. But the seven Ely sokemen at Islington (213) had eleven bordars and three slaves on their two-teamed carucate. On the other hand, we find a high proportion of sokemen with holdings expressed as a very small number of acres, and apparently devoid of beasts of the plough or of helpers. To differentiate free men and sokemen on the score of their respective properties is obviously impossible, and we can hardly say that the sokeman is plainly less free than the *liber homo*. Perhaps Stenton's suggestion that the free man 'may have been able to claim an ancestry which gave him higher rank than the sokeman' is the correct clue.[1] The term 'sokeman', as he has further said (*op. cit.*, p. 508), 'is indefinite as is *villanus*'.

While many an anonymous *liber homo* was no doubt not only

[1] Stenton: *Anglo-Saxon England*, p. 509.

of thegnly status but was as prosperous as a minor thegn, and many sokemen differed from free men only in the terminology employed, we have none the less to visualise East Anglian society as composed in great measure of 'large numbers of men maintaining themselves as independent members of society on resources which can have been little more than adequate for their subsistence'.[1]

[1] Stenton: *Anglo-Saxon England*, p. 510. He further points out that these could not always have supplemented their resources by occasional labour, 'for the demand for labour must have been limited'.

CHAPTER XI

Commendation, Sokeright, and Services

COMMENDATION

The preface to the IE does not require that pre-Conquest tenurial relationships shall be recorded by the Inquest officials. But since they were supposed to note how much land each free man and sokeman had, though they did not do so, and principles of succession to estates had been established, it was an obvious precaution to try to discover, however broadly, the conditions under which land was held. Their inclusion in the formal record of the Inquest would, in view of the many divergent claims to lawful succession, form valuable evidence when future disputes had to be considered.

Maitland long ago warned us of some of the difficulties inherent in what was in fact recorded in DB. 'We cannot', he wrote, 'expect that men will be very accurate in stating the legal relationship that existed twenty years ago.'[1] We can never be sure, from the character of DB, whether the man said to have held an estate did so directly from the king, or from some unnamed intermediate lord. We do not as a rule know what protector, in the early years of Anglo-Norman England, a man whose lord was recently dead or exiled might have adopted. Sometimes we do; Godric the priest, who had been commended to Edric of Laxfield before the latter was outlawed and exiled, afterwards became the man of Northmann.[2]

We hear much of commendation, but we are never told exactly what this implies, though we can guess that the relationship between lord and man was a highly variable one. Maitland sketched for us some of the implications of the word, reminding us that by Æthelstan's law (ii.2) every man must have a lord.

[1] *DBB*, p. 63.

[2] After the Conquest a sokeman 'turned to Wigot of Wallingford for protection' (137b2), and a thegn who could go to what lord he pleased turned of his own accord to Arnulf of Hesdin (70a2); see also fols. 32bi, 58a2, 36ai.

The association of a minor landholder with a great thegn, an earl, or a powerful religious house would furnish advantages to either party to the contract. The small man would have someone to help him preserve or obtain his lawful rights, support him where possible in a court of law, and generally act as his protector: 'for his defence', as DB occasionally says.

Ballard claimed that the free man could commend himself to a lord, whereas the sokeman could not.[1] But this definition is not valid: the sokemen of DB are the *liberi homines* of early charters, we have been reminded by Douglas. We meet many instances where men were free, but Stigand had their soke: these are not instances of differentiation, for all but the greatest men were in someone's soke or that of the Hundred, and no man was outside the king's justice.

A large number of entries unfortunately do not tell us to whom the tenants of an estate were commended; we hear merely of *liberi homines commendati*.[2] Often we find a long consecutive string of such entries, and are inclined to wonder if those concerned were in fact commended to the last person previously mentioned as having possessed commendation. Yet we apparently hear of the commendation of a bordar with 1½ acres to Burgheard (Cotton, 286).[3] But the phrase at Sparham (270), '. . . a free man with one bordar over whom his predecessor had only commendation' probably implies the commendation of the free man, not of the bordar.

Certainly the practice of commendation extended far below the level of the great men of a province or shire. At Cove (313b) two free men were commended to a certain Edric who was himself commended to Edric the predecessor of William Malet.[4] Vigulfr had the commendation of a number of free men, but for one of his Coddenham holdings he was commended to Toli the sheriff. Besides high-ranking and well-endowed women such as Queen Edith and her namesake 'the fair', 'the rich', we hear of lesser female possessors of commendation, e.g. Æthelgyth

[1] A. Ballard: *The Domesday Inquest*, p. 122.

[2] e.g. at Ashfield (306), Benhall (309), Thorpe (360b).

[3] Could he have been a formerly free man reduced in status? Two bordars of 1086 are said to have held a quarter of a virgate freely in King Edward's day (84b2).

[4] See also Winston (305b).

(415b), who had held also under King Edward, and Quengeva (369b), who at Waldingfield (424b) shared a man's commendation with her son Beorhtmær.

We could reasonably expect the commendation-tie to be indivisible. But equal shares of a man's commendation are frequently noted, while Robert Malet's tenant Walter of Caen had 'a quarter of a free man', and St Edmund three-quarters of Wulfwine's commendation.[1] We even find lords with one-third and two-thirds, and one-sixth and five-sixths of a man's commendation.[2] The number of occasions on which men are said to be *integri* or *dimidii* is large.

We might have expected, too, to find the commendation-tie invariably indissoluble, but unless he was in no position to argue the man who, in Maitland's phrase, 'goes with his land to his lord' could not commit himself to that extent for fear that his protector would not keep his share of the bargain, or might fall out of favour with a greater man.[3] We have seen in DB degrees of freedom; men could or could not sell their land. Sometimes we hear of qualifying clauses; a man could sell only if he first offered the land to his lord, or if he gave his lord 2*s*. for the privilege of doing so.[4]

Remarkably little directly referring to commendation appears in the Essex text; the term indeed is found only half a dozen times. Two instances are straightforward references to the persons to whom pre-Conquest free men had been commended; one stresses that the holder's predecessor had no customary service from the tenant, but only his commendation.[5] The other three mention that a lord had the commendation of the persons recorded, but that they held freely, or could sell their land, or go to what lord they would.[6] Here as elsewhere commendation is a terminable association.

[1] e.g. Thornham (322); at Boulge (411b) a free man with only six acres was commended to both Haldein and Wulfric: see also Bredfield (318, 387) and Wyverstone (321b).

[2] Cookley (333b), Wyverstone (309).

[3] Maitland: *DBB*, p. 71. He added 'we dare not say a man may commend himself without commending his land also'.

[4] Islington (207), Fritton (260); also Dersingham (278b), where only 18 of the 21 free men could sell.

[5] Nayland (47), Hasingham (102b); Maldon (6).

[6] Fols. 25, 40b, 75.

Commendation must, however, surely be implied when we are told that the holder of an estate was someone's 'man', e.g. *Coleman homo Wisgari* (40b). The instances of Leofhild and of the man of Ansger whose land was no part of his fief have already been quoted (pp. 19, 28). Twice we read of the act of commendation; a free man 'came of his own accord' to Westminster Abbey (100), and another 'put' a half-hide at Wennington in the same abbey (15). The practice apparently continued after the Conquest; an Englishman voluntarily became the man of Geoffrey of Manneville (62b), and 'in the time of King William' a free man was 'made the man of the predecessor of Ralf Peverel, but did not give him his land' (71b). We cannot imagine that after the Conquest men possessed such liberal opportunity to change their lord at will as before. Indeed, it has very properly been said that the essence of the Norman conception of tenure was that men should hold 'of', not 'under', their lords; *de*, not *sub*. The privileges of men of relatively humble position, it has been said, implied 'a freedom that could not be tolerated . . . they represented anarchical tendencies that might well have disrupted the community'.[1]

An examination of two small Suffolk fiefs, those of Robert of Mortain and Earl Hugh, which occupy only 2½ and 9 folios respectively, will show the extraordinary complexity of pre-Conquest associations. The holders of the lands which ultimately became the count of Mortain's, who total just 100 persons, had been commended in eleven different ways; the lords listed include the king, Earl Harold, Bishop Æthelmær, the abbot of Ely, Ælfric the priest, and 'Godemann the *antecessor* of Roger Bigot'. Wulfnoth had held the manor of Combs (291) under King Edward, where he himself is said to have had 50 free men. How did Brian of Brittany, here said to be the predecessor of Robert, come to acquire the lands of persons so variously commended? Why did not those commended to the forerunners of Robert Malet and Roger Bigot (290) have these barons for their lords in 1086? Acquisition of a few of Ely's free men cannot have been the result of their incorporation in an adjacent manor, for Robert of Mortain had little property in the Hundreds in which these had been. But he or Brian may

[1] H. R. Loyn: *Anglo-Saxon England and the Norman Conquest*, p. 329.

at one time have had more, for the C3 Schedule in IE accuses him of having six 'men of the soke' at Drinkstone and 40 acres of sokeland at Rattlesden (DB fol. 291; H, p. 194).

We are not told who had the commendation of a number of the free men mentioned in Earl Hugh's *breve*, though his anonymous *antecessor* is referred to (298b, 302b), and perhaps we should assume that those named who were commended to him, and are often styled 'thegn', had no lord but the king.[1] Eighteen persons are mentioned as having had the commendation of those whose lands the earl, whose *antecessor* is nowhere named in vol. ii, had acquired. They include the countess Ealdgyth, Toli the former sheriff, Earl Gyrth, and an Ely free man whose acquisition by the earl is not listed in either Schedule. The figure appearing most frequently is a certain Burgheard, who in five holdings had had 71 free men and women commended to him.[2] This may be the 'Burgheard of Mendlesham' who held land in Lothing and Hartismere Hundreds, which passed to the king and St Edmund and Hugh de Montfort, close to Wangford Hundred in which most of the properties attributed to a man of this name lay. But again, on what principle these people's lands, in eight different Hundreds, were allotted to or acquired by the earl, is a mystery.

SALE OF LAND

Another contention relative to a potential differentiation between free man and sokeman might be that the free man could sell or grant his land and leave his lord, while the sokeman could not. This might well have an element of truth about it, but DB can show a number of passages denying the inevitability of such a differentiation. Ballard, who claimed that holding *libere* implied that a man so holding could sell his land, gave his figures for Essex, where, he stated, of 49 free men only two could not sell their land, while of 112 sokemen only five could do so.[3] One Essex exception to such definition would

[1] Skúli, who held the manor of Barnham, is called 'a thegn of King Edward' (299).

[2] It is of course quite likely that these do not represent seventy-one different persons. A man of this name was a relative of the former Earl, Ælfgar.

[3] Ballard: *The Domesday Inquest*, pp. 113–14.

certainly seem to be Leofhild, for though she held Abbess Roding (57b) as a manor, could not hold it of anyone but Barking Abbey.[1]

The number of Essex entries which mention power to transfer land or the reverse is only about forty. Norfolk shows appreciably fewer, and there are only about half a dozen instances in which the tenants could sell their land.[2] One passage is of such a character that if we had more parallels to it we might presume a general rule. Certain free men at Brockdish (139) could not give or sell their land without Stigand's leave, 'for he had the soke'. But sokeright over a man does not seem to have bound him to the lord who possessed it; 'the lord's right was superiority, not ownership'.[3] Over and over again in the Essex Domesday we are informed that someone could 'sell his land', 'go where he would', 'recede', or 'depart', but if he did so, the soke 'remained in the manor' or to its lord.[4] There is an odd instance in which we are told that Coleman was 'so free that he could go where he would, with his sake and soke', but none the less he remained Wihtgar's man.[5] Wihtgar must have guarded himself against the total loss of an adherent.

Suffolk furnishes about 150 reports of power to sell land or the reverse. What is marked in that county is that of the groups of free men in a village treated as a whole, some could sell and some could not.[6] We find plenty of free men without power to sell their land, or to sell it without licence to do so, and while most of the sokemen were similarly restricted, the occasional man so categorised could sell.[7]

Round long ago commented on the variety of formulae used

[1] Holding this estate 'for a manor' probably implies no more than that she, not the abbey, was liable for the geld due from it.

[2] Four of these are the instances quoted on p. 132, where the land had initially to be offered to the lord, or a fine of 2*s*. paid for leave to sell.

[3] Stenton: *Types of Manorial Structure in the Northern Danelaw*, p. 12.

[4] e.g. fols. 10b, 44, 50b, 78, 92b. So might the 'custom', e.g. at Hudeston (181b).

[5] Roding Morel, fol. 40b.

[6] e.g. at Bedingfield (368) or Acton (416).

[7] e.g. at Finningham (309b), Boxted (350), Onehouse (291), Bures (360), Beccles (369b), Middleton (238). There was disagreement about a Whinburgh sokeman (208); the Midford Hundred jury said he could not sell his land, but the sheriff contradicted them and said he could sell without his lord's leave. Another instance of a sokeman (but only one out of half a dozen at Standon) with power to sell his land appears on fol. 142b2.

by the clerks when noting whether men could or could not sell their land, and on what conditions.[1] It may be that we are not always told all that might have been said of the conditions governing such transactions. It is not infrequently mentioned that land could not be sold without the lord's leave (e.g. at Thorpe Abbotts, fol. 139). Sometimes we are given additional information. The free men of Pirleston (263) could not give or sell their land without St Edmund's leave, but they also had to obtain that of Stigand, who had the soke over them, which reads like a parallel to the Brockdish case quoted above. A Norwich burgess was so much bound to the royal demesne (*ita dominicae regis*) that he 'could not withdraw or do homage without leave' (116).[2]

Sometimes we obtain detailed statements about the conditions under which estates were held. Guthmund, brother of a former abbot of Ely, had been granted a competence to furnish him with adequate status and income. Among his lands was the manor of Nacton (406b), but he could not give or sell it away from the abbey, to which it was to return if Guthmund no longer held it. Bjorn bought an estate at Little Bealings (373), which the abbey was to recover on his death: the IE (H, p. 151) adds that he was not empowered to sell it.

Purchase, indeed, was frequently not outright purchase, but more in the nature of a lease, for life or lives. Such a system was probably adopted more often by ecclesiastical than by lay landholders; the former possibly both got more in the way of services out of their tenants than the thegn or baron could hope to exact, but they also stood more chance of losing control over the land. Certainly the religious houses lost, at least temporarily, a good deal of land after the Conquest. We have seen how the newcomers took over estates which in 1066 were in the occupation of their predecessors, even though they were being held of a local abbey (p. 87). Several times it is recorded in DB, either because usurpation had occurred or it was feared it might occur, that land was to return to the grantor on the tenant's death; his heir, English or Norman, was to have no automatic right of

[1] Round: *FE*, pp. 22–6.

[2] Thirty-six Thetford burgesses could be the men of no one except the king: it was not only in the rural districts that men commended themselves or did service.

succession. Gislingham (444b) had been part of the demesne of St Edmund in King Edward's day. Abbot Leofstan leased it to a free man called Ælfsige and his wife on condition that after their deaths it should return to the abbey. A priest, Edmund, who had commended himself to the abbey of Ely, obtained land from his wife (perhaps a marriage-portion), and with her consent agreed not to sell or bequeath it to any but Ely Abbey (Brandeston and Clopton, 431b). In King Edward's reign Leofgifu was holding half a carucate at Topesfield (372b) from the archbishop of Canterbury, and arranged that his church of Holy Trinity should receive another half-carucate after her death. She lived into King William's reign, and was indeed then seized of the land, but at the Inquest John fitzWaleram claimed it, and St Edmund the soke over all of it.[1] But where a free woman with a small estate, said to be *libera terra*, at Mellis (419) bestowed (*concesserat*) it before the Conquest on St Edmund, Aubrey de Ver had somehow obtained it by 1086, for his predecessor had had the soke and the commendation of a number of free men and women also holding land in Hartismere Hundred.

Some of these transactions imply what Maitland described as the occupier 'carrying his land to his lord'. He did so, no doubt, in part to acquire the patronage and protection of a powerful establishment (and possibly to acquire working capital on loan); he may have had to furnish in return rent and certain services. But there must, even before the Conquest, have been numerous bargains by which the land proceeded from above. The religious houses at least, sometimes perhaps because they found it more convenient to draw rent from a tenant than to administer an estate through their own reeve, sometimes to acquire the military and other services of a dependant, would lease a holding or component of a manor which, however, was to remain inalienable. These, the abbey thegnlands, are not frequently described in vol. ii by this name, as they are in the south-western shires, though they are often so styled in the IE. Thegnland was not necessarily confined to ecclesiastical estates; there are instances of its occurrence on, e.g., royal

[1] Similar arrangements are reported for Norton (286) and Pakenham (361b); see also Livermere (363b).

manors. Robert d'Auberville had holdings which the Inquest adjudged to be thegnland of the royal manors of Winsford and Dulverton (98bi). The omnipresent and inherent danger in thegnland was that it had to be created out of demesne land or the *terra villanorum* (e.g. at Wellington, fol. 89a2), and the lessee might refuse to observe the terms of the lease or even claim that he held it in chief; in either circumstance rents and services were liable to be lost, and to be recoverable only at considerable trouble, expense, and delay.

SOKERIGHT

Maitland, summing up the provisions of the *Leges Henrici*, that 'treatise on soke', confessed that 'the picture that is left on our minds is that of a confused conflict between inconsistent and indefinite principles'.[1] To attempt to delineate eleventh-century legal systems by means of DB would produce no more satisfactory result, for DB is no legal treatise, and merely affords us glimpses of who possessed sokeright, indications of whom lesser men were the justiciables, and statements about the proceeds and certain limitations of judicial powers.

The principle from which one is obliged to start is that adopted by Maitland; that in the Conqueror's eyes all justice was ultimately royal justice, though both he and his predecessors had granted to certain religious houses and lay magnates the right to administer justice to their dependants or to retain the profits of such administration, and to receive the fines exacted from their justiciables in the Hundred- or manor-court where they did not themselves operate a court. But just what was a dependant? Was he such because he lived and worked in a certain district over which local judicial powers had been conferred, or because he was the tenant or servant of the lord? Was sokeright, indeed, inherent in the man or in the land? – a problem which confronted us also when considering commendation. Further, if a lord enfeoffed an inferior, did the beneficiary acquire also sokeright over his tenants on his sub-fief? And to what court did a man owe suit? Private courts of justice do not seem to have been numerous at the period, and indeed it would

[1] Maitland: *DBB*, p. 80.

be absurd to try to institute a court for the smaller holdings, or for a multiplicity of holdings scattered over a wide area. So long as the possessor of sokeright gets the fines exacted from his dependants, he will not greatly trouble himself as to the court in which judgment is given. It is highly unlikely that Holy Trinity, Canterbury, or St Mary of Grestain, who possessed sokeright in just a few places in East Anglia, held courts for their dependants.[1]

The number of individuals and institutions said to have possessed sokeright in 1086 is naturally also comparatively small (see Appendix B). We should expect that enjoyed by King Edward or by the Godwinesons to devolve upon King William, but sometimes this seems to have been acquired by Earl Ralf, e.g. at Bedingham (131) or Cautley and Hassingham (122b). In Norfolk a vast amount had been enjoyed by both Earl Ralf and Stigand, but we are not always told whose it was in 1086.[2] Occasionally we are: William of Warenne seems to have the four free men of Methwold (162) who had been Stigand's, and the soke of his North Elmham sokemen (191b) had been transferred to the royal manor of Milcham. The soke of those inhabitants of Cautley and Hassingham which Ralf had enjoyed after he became earl had, however, returned to the Crown: Godric was holding them *in manu regis*, and it looks as if at Hethersett (150) Ralf's right had passed to Earl Alan.[3] Sokeright is said in a few entries to have been bestowed since the Conquest. The king had given that of Gyrth's freemen, whom he had stolen from King Edward, to St Edmund, and also that of Brook 'when he first visited Edmundsbury' (210). Earl Ralf gave that which he had shared with Stigand at Coltishall (133), and Belaugh (229b) and the soke of Shropham (152) to his follower Walter de Dol.

The Essex text does not give us a great deal of information about sokeright. Frequently we are told merely that it was inherent in the manor concerned; e.g. we hear of 'the king's soke

[1] e.g. fols. 373, 416b; 291b.

[2] See, e.g., the entries for Mintlyn (197b), Norwich (116); Beighton (264), Brundall (200).

[3] Soke at Horningtoft and Kipton (120b) which had been Stigand's, but 'invaded' by Ralf, was 'therefore' in Godric's hands: William de Noyers had that which had been Stigand's at Weasenham (121).

of Lawford' (40b), of money paid 'from the soke of Waltham' (64), that a man's soke 'lay in Warley' (92b). Apart from the king and the above instances, only eight landholders are mentioned as having sokeright, all of whom are pre-Conquest figures.[1]

In almost every instance it is only the most influential of men, besides the king and the earl, or of ecclesiastical institutions, who are said to possess or to have possessed sokeright. This is only to be expected, for sokeright was not something to be lightly granted. Comparatively few thegns are said to have possessed its privileges in 1066; it would be interesting to know if any or all of these were serving or had at the material time served as royal *ministri*. For they include Wihtgar, and the atmosphere of the entries concerning him suggests that he may well have been a sheriff's deputy in south Suffolk and north Essex, and also Northmann, who is probably the former sheriff of that name.[2] Certainly a former sheriff, Robert fitzWymarc, had had the privilege (401), and Siward of Maldon (416, 416b) seems to have been influential enough to have been a royal official.[3]

There must, however, remain some doubt regarding the position of those who are said to have possessed soke 'under' someone, e.g. Scalpi the housecarl 'under' Harold (Churchford, 419b), Ælfgar *sub* Siward of Maldon (Kentwell, 355), and Ælfgifu of Stigand, to whom she was commended (Rishangles, Thorndon, 322 *bis*). The phrase might suggest that those concerned had been appointed by their superiors to oversee justice and collect the profits thereof, doubtless for a consideration. Northmann held Cavendish (428) with sake and soke, but 'under' King Edward, and he certainly was then a royal official.

Sokeright was purchaseable, though doubtless the royal

[1] Holy Trinity, Canterbury (99b), St Ouen (22); Queen Edith (54), Ansger the marshal (61b), Robert fitzWymarc (45b), Wihtgar (41 *ter*), Wulfwine (58), and another Wulfwine the *antecessor* of Aubrey de Ver (78).

[2] e.g. fols. 348b, 391, 428b; 349b, 428.

[3] Did their successors, e.g. Richard fitzGilbert and Ralf Peverel, inherit their sokeright? It rather looks as if they did; Wulfric the king's thegn had the soke of Waldingfield (425) and Ranulf the brother of Ilger who was his successor obtained the land 'by the king's gift, with sake and soke'.

licence for the transaction had to be obtained. Bishop Æthelmær had bought the soke over the bordars and those who 'sought the fold' at Beighton (194b) from Earl Ælfgar. One of the four sokemen at Oulton, part of the royal manor of Causton (114b), had been sold by the reeve of the vill for 10*s*., probably to Earl Ralf. It may have been his services which were sold, but sokeright over him may have been included also. But it is also made clear that at Bradfield (362) – and probably this would be true of all St Edmund's manors – sokeright would remain the Saint's 'whoever bought the land'.

Infringement of sokeright is quite frequently mentioned. The bishop of Thetford's man Ralf was 'detaining the soke of two sokemen' at Cressingham (197b). Lisois de Moustières 'retained' the soke over Shropham and Brettenham free men (239b), and his successor Eudes fitzHerbert had retained it also.[1] The free men of Barton Turf (159) over whom St Benet of Holme had enjoyed soke seem to have become William of Warenne's by the dubious process of 'exchange'. But the soke over the men who seem to have been appropriated by various barons from royal manors, e.g. Hingham (110b) and Croxton (136b), may not have been acquired also by those who obtained them.

Sokeright would seem to have been inheritable: so much we might suspect from those numerous instances of men who could sell their land but not the soke over it. We are told that soke over the men of Weston (147) lay in the royal manor of Foulsham, but in 1086 Earl Alan had it 'because' his predecessor Ralf had it. But it can be argued that 'the king's soke' really implies that of the king and earl, and so we might expect Alan to acquire automatically soke said to have been Ralf's although the king is unmentioned.[2] Raymond Gerold had had soke 'over the land only, when he departed', and this is said to have passed to Roger of Poitou, styled his successor (139b).

But it is hard to say what lies behind the occasional instance of the possession in 1086 of sokeright which can hardly have been inherited. Soke which lay in Foulsham, a royal manor,

[1] See also Pirleston, Redenhall, and Denton (139b).

[2] Passages quoted above, where Godric and William of Noyers had acquired Ralf's sokeright, may mean only that they collected the customary royal share of two-thirds in their master's interests. On the other hand, the soke of eight Witchingham men is said to lie in the royal manor of Foulsham, 'but the earl has it'.

had become Walter Giffard's (Ringland, 241b) or was in the hands of William d'Écouis or Humfrey fitzAubrey (240b, 241, 149b, 262b). Ralf Baignard had sake and soke at Hempnall and Boyland (248b, 249); here, perhaps, in right of his predecessor's possession of it. The king had sake and soke over the whole Hundred of North Erpingham except over the land of Siward Barn (128, 185), which William d'Écouis had acquired (223b).[1]

As with all other Domesday topics, the phraseology regarding sokeright is highly variable. The Boughton sokemen (251) *jacent ad socam*, the free men of Fincham (159b) *ad socam abbatis de Rameseia*, and Ralf of Beaufoy seems to have had the soke of men at Mattishall and elsewhere (228) 'from the abbot'. Some statements are not readily to be fully explained. The men in a variety of holdings (129b–30) were 'all free with soke when Godric received them', but in 1086 they had to pay £7.[2] At Upton (129) the king and the earl had sake and soke over twenty sokemen, and 'commendation in (? and) soke' of seven more. Fifty-five acres at Rollesby (272) were 'in soke'. The wording of a Brockley entry (349b) suggests that the king's two free men could sell their soke (*sed poterant vendere in soca Sancti Edmundi*), but I suspect that the interpretation should be that they could sell, but the sokeright over them would remain St Edmund's, who had the soke of the other free man recorded. Sometimes we encounter contradictory information; at Aveley (401b) sokeright is at one point in a single entry ascribed to Robert fitzWymarc, at another to St Edmund.

References to soke are normally of four kinds; to the soke of the individual, to that resident in a particular Hundred or vill or manor, to a division of sokeright between two or more lords, and to the retention of soke by the lord if a man sold his land or withdrew his commendation; occasionally it is noted that a man so doing could carry his soke with him to his new lord.[3]

Quite often entries make no mention of sokeright. We would, for example, expect to find St Edmund with soke throughout

[1] The statement about the king does not seem to be correct, unless it should be limited to free men (fol. 185), for St Benet of Holme had soke over forty-nine Thurgarton sokemen (216)

[2] This could mean that there was no obvious inheritor of them, and Godric had them 'in the king's hand'.

[3] See p. 135.

his fief within his peculiar Hundreds, but though he is said to have the soke of Tuddenham (355), sokeright is unmentioned in the Worlington entry which precedes it. There are also many entries in lay fiefs where we can only guess or deduce who had the soke.

SOKE 'IN THE HUNDRED' AND 'IN THE MANOR'

The frequent references both to 'soke in the Hundred' and 'soke in the manor', often to a named manor, and occasionally to 'soke in the vill', encourage us to consider whether in addition to the Hundred-courts there were in 1066 and/or 1086 fairly numerous manorial courts of justice in East Anglia.[1] The fact that the majority of the manors concerned are royal rather suggests that the court concerned would often be the Hundred-court, held at a royal vill. A number of Essex entries refer to the 'soke of the manor', or of 'the king's manor', e.g. of Lawford (40b), Great Chesterford (3b), and Writtle (5b). Writtle seems to have been the Chelmsford Hundred-manor, but Lawford would be inconveniently situated as the administrative headquarters of Tendring. But there are besides a number of entries which suggest the reverse. The soke of a Childerditch sokeman 'lay in the land of St Paul at Warley' (92b), and Warley was a St Paul's manor. Two free men were in the soke of the manor of Stapleford Abbots (20), a manor of St Edmund. A Copford free man and a Theydon Gernon sokeman could 'go where he would', 'sell his land', but the soke of each would remain in the manor if he did so. The holders of these manors were the bishop of London (10b) and Eudes fitzHerbert (50b), succeeding Wulfmær. But while St Ouen (22) had two parts of the soke of West Mersea (the king had the other third), it is to be presumed that the inhabitants attended the Winstree Hundred-court, not a manorial court. They were, it is said, the king's sokemen.

It is, however, made plain by DB that sometimes the whole soke of a Hundred was in a single hand. Ely had the soke of $5\frac{1}{2}$ Hundreds (Kembrook, 385b). In this entry it is said also that

[1] 'Soke in the vill' of Sudbury occurs on fols. 286b, 287.

the abbey possessed soke in the whole Hundred of Colneis in which Kembrook lay (see also fols 292, 406, and 424). But, as not infrequently happens, the statement is qualified elsewhere; on fol. 343b St Audrey is said to have soke 'over all this land except the hall of Walton'. On fol. 413 Ely is said to have soke throughout the Hundred of Wilford, but it looks as if at Hollesley on the same folio Robert Malet had received that of his holding at the king's hands. On the same folio it is also stated that Ely has the soke of the whole Hundred of Carlford, but certain entries seem to deny it.[1]

For Bury, out of the $8\frac{1}{2}$ Hundreds over which St Edmund had sokeright, the whole soke of Blackbourn (Rushford, 421) and Bradmere double Hundred (Sapiston, 436b), separate in DB, but later one, is mentioned. The 'whole soke' of Guiltcross Hundred is said to be in the royal manor of Kenninghall (Gasthorpe, 127b). The soke of the Hundred of North Greenhoe was attached to the royal manor of Wighton (113b) 'whoever holds there'.[2] Guthmund had been given 'the whole soke' at Occold (410b) by his brother Wulfric, abbot of Ely.

We might then think that 'the whole soke' implies that of the villagers and the sokemen, that of the free men being reserved for the king, or the king and the earl, or 'the Hundred', which all seem to mean very much the same thing, especially in view of the statements about men having soke only over their demesne or 'hall' (p. 147). But this is very doubtful, though it is not impossible that those to whom sokeright had been granted did not receive the fines for trespasses in full, the earl's third penny and perhaps a royal share also being first deducted.

That men's soke lay in a royal manor may merely imply that their soke was 'in the Hundred', and that justice was done at the

[1] Playford (314b), Otley (433), and Little Bealings (442). The other Hundreds concerned were Loes (where in one place the *antecessor* of Earl Hugh had the sokeright, but of Ely; fol. 302b); Plomesgate (where in three holdings soke does not seem to have been Ely's, fols. 297, 316, and 338b); and the half-Hundred of Parham, where, at Parham itself (285), Thormond had enjoyed the soke of three free men, Ely of another three.

[2] This phrase does not imply that if the king granted such a manor to one of his tenants-in-chief the Hundred-soke, previously divided between the king and the earl, would pass with it; it must refer to sub-tenancies, whose holders might be the men of a variety of barons.

royal manor named, which presumably was the headquarters of the Hundred. The instance of Wighton quoted above would certainly suggest this. But to this hypothesis the text of DB vol. ii furnishes certain objections. In Forehoe Hundred soke is said to have been in the royal manors both of Wymondham (166) and Hingham (227, 227b, 252b). The soke of Starston (139) was 'in the half-Hundred of Earsham', of which half-Hundred Stigand had, with certain exceptions, possessed the soke (139b).[1] It is possible that, as for other factors, several Hundreds were treated as a group.[2] We hear of the soke of Walsham Hundred (113b), but also that free men in Blofield Hundred produce £13 'in the outsoke of Walsham' and that a few of those at Thrigby in East Flegg Hundred (135) are 'worth 9*s*. in the outsoke of Walsham'.[3] But it is true that the Witton entry (123b) records that the soke of its free men is 'in the Hundred to the third penny'; still, the Hundred might be Walsham, and not Blofield in which Witton lay; the third penny is presumably the earl's share. In Great Yarmouth (118) is said to lie 'two parts of the soke of three Hundreds', and since Yarmouth was geographically in East Flegg, the three might be this, Walsham, and Blofield.

Just as commendation was divisible, and not necessarily equally, so was sokeright. At Thornham (437b), St Edmund had three-quarters, the king the other quarter. At Wimbotsham and Stow Bardolph (274) it had been equally divided between St Benedict of Ramsey and the predecessor of Hermer de Ferrières, as at Stalham (148b, 180) it had been between Edric and 'the king and the earl', and at Herringswell (385b) between St Edmund and Wihtgar. The division of soke between the king and the earl is of frequent mention. At Cranley (429) the king had shared the sokeright equally with Ælfric, while at Stoke (382b), 'beyond the bridge', Ely had half the soke.

There is a further complication. Sokeright has its additional

[1] The soke of Mundham (140) and Pirnough (177b) in Loddon Hundred seems to have been 'in Earsham', and possibly that of Gillingham (141b) also, for it was *in censu de Ersam*.

[2] For one group of Hundreds, Gallow, Brothercross, and Holt, the entries for all of which come in sequence in DB, sokeright is unmentioned.

[3] Free men in Freethorpe in Blofield Hundred are said to be 'valued in the £13', and I think this £13 must also be 'the outsoke of Walsham'.

limitations. Certain pleas, though not in uniform fashion, are frequently reserved to the Crown. But not invariably; in Yorkshire neither the king nor the earl received the profits of justice where certain ecclesiastical institutions held land.[1] Note that though the king may claim that all justice, and all right to the profits of jurisdiction, emanate from the Crown, often it is the earl who receives a proportion of them, often one-third, for it is the earl or his deputy who is responsible for the maintenance of the king's peace, and very largely for the collection of the profits of justice.

Occasionally in the Norfolk text, more frequently in that of Suffolk, but never in the Essex section, we hear of the 'six forfeitures'. These, according to the so-called 'Laws of William I', were for the crimes of failure to serve in the fyrd when summoned to do so, breaches of the peace, homicide, housebreaking, and being deserving of outlawry and succouring outlaws, and were reserved to the Crown.[2] There were, after all, crimes which could not be expiated by means of a money payment. When King William confirmed the liberties of Ely, his document stressed that they included only 'all forfeitures which are emendable' (H, p. xviii). Sometimes we are told that while someone other than the king, or the king and the earl, had sokeright, the king (or the king and the earl) 'has the six forfeitures' (e.g. Calthorpe, 179b; 'the other Snareshill', 178). But this is not invariable; at Blofield (194b) the bishop had them. We find Ely Abbey and Wihtgar as having possessed men's commendation and soke, but St Edmund had the six forfeitures, e.g. at Clopton (384b), Stoke-by-Clare (391), and Wixoe (414), while Chedburgh (384b) was in Ely's demesne 'with all custom', except the six forfeitures of St Edmund. Over twenty-four of the Tunstead sokemen St Benet had only three forfeitures (244).

[1] Fol. 298bi. This also lists certain persons who had sokeright in 1066, as does fol. 280bi for Nottinghamshire and Derbyshire; see also fols. 238bi and 1bi.

[2] DB 252ai implies that the pleas of three – breaches of the king's peace given by the sheriff, *heinfare* (housebreaking), and *forestal* (ambush) – were reserved to the royal demesne throughout England, but it is highly doubtful whether this is the correct interpretation of the text; see Ballard: *The Domesday Inquest*, p. 85. These three are mentioned also as the king's in the entry for the city of Hereford (179ai). The various versions of the legal codes vary.

LIMITATIONS OF SOKERIGHT

But we hear further of certain forms of limitation of sokeright. Burgheard had the soke of his free men as of his villeins (Cotton, 285b), and Leofwine Croc over his 'hall' or demesne and his bordars (Buxhall, 350): the inclusion of such information suggests that it was not inevitable that a man should have the soke of his free men and peasantry. Indeed, at Wenham (425b) Auti had soke over his demesne, but the soke of the villeins was in Bergholt.[1] Guthmund, too, is said to have had soke only over the demesne of his hall (Haughley, 408b). But at Burstall (377) Godwine, Stigand's man, had had the soke of his house (which surely implies the demesne) and of three acres, though the remainder lay in the royal manor of Bergholt. This phrase must be intended to stress that while a man might have soke over his villagers, that of the free men and sokemen attached to the manor might be another's. In the Hundred of Stow, from which the first two examples are taken, the soke of most men was the king's, or the king and the earl's, or 'in the Hundred'.[2] The bishop of Rochester had soke of his manor of Freckenham (381), but St Edmund that of the free men added to it by Earl Ralf. In Diss Hundred (130b) the soke of those who had less than 30 acres lay in the royal manor of Fersfield, but if they held more, in the Hundred.[3]

The soke of the half-Hundred of Diss was in the Hundred except in so far as the land of St Edmund, where it was shared equally between king and Saint, of Wulfgeat, and of Stigand, was concerned (Burston, 114). That of Stigand's half-Hundred of Earsham was reduced by reason of St Edmund having the soke of Thorpe and St Audrey that of Pulham (139b). The king had the soke of Henstead (399b) except over the demesne of Haldein. In North Erpingham Hundred the king had soke

[1] Who were in his demesne? – there were villeins, bordars, and slaves at Wenham, but no free men or sokemen are mentioned.

[2] e.g. Buxhall (355b), Dagworth (408b), Creeting (350b).

[3] Does this imply that in the first instance the king got all the profit, while in the latter the earl received one-third? A writ of William II (*FD* no. 16, p. 59) may refer to this distinction: St Edmund's men were 'not to go to shire or Hundred unless in the time of King Edward they held so much land as made them worthy of it'.

except over the land of Siward Barn (Beckham, 128); this had passed to William d'Écouis.

THE PROFITS OF SOKERIGHT

Sokeright was a privilege which could be of considerable value. It is improbable that Sweyn had soke over all the men of the Hundreds of Clavering (46b) and Rochford (45b), but from the first he received 25*s.* and from the latter 100*s.* The annual fines, it is to be presumed, came to more than these sums. The soke of the Hundred-and-a-half of Midford, which belonged to St Audrey, was worth 60*s.*, and that of the Hundred of Clackclose brought St Benedict of Ramsey ten shillings more (214, 215b). The outsoke of the free men of Walsham brought in £13 (123b; see also 135), and the Hundred of Walsham rendered 40*s.* to the king and 20*s.* to the earl. 'The whole Hundred' of Shropham paid 40*s.* (177) and of Guiltcross 20*s.* (128). We are not told what proportion of the sum of £9 was contributed by the sokeright of West Flegg Hundred (146b); this may be connected with the pre- and post-Conquest sums noted under Great Yarmouth (118).

FOLDSOKE

There are references also to foldsoke. This looks as if it must have been one of the obligations concealed under the title of *consuetudines*. It is never mentioned in the Essex Domesday, and in the Suffolk text, save for three instances, only for the land of St Edmund. It is improbable, however, that the peasants' and peasant farmers' duty of penning their sheep in the lord's fold, so that he might have the benefit of the manure, was not exacted elsewhere also. In Norfolk it appears in the *breves* of only fourteen landholders, of whom St Edmund, oddly enough, is not one, while it is recorded only once for Ely Abbey. This suggests that this right was reported or recorded only spasmodically. Its occurrence is limited, too, to eight Hundreds, and it has been pointed out that these are not those in which the incidence of sheep is heaviest, from which the deduction has been drawn that its absence encouraged an increase in peasant sheep-breeding.[1]

It was not a post-Conquest innovation, for at Kirby Bedon (124) there had been twelve men whose duty it was to 'seek the fold' of Edric (*sequentes faldam Edrici*).[2] The formulae noting this obligation vary: the free men at Stow Bardolph (206) were *consueti ad faldam*; at Beighton (194b) Bishop Æthelmær had had by purchase sake and soke 'over the bordars and those who owe suit to the fold', while Earl Ralf had had this power over all the men of Walsham Hundred who 'sought the earl's fold', but over the remainder it was divided with the king.

At Hillington (203b), of a dozen men half were 'in foldsoke' and the other half free. St Benedict of Holme had soke over the Reedham men who 'sought the fold', but the soke of those not so bound was in the Hundred (216).

The possession of foldsoke did not also confer full sokeright, for while Ely had the commendation and foldsoke of two sokemen of Hoe (214), their soke was in the royal manor of Mileham (214).

SOKERIGHT AND THE GROWTH OF MANORIALISATION

The possession of sokeright was a factor which must to some extent have accelerated the manorialisation of East Anglia after the Conquest. The impression the text of DB often gives is of large numbers of groups of free men and of sokemen very loosely attached, if attached at all, to a particular manor before the Conquest. How slight the connection may have been cannot be determined, but it is conceivable that often rents and labour services can have entered into the matter very little. One might indeed expect these to be enjoyed by the possessor of commendation where sokeright and commendation were not in identical hands. But we are so frequently told of the addition, 'in the time of King William', of free men and sokemen to a manor, that we can only think that ties were being created or strengthened.

[1] *VCH: Norfolk*, ii, p. 31.

[2] See also fol. 129b.

Douglas has pointed out, for example, the tendency for the soke of all unattached free men to be regarded as the king's.[1] It is surely significant that we find *breves* for the free men of the king, and of his sheriff Roger Bigot. Their attachment to a manor may have been so recent, or even undetermined, that they had to be given sections to themselves. But no doubt they would ultimately be incorporated within a neighbouring royal manor.

Free men and sokemen so often lived at such considerable distances from the headquarters of manors that it may not have been easy to decide where their services should be employed. Sometimes, for the older-established manors, we are told where their services were required: those noted for Flempton 'owed service in Risby and Lackford and Hengrave' (358b); this is a St Edmunds manor.[2]

We do not, however, in vol. ii, as we do in vol. i, find first the description of a manor and then, headed 'soke of the manor', a long list of properties. But there are many occasions on which we cannot help feeling that no injustice would have been done, no error committed, by the adoption of such a system.

The thegnland of a manor was simultaneously becoming the land of the *milites*, those who discharged the military service demanded from a tenant-in-chief by the king. This is perhaps hardly the strengthening of a bond, for the essence of thegnland is that it is inalienable, though the duties demanded may have become more closely defined in post-Conquest times. Here, too, one can imagine the creation of demesne land where none had existed earlier. We do not find demesne on the East Anglian sokelands (though we find sokemen with demesne teams), but it is frequent in, e.g., those villages forming thegnland of Glastonbury Abbey which were physically separate from the *caput manerii*.[3]

[1] *Soc. Stud.*, p. 190.

[2] See also fols. 364–6.

[3] See the Wiltshire, Dorset, and especially the Somerset Domesdays, and the Summaries in the *Liber Exoniensis*. Miller (*The Abbey and Bishopric of Ely*, pp. 56, 58, 63) has pointed out how sokeland was being turned into thegnland and any difference between them being obliterated, and that soke was becoming a territorial burden.

CUSTOMARY DUTIES

Students of Domesday Book constantly find themselves reading that a lord holds a manor 'with all custom', or that lesser men owe 'all custom' to their lord or to the manor to which they were attached. But exactly what these obligations imply is very rarely specified, and when the nature of the due is stated, it is never definitely said that no more than this is required, and rarely who is obliged to render it. In vol. i we are told, for example, of villeins who have to render blooms of iron, of holdings which owe dues of swine and sheep and lambs to a manor, of churchscot and burial fees and obligation to military service and attending a court of law, of renders of a variety of fish.[1] But rarely can we feel that we are being told the whole story, and we hear so little of agricultural services that our knowledge of those demanded in the England of the Confessor and of the Conqueror is disappointingly scanty. We do, however, know that it was not only the villeins and bordars who had to perform them.[2] This is true of the eastern counties also.

Two terms which to some extent bear on the above recur in DB vol. ii. The one is *consuetudo*, and the other *servitium*. Both, we may think, imply the dues and/or services owed by a man to his lord in respect of tenure of land or of being his justiciable. Neither, it seems, is the automatic product of commendation or sokeright. Sometimes soke and commendation and 'service' or 'custom' do go together, as can be seen from the account of the Bury St Edmunds fief in Suffolk. But of eight men who were connected with the manor of Barton Bendish (250b), four were bound by 'all custom', while the other four were merely Ralf Baignard's sokemen. Again, Robert Malet was claiming some free men, three because of their commendation to his predecessor, the rest for 'all custom', and while a sokeman had been paying Ralf Peverel 3*s*. a year, the man had only been commended to Ralf's predecessor.[3]

[1] e.g. fols. 86bi, 91a1,2, 97bi, 42a, 175bi, 87bi; see also Finn: *An Introduction to Domesday Book*, pp. 237–9.

[2] See, e.g., fols. 163a2, 166a2, 174bi,2, 269bi,2, for some of the services rendered by thegns and radmen and free men. The burgesses of Steyning 'worked at the court' – on the demesne – 'like villeins' (17a2).

[3] Thorpe (171b), Maldon (5b).

But neither of these terms is capable at any time of strict definition. It has been said that they have 'different meanings for different sorts of men', and it could have been added that interpretation must surely depend on the fief or the manor to which customary services were due.[1] As Maitland said, the impression to be gained from what information we have is that it is occasional rather than regular labour which is obligatory, 'boon days' rather than 'week work'.[2] Some Ely sokemen, between the Conquest and the Inquest, had to plough and thresh, others to weed and reap as well; some had to furnish horses and transport the monks' provisions.[3] In DB we hear of a miscellany of services rendered by the free men and *radchenistri* of the west Midlands and the king's thegns and drengs and free men of south Lancashire.[4] The west Midland obligations include ploughing, harrowing, and reaping; those in south Lancashire making the king's house 'as the villeins do' and barriers to confine the deer.

It was no part of the inquisitors' duties to cause to be recorded what services were due, nor would there have been space in DB regularly to include them. Thus what information we find therein recorded is the result of information spasmodically supplied by the representatives of fiefs and manors, anxious that their powers should be recorded, though it does at times look as though inquiry had been made as to whether all or only some of the ties of commendation, soke, and customary duties were being claimed.

It is only in the Norfolk *breve* of Hermer de Ferrières that we have mention of *consuetudinarii*, as if these could be categorised as neither free men nor sokemen.[5] It is only very occasionally that we are told what the particular customary obligation is; some men of Stow Bardolph were *consueti ad faldam*, and those of Fodderstone were paying a novel customary due 'because they cannot do without their pasture', the common right to which

[1] Miller: *The Abbey and Bishopric of Ely*, p. 49.

[2] Maitland: *DBB*, p. 77.

[3] H, pp. 193–5: IE MS. C fols. 211b, 212b, 213a. The information is so fragmentary that we cannot say that these were all the services due, or that those for whom only ploughing and threshing is mentioned had no other duties.

[4] Fols. 163a2, 166a2, 174bi,2; 269bi,2.

[5] Fol. 273b – but they are 'bound by custom to the fold of Hermer's predecessor'.

seems to have been taken from them by Hermer.[1] Sometimes we hear merely that men were *consuetudinarii ad manerium*, with no hint of what their duties may have been, or bound by some customary tie to the Hundred.[2] Often enough it is said that the lord has 'all custom,' or 'service and custom', but there is record also of the customary dues being only partial, and that men are 'in demesne, quit of all custom'.[3] The variety of phrase and import is considerable; again at Garvestone (207b) the predecessor of Hermer de Ferrières had 'no custom except commendation', and at Chedburgh (384b) Ely had 'all custom except the six forfeitures'.[4] Certainly customary obligations seem sometimes to be contrasted with sokeright. At Thorpe (171b), of nineteen free men three owed commendation, and the rest 'all custom'. At Barton Bendish (250b) there were four men 'of all custom' and four others *ad socham* only. We find, too, men who could sell their land, but if they did so, their soke and service, or their custom, would still remain their lord's.[5] Roger de Raismes was holding 85 acres at Feering (14b) of the abbot of Westminster and paid him 10*s*. *pro suo servitio*. This may imply that Roger had the advantage of the services of the inhabitants of his holding, in respect of which he paid the owner of them an agreed sum.

It is, our text strongly suggests, that it is chiefly of labour services of which we are reading. But here and there we are told also of customary renders, especially in connection with the boroughs, and sometimes these are included with the total value of the property, and need separate consideration.[6] They include 'a custom of 22½*d*.' due from the Suffolk borough of Sudbury to the Essex manors of Henny and Bures St Mary

[1] Fols. 206, 274; on 110b we hear of 'a certain custom in pasture'.

[2] Fols. 215, 370b; 291 (Combs). The last rather suggests that all that is implied is that their soke was in the Hundred. *VCH: Norfolk*, ii, p. 31, would differentiate custom and sokeright by reason of the passage (Merton, 252) *cum omni consuetudine praeter vi*, but I think this implies six of the twenty-nine sokemen, not the 'six forfeitures'.

[3] Garvestone (207b); at Thetford (173) there was land 'quit of all custom', and men of whom Roger Bigot had no custom, except commendation.

[4] The last again suggests that sokeright is implied.

[5] Fornham St Martin (362), Theydon Gernon (50b), Radwinter (78). But sometimes a man could sell his land and his soke (Standon, 142b2).

[6] See pp. 175–6.

(84b), the heriot payable at a landholder's death, and renders of honey (119, 110). Ipswich men 'living on their own land' owed 'service and custom to the king' (290). The 'king's service' is described as a 'custom' (Wethersfield, 4); the sheriff had customary dues (Witham, 2; see also *Bineslea*, 79), and Leyton sokemen owed them to the royal manor of Havering (85).

But we can, of course, never be sure just what payments or services the term *consuetudo* may imply.[1] *Consuetudo* is once contrasted with *census*, rent (Fersfield, 130b), and once with geld (Bardfield, 41b), but it may be that often 'custom' included a certain amount of rent and payments for socage land. The majority of the customary dues and services would seem to date to before the Conquest. But we hear of the imposition of novel and heavy obligations, sometimes at the instigation of Roger Bigot's reeve Ælfric.[2]

[1] For a discussion of some aspects of customary dues, see E. B. Demarest: '*Consuetudo Regis*' (*EHR*, xxxiv, 1919, pp. 63–71).

[2] e.g. Ringsfield (282b), free men connected with Mutford (283); but the £30 to which the 13*s*. 6*d*. due had increased may well be a mistake for 30*s*.

CHAPTER XII

The Manor and Manorial Values

The essence of the arrangement of the material forming Domesday Book is organisation thereof in terms of the fief and of the manor. Nowhere was the supervisors' intention more difficult to achieve than in East Anglia, for in some ways the system adopted in the shires of the Danelagh for manorial components and 'soke of the manor', confused and confusing though it is, makes the material more intelligible and easier to handle. So often, in the Norfolk and Suffolk texts, the various items relating to the individual manor, especially when the holdings comprising it lay in several Hundreds, are dispersed over several folios. Moreover, it is often impossible to discover whether any or all of a string of holdings which immediately follows the account of what is said to be a manor are components thereof, portions of some other manor, or (though not so designated) themselves manors. Often the entries separate the bulk of the account from the information which usually ends the record of the manor – the value, the dimensions, and the geld-liability. Moreover, an appreciable number of small estates do not seem to have been incorporated in a manor by 1086, and this category may include several which are not inscribed under the headings of the king's or the sheriff's free men. But what is noted as having been classed as a manor in 1066, e.g. the many 30-acre holdings in the east of the region, may well have lost its manorial status by 1086. There are numerous oddities: St Peter's, Ipswich (382b) counted as a manor; the vill of Watton (174) had been 'in two manors' T.R.E.

ESSEX MANORS

About 600 Essex holdings are said to be manors, and the number would be appreciably increased if those which are not specifically said to be manors, but which quite obviously were such, were also counted. It is plain that, e.g., Runwell (13b), assessed at eight hides and 'always St Paul's', and Moulsham (15), were manors. This, however, leaves over 200 entries and sub-entries which also are not said to be manors, and most of these probably were not thought of as being manors. For many such entries the text says that *Y* held in *Z*, not that *Z* was held by *Y*, but, as for other shires, it is unsafe to presume that the ninety holdings 'in' somewhere were necessarily not manors. It is highly unlikely that the second Wickford entry on fol. 43, for example, where except for the tenancies we are told nothing except that it is of 30 acres, and the value, counted as a manor.

There is no instance in Essex of a man said to be a sokeman having held a manor in chief. Either the holder of a manor is named, or is categorised as a thegn or a priest or a free man, or is said to have held freely. Wherever we are told of what in 1086 was a manor, but which sokemen are said to have held, they are described as having been sokemen of some pre-Conquest magnate, or as holding 'under' or 'of' a lord.[1] Sometimes, indeed, the holding is not said to have been a manor.

We are, however, very rarely told to which manor a holding might have belonged. We are indeed told that a holding at Stifford (24b, 90), held by Gilbert the man of the bishop of Bayeux, had mostly lain in William Peverel's manor of Grays Thurrock, that Sweyn took 30 acres from Geoffrey de Manneville's manor of East Tilbury and put it in his manor of West Tilbury (59b), and that a virgate added to Nazeing and Epping belonged to Waltham (80b, 15b), but with the majority of the holdings which are not said to be manors there is no clue to any connections which they may have had. We are, however, told that *Siriceslea* (55) had been held by Harold *ad manerium de Hatfelde*, and so may have been treated since its occupation by Ralf de Marci, Hamo the steward's tenant, as a manor. But it could not be divorced from Hatfield Broad Oak, for while we are told that Ralf holds it *ad feudum Hamonis*, this sokeman's half-hide is said to have been 'recovered' by the Inquest (2b).

[1] In Suffolk, however, Wulfric, Edric's sokeman, had held Aldeburgh *pro manerio* (316), and Edwin, a sokeman-priest of Ely Abbey, had similarly held *Nordberia* (353). Sokemen are indeed quite commonly said to have held manors in East Anglia.

A holding in Shellow Bowells had lain in 1066 in the manor of Rodings (62), and is not said to be a manor. Since it was being held by Geoffrey de Manneville but properly lay in a manor which Eudes fitzHerbert had obtained, and was claimed by Ely abbey with the support of the jurors of Dunmow Hundred as being part of their Rodings manor (49), it surely was not a manor. A Leyton holding, again, is not described as a manor (85), for the sokemen who had held it had before the Conquest rendered their customary dues in the royal manor of Havering (2b).

In Essex, as in many other parts of England, the manor must have been the gelding unit, and probably those holdings which do not appear to have been considered to be manors had to produce their liability at one of the lord's manors. But though the manors of Norfolk and Suffolk may also often have been gelding units, the true unit here was the geld-collection centre.

THE MANOR IN EAST ANGLIA

East Anglian manors seem in one respect to have been of normal eleventh-century character, for demesne is often mentioned, as are sub-tenancies which often suggest former thegnland, and *terra villanorum* is implied if not specifically so described. But the total amount of manorial demesne is not given as it regularly is in the Exeter Domesday, and intermittently in the Exchequer text.[1] When quantities of demesne are noted, it is usually because they are situated in a village other than that which holds the *caput manerii*, or because free men have been brought into demesne.[2] Thus 24 acres of the demesne of Eye were at Thrandeston (319b) and 180 of the demesne of Frettenham at Coltishall (244). We are occasionally told that the 'hall' (*aula*), which typifies the demesne land, is

[1] At Mundham (270) Ely had 20 acres 'in her demesne', but such a phrase may imply that they were unlet, not that they were the demesne portion of a holding. Once we find the unusual phrase *terra v carucis in dominio*, suggesting demesne ploughlands.

[2] We are, however, told that of the 100 acres of Happisburgh (150), 60 were on the demesne when Earl Ralf lost his lands, but Edric seized them. Happisburgh, it happens, is not styled a manor. The Middleton free men (222) were absorbed into the demesne.

'in another Hundred' (Fornham St Genevieve, 362; Woolpit, 363b); we hear even of the *dominium hallae* (Haughley, 408b), and *halla* or *aula* is consistently used when recording the livestock on the demesnes (e.g. Kentwell, 355; Tuddenham, 403).

What we are frequently told is that a newcomer has abstracted part of the demesne. The fact that this could so readily be done rather suggests that it represents thegnland, though as a rule no 1066 tenant is mentioned, or a distant manorial component. Thegnland had not infrequently been created out of demesne. At Saxlingham (217) 10 acres of the demesne had been leased to Edric, Stigand's free man, by St Benedict of Ramsey. The predatory Breton Wihenoc had acquired 30 acres of the demesne of Beechenwell (190b). Seven acres of Ely demesne had been 'invaded' (Rattlesden, 303).

Occasionally we are told the value of the manorial demesne. Of the £10 at which Helhoughton (169b) was valued, the demesne was worth 20*s*.; the demesne of Deopham (*caput manerii*) was 'then' worth £4, and it had been let first for £12 and then for £6 (227); that of Plumstead (269) was valued at 5*s*.

The Norfolk fief of Earl Alan (144–51) furnishes a good example of the treatment of manors. Only eight of the numerous properties are actually styled 'manors', though some not so categorised must surely have been manors, e.g. Narford and Somerton and Hickling.[1] When a holding is said to be 'in the valuation of' a manor, it is to be presumed that it was part of that manor.

The difficulty is to determine the status of properties not styled manors which do not immediately follow the entry for a manor in the text (when they do so, it often appears that they were part of it), such as the Palgrave entry, or are the only properties of the earl in a Hundred, e.g. Mileham and Stanfield. But it is possible that each was an outlying component of a manor not named in connection with it, especially as they had been or were still tenanted by anonymous free men and sokemen. One might expect to find manors and their berewicks only in those vills which were geld-collection centres, or for which dimensions are given, which would make, e.g., Pickenham

[1] Swaffham, which had been royal, had been received as two manors.

a manor. The curious order in which many entries appear makes this difficult to establish, for of Felthorpe it is first said that it is valued in Costessy, and then dimensions and geld-liability are given. But these last, I think, refer to Taverham, entered immediately before Felthorpe, which may well have had manorial status. But unless the information was omitted from the text, this principle would deny Saxthorpe and Hickling manorial status, and also Happisburgh, where we are told of demesne land. The presence of livestock on the demesne, too, probably indicates manorial status. But as Happisburgh had been seized by Edric, the earl's spokesman may not have regarded it as a manor. Also, dimensions and geld-liability may have been recorded in entries for other holdings in the vill concerned.

The arrangement of entries is so unsatisfactory that thence to deduce manorial components is a most difficult task. Hunworth in Holt and Matlask in North Erpingham (146, 146b) were both valued in Saxthorpe in South Erpingham Hundred, but the Saxthorpe entry does not appear until fol. 148. The entries for holdings in both Holt and Happing Hundreds are each in two groups. The first Bawdeswell entry begins on fol. 147, l. 9, but its dimensions are on fol. 147b, l. 9. Thus the dimensions given at the end of the first Bawdeswell entry (l. 11) must really refer to Lyng (ll. 5–8), and those given on fol. 147b, l. 8, must be those of Foxley (fols. 147, 147b; ll. 24–5, 1–5.)

On these principles, we might reckon twenty-two manors in all in the fief, the eight which are styled manors, and fourteen which, according to the above principles should have been said to be manors. Possibly Waxham (149) should be added, for it has demesne livestock.[1]

The accompanying map of Earl Alan's manor of Costessy illustrates a largely typical dispersion of the components of a manor. These are ascribed to six different Hundreds, and are

[1] Swaffham (144), Costessy (144b), Syderstone (145b), Ingham (148), Stalham (148b), Ingham (148b), Shelfhanger (149b), and whatever manor it is which is referred to on fol. 145b, l. 5; Narford (144), Pickenham (144b), Westfield (145b), Somerton (146b), Lyng, Bylaugh, Foxley (147), Taverham (147b), Saxthorpe, Worstead, Hickling (148), East Walton (149), Little Harling (149b), Hethersett (150). It is more than possible that Mileham (144b), Waxham (148b, 149), Ilsington (149), and Happisburgh (150) also counted as manors.

The components of the manor of Costessy
Places underlined are not said to be 'in the value of Costessy'.

scattered about an area comprising over 80 square miles. Within this area, a number of the earl's holdings were not part of Costessy, and the components themselves fall into two groups.

For about one-fifth of the Norfolk manors we are given information enabling us to identify at least some of their components in 1086 without experiencing the doubts as to their composition referred to earlier. In all but about fifty of the passages a holding is plainly stated to be a berewick of a manor, or 'in the value of' or 'belonging to' a named manor. A variety of alternative phrases include statements that a holding 'lies in' a manor, is in the rental or in the *firma* of a manor, or 'pays in' a certain manor.[1]

Normally, as might be expected, references to the components of a manor come at worst within a few folios of each other, though the relevant entries may indeed be widely separated. But this is far from invariable.[2] Tracing such manorial ramifications demonstrates how curiously the various holdings in a vill were attached. Sco Ruston seems to have been an unmanorialised village. Four sokemen of Stigand's were 'in the value' of Bishop William's manor of Coltishall (159); three of St Benet of Holme's 'in the value' of Scottow (219b), and a free man 'in the value' of Roger of Poitou's manor of Tunstead (244b). The unmanorialised village is no rarity in Norfolk. There were six holdings recorded for Dunston, which had been held by 13½ free men and had passed to five different owners, rated in all at less than two carucates, with only four recorded teams and eight bordars. There is not the smallest suggestion that any of these holdings was a manor; indeed, one was 'in the value' of Markshall.[3] Yet 6½*d.* in the £ of geld has to be produced at this village. In the same Hundred of Henstead Poringland furnishes a similar example. The eight lay holdings range from 12 to no more than 30 acres, and the inhabitants below the status of free men or sokemen seem to number only a couple of bordars.[4]

About some villages or hamlets, indeed, we are given virtually no information. All we are told of Clenchwarton (221b) is that Richard holds 40 acres of William d'Écouis, worth 6*s*. Of

[1] e.g. Caston (126), Ellingham and Gillingham (141b), Somerton (138), Runham (116).

[2] See, e.g., the connections of Stratton Strawless with Marsham (196b, 241b).

[3] Fols. 150 *bis*, 188, 205, 230, 273.

[4] Fols. 124, 143, 176, 182b, 186, 203, 210, 278. On fol. 182b 2½ bordars seem to be mentioned, but could well be an error for 2½ acres of meadow.

Quarles and Egmere (113), berewicks of the royal manor of Wighton, it is said that in each there is half a carucate of land, but 'there is nothing there', though there could be a team at each. Yet each is responsible for the production of geld to the value of 6*d.* in the £. Holkham, also a Wighton berewick, preceding these entries, is said to be waste, and doubtless Quarles and Egmere were also. From these the king must have lacked his geld.

MANORIAL AND OTHER VALUES

The values of manors and holdings as recorded in DB have everywhere provided difficulties. Round, when editing the Essex text, confessed himself puzzled by the stated rises and falls over the twenty years since the Conquest, which frequently seem to bear no possible relation to changes in the number of teams, inhabitants, livestock, or other manorial appurtenances.[1]

A general, and on the whole considerable, appreciation in the value of manors is marked. This is certainly not always due to an increase in the labour available or to the employment of additional plough-teams, for where we have comparative figures these show a considerable decline in the latter, and many a holding the value of which had increased shows fewer inhabitants in 1086 than in 1066 or later. For an explanation of this general rise in 'values' we must not necessarily look to post-Conquest improvements in manorial economy, though it has been pointed out by Lennard that some landlords among the newcomers took pains to ensure them.[2]

We are going to see that many Domesday statements regarding values may be altogether deceptive. The enlargement of a manor would make it more valuable, and the figure given for it for 1086 not comparable with sums recorded for earlier dates. Moreover, there are items of profit contributing to manorial values which well may not have been reckoned in, or were inappropriate to, pre-Conquest valuations.

The Kalendar of Abbot Samson perhaps furnishes an explanation of some of the valuations. *Carrucatae de socagio* and

[1] *VCH: Essex*, i, pp. 364–5.

[2] Lennard: *Rural Eng.*, pp. 210 *et seq.*

the free men and sokemen who hold them are recorded for each vill, though the land is not said to be a portion of a particular vill or manor; it is indeed made plain that they belong to the Hundred, as do the revenues derivable from them. The carucate was made up of 120 *ware* acres, and since *ware* implies 'defence' they must have been holdings assessed for the purposes of some royal exaction. The text makes it plain they are units of assessment and not areal units.[1]

The 'carucates of socage land' of the Kalendar also owe their origin to the provision of a *feorm* by each of a large number of divisions of the shire. Socage land has been defined as 'belonging to the men seated upon it, but carrying a liability to services and dues to be rendered at the manorial centre to which it was appendant'.[2] Services seem to have been the prerogative of the manor, but dues were not manorial but hundredal, though collected at a convenient manorial centre. Davis has quoted passages from DB recording the payments of free men 'in the Hundred' and 'by the Hundred', which would seem to be these customary dues from their land.[3] The holders paid also a relief on succession to the land, 'hidage', a payment additional to rent, and a *gersuma*. Thus when we read in DB, as we often do, of freemen and sokemen being 'added to the manor', the phrase may imply divorcement of their dues from the Hundred and their transference to a particular manor. If so, it is plain to see why the Inquest officials recorded these incidents, for often one lord would lose revenue and services where another gained them. The numerous losses of free men and sokemen from the royal manors (p. 48) are probably instances of diminution of the Hundred-dues. *Gersuma*, Davis points out, can indicate any type of extraordinary payment, and since in the eleventh century the value of land was increasing steadily while socage dues remained fixed, a *gersuma*, an increment, had to be added to these dues to obtain full value from socage land. These two factors may well account for some of the huge apparent increases in manorial values.

King William's greed for gold is stressed by the chroniclers of

[1] For full details, see Davis: *Kal.*, pp. xxxii–xxxiii.

[2] Stenton: *Types of Manorial Structure in the Northern Danelaw*, pp. 13–14.

[3] Davis: *Kal.*, pp. xli, xlii.

the time.[1] Domesday Book copiously indicates his leasing of royal manors *ad firmam*, in the majority of instances to sheriffs and other royal officials, though this was probably no innovation.[2] It indicates, moreover, the formidable increased sums expected, which the lessees would hardly have been prepared to pay unless there was the probability of securing a profit for themselves. Appointments to official positions may to some extent have been contingent on agreement to farm a group of royal manors. Many a sheriff must have had to decide before accepting office that his receipts would show a surplus against the *firma* of shire or borough.[3] It is, too, reasonable to suppose that while some of the *valet* figures represent an actual rent being charged to an unnamed tenant, others indicate, not the immediate value to the owner, but the sum at which he was prepared to rent the holding. When tenants-in-chief organised sub-infeudation, they may also have demanded sums in excess of previous values from their *milites*, though it is not normally indicated that the sub-tenant paid rent to his feudal superior. The *Domesday Monachorum* shows that often, where DB gives us a *valet*, the holding was in fact being rented for a sum higher than this.[4]

We find, in addition to the apparently extraordinary figures for 1086 against 1066 numerous instances of inability to pay the rents demanded, of premiums demanded for the privilege of farming or renting manors, of disagreement as to the fair value of a manor, and indications that a good many of the figures of DB may indeed be altogether deceptive.

ESSEX VALUATIONS

The Essex valuations are less complex and difficult to interpret than those of East Anglia, and the extent of royal property was here less. No Essex royal property is said to have been King

[1] See p. 30.

[2] Lennard: *Rural Eng.*, p. 155, points out how many people said to be farming manors in 1086 had English names.

[3] In 1066 the farm of Bromsgrove (172a2) had been £18; King William's sheriff paid £24 'so long as he held the woodland'. The loss of this might have made the difference between profit and loss.

[4] Lennard: *Rural Eng.*, pp. 204 *et seq.*

Edward's, and a number of the manors which became King William's are said to have been held by Harold, though some had surely been royal in Edward's day and had then become Harold's in 1066.[1]

Terra Regis, throughout DB, invariably requires special investigation. The amounts given often arise here from peculiar circumstances, and as a rule are more detailed than those of the average lay holding. In Essex they fall into four groups. Five manors are said to have furnished a *firma noctis* in 1066, which in each instance seems to have been commuted for a cash payment by 1086, though it is not possible to make a comparison from the figures given.[2] Such a *firma* is rarely recorded in DB for a lay manor, though a number of religious houses received it.[3]

Eleven manors and the borough of Maldon were being farmed; those which had been Harold's by Ranulf brother of Ilger (Benfleet, 1b) and by Peter de Valognes the sheriff of the county, who had Maldon and six manors. Those which Earl Ælfgar is said to have held were farmed by Picot the Cambridgeshire sheriff (Westerfield, 4) and by Otto the goldsmith (Shalford, 5b; Finchingfield, 4). Godric, the farmer of East Anglian manors, had Great Sampford (7), which had been first Edith the Fair's and then Earl Ralf's. There seems to be a somewhat geographical basis for this distribution. The small manor of Childerditch (5), which like Finchingfield had been Queen Matilda's, was in the hands of Hamo, the sheriff of Kent.

There are a number of minor properties, not in the hands of magnates in 1066, but the most significant results are to be drawn from the score of manors dealt with above. For six we are given figures for 1066 and for a date later than the Conquest but before the Inquest, and these had appreciated in value from £85 to £124. For all except those where the earlier *firma noctis*

[1] So Round suggested (*VCH: Essex*, i, p. 336). But Writtle and Newport, it is said, had been held by Harold *tempore regis Edwardi*. Perhaps he farmed or administered them, or the phrase might really relate to the hidage or to manorial status.

[2] Brightlingsea, Lawford, and Newport had been responsible for two nights; Writtle for ten. Great Baddow (21b), though Earl Ælfgar's, and not royal in 1086, had furnished a farm of eight nights.

[3] See p. 175.

makes comparison impossible, the increase was from £216 2*s*. to £327, and *gersumae* or premiums would add another £27. Writtle (5) and Maldon (5b) are said to pay 'by weight', and this implies a higher return than if counted coin was accepted.[1] Since holdings and services seem to have been abstracted from a number of the royal manors, e.g. Witham, Hatfield Broad Oak, Writtle, and Lawford, such an increase is formidable evidence of the king's lust for money, and even so three properties had declined in value since Peter and Ralf Baignard received them.[2] Fingrith (5) is said to have increased in value by 250%, from £4 to £14. It is of course possible that the 1086 values include factors which are not included in those of 1066; e.g. the value of Witham (1b) seems to include whatever sum the pleas of the half-Hundred produced, which are unmentioned in the 1066 statement.

Though the clerk's normal verb is *valet*, *reddit* is not infrequently used, showing that it is actual rents which are being recorded. Occasionally phrases occur which show that the sum mentioned represents a rent. The value of the houses in London belonging to the manor of Grays Thurrock (63) was included in its *firma*, and the thirteen sokemen at South Ockendon (57b) *iacent ad firmam de xvi libris*. Mundon (49b), worth £10 in 1066 and £17 at the time of the Inquest, had been leased since Eudes succeeded Lisois (*fuit ad firmam*) for £30.

Though increases in the individual manor are elsewhere often large, totals can show nothing which compares with those of the royal manors. Of 61 holdings of Earl Eustace where we have comparative figures, 47 show an increase and 11 a decrease, with a total gain of some 17½%. Ralf Peverel's have appreciated by 21½%, John fitzWaleram's by 11%, but those of Robert fitzCorbucion show a decline of 26%. Yet the royal manors have more than doubled in value, and the king had many other sources of revenue besides these, including those of the borough of Colchester.

It is unfortunate that we are given intermediate values for only about a couple of hundred Essex holdings. The number of those which appreciated between 1066 and *post* or *quando*

[1] See p. 171.

[2] Maldon (5b), Brightlingsea and Lawford (6); from £63 to £49.

recepit is very much the same as that for those which declined. On balance there is a slight fall, of less than 1½%. It looks as if the inevitable consequences of the occupation did not at once necessitate a general lowering of rents, or induce difficulties where letting manors to be farmed. The royal manor of Shalford (5b) had been worth £12 in 1066, but went up to £22 *post*.

Between 1066 and 1086 values rose, on the average, by 17%. Figures much in excess of this obtain in the western Hundreds, where proximity to London may over twenty years have made the manors more profitable. But what increase there is in the coastal Hundreds is very slight, and while Rochford displays an average rise, these six Hundreds can show one of only 4½%.[1] Here again we may be seeing the results of deliberate devastation in 1085 to ensure that the expected Danish invaders could not find the means of sustenance, or of unrecorded raids or the threat of raids. Two large coastal manors show serious decline in values, Clacton and St Osyth (11), from £40 to £26 and from £12 to £10, though St Osyth had recovered well from the figure of £2 to which it had fallen 'when received'. Some of the appreciations are considerable, amounting in one instance to about 150%: Weeley (57), worth £8 in 1066, was at the time of the Inquest valued at £19 and an ounce of gold.[2]

There can be no doubt that frequently manorial lords were here demanding greatly increased and excessive rents. Coggeshall (26b) and Rivenhall (27) was each producing £20, but were worth only £14 and £12, while in 1066 they had been worth £10 and £9. Thaxted (38b) had been worth £30 in 1066 and when received. In 1086 it was being rented to an Englishman for £60, but the rent was short by at least £10 a year, and both the English and the foreign jurors valued it at only £50. Rents may indeed not infrequently have proved to be in excess of what could reasonably be paid; Kelvedon (14) in 1066 was worth £5, £12 'when received', but in 1086 was valued at £8 only. Yet though Harold had received £36 from Waltham, the bishop of Durham's men valued it at £63 5*s*. 4*d*., while the

[1] Rochford was largely under the influence of Sweyn, who seems to have kept his manors everywhere at a high standard of equipment and profitability.

[2] See also Saffron Walden (62), where the population had increased considerably, Feering (14b), Henham (71), Stanford Rivers (30b), Felsted (21b), Walthamstow (92).

Hundred-jury said it was worth as much as £100. Perhaps Harold had treated a church with which he had intimate connection generously, or perhaps the composition of the manor had changed.[1] Among other manors where the receipts were grossly in excess of the value were Laindon (9b) and Amberden (73b), where from a manor worth £12 Ralf Peverel, who had appropriated it from Ely Abbey, had for three years been obtaining £18. The classic instance is Barking (17b), worth £80 in 1066 and still, according to the English (interested parties, perhaps, but probably also the best judges of true worth), to be valued at that sum. But the *Franci* said that it was worth £100; presumably, if anyone wished to rent it from St Mary.

Premiums for leases, which show that these must have been in demand, are, it would seem, recorded also for manors which are not royal ones. In addition to the instance of Weeley just mentioned, Walthamstow (92) was worth £28 and two ounces of gold. At Stevington (82) and Grays Thurrock (90) the ounce of gold additional to the greatly increased values also looks like a *gersuma*, as does 5*s*., plus perhaps a silver mark, worth 13*s*. 4*d*., surplus to the £30 value of the Sokens (30).[2]

Rents of one penny per acre are frequently apparent throughout vol. ii, but seem to occur in Essex less often than they do in East Anglia. But this was the sum paid in a number of instances; a sokeman paid 8*d*. for 8 acres at *Careseia* (100b) on Northey Island, another at *Wringehala* (100b) 20*d*. for 20 acres, while a free man's 30 acres at Thorndon (23b) were worth the same number of pence, and the villein's 40 acres at Fanton (17b) were worth 3*s*. 4*d*. We find also acres valued at 2*d*. each (Hutton, 20b) and at 3*d*. (held by a king's servant in Chelmsford Hundred, 98b; in Uttlesford Hundred, 100b).

The *ora* of sixteen or twenty pence, also of occasional occurrence in vol. ii, does not appear by name in Essex, though Round showed it entered into the payment for 'feeding the

[1] We are not told here of additions to the manor, but there had been post-Conquest additions to many Essex manors.

[2] For the *gersuma*, see Lennard: *Rural Eng*., pp. 180–2, but he (and also R. H. C. Davis (*Kal*., p. xxxvi)) doubts if it always represents a premium for a lease. The curious sum of 13*s*. 4*d*. + 5*s*. = 18*s*. 4*d*. recurs in the values of the Cornish demesne manors of Robert of Mortain.

prebendaries' at Colchester.[1] But sums which appear to be based on the *ora* of 16*d.* are not infrequently to be found; 1*s.* 4*d.* in Rochford Hundred (4b), at Crishall (33), and on Godwin the deacon's land (98b); 2*s.* 8*d.* at Ockendon (5) and West Bergholt (102b): 5*s.* 4*d.* at Debden (16). So are those for the *ora* of 20*d.*; 1*s.* 8*d.* in Thurstable Hundred (7b), Chadwell (98), and in Rochford Hundred (103b); 3*s.* 4*d.* at Loughton (2b) and Nevendon (96). Figures such as 6*s.* 8*d.* (Debden, 16; Fordham, 38) or 8*s.* 4*d.* (Uleham's Farm, 29b) could derive from either.[2] But from the number of acres concerned several of these look as if they might really be derived from rents of 1*d.* or 2*d.* per acre.

EAST ANGLIAN VALUES

An increase in the value of holdings, or in the rents demanded, is equally apparent in East Anglia. Again, this appears to be largely unconnected with such manorial resources as are detailed in DB. Some of the figures given show gigantic rises: Wood Hall (388b) from £2 to £12, Witnesham (427b) from £3 to £12, Wortham (354b) from £2 to £5. It is not only the smaller manors which display these vast increases: for Hitcham (384b) the figures are £20 and £40, for Thorney in Stowmarket (281b) £15 rising first to £35 and ultimately to £40. In none of these are we told of appreciable increases in both population and teams. At Hitcham the number of recorded inhabitants grew from 56 to 70, but the 19 teams were five fewer than they had been in 1066. The Witnesham figures remained unaltered except for the loss of a slave.

But it is possible that some of the information is deceptive. The value of Pakenham (361b) had risen from £10 to £25, but 31 + 3 + 1 free men are separately mentioned, and it may be that these were not included in the 1066 value, but were absorbed into the manor later. Collation of the Exeter Domesday with *Terrae Occupatae* shows that sometimes the value given

[1] *VCH: Essex*, i, p. 420.

[2] Also noteworthy are 10*s.* 8*d.* (8 *orae*; Matching, 20b) and two acres of *libera terra* worth 4*d.* (Lammarsh, 99b). Note that these are almost all very small holdings, suggesting the sums represent actual rents.

for the time of King Edward is for the manor as it was in 1066, that for the time of the Inquest for the manor after the addition to it of various local holdings. Hollesley (317) had appreciated from £5 to £13, but we are told further that certain holdings are valued in Hollesley, e.g. Sutton and Bawdsey. Thus at Barrow (289b), which had doubled its 1066 valuation of £10, while the teams had increased from 7 to 17 and the recorded inhabitants from 12 to 26, the sums may for each item give the 1066 figure as the composition of the manor then was, but for 1086 for an organisation which had been enlarged. If so, large increases in value have everywhere to be viewed with reservations.

On fol. 111b Holt is said to be worth £50 by tale, on fol. 112b, £66. The latter figure must include the holdings apart from Holt comprising the manor. We are not given all their values, and indeed it is only in certain Hundreds, which include Holt, that the values of berewicks and manorial components are given; as a rule they are invisibly included in the value of the *caput*. If only we always had information about the values of the components of the large dispersed manors we could form a much better idea of the real values in 1086 of their administrative headquarters. For all we know the values given for these may often include values given also separately for components.

In many of the relevant instances we are told that the sum is *de firma*, or that the manor is *ad firmam*, again showing that it was being farmed in the expectation of a profit being made by the lessee. Many an entry shows that the rents charged were extortionate, and reports the inability of lessee or inhabitants to produce them. Blakenham (353) had been valued at £3 both *tunc* and *post*, but for three years it had been at farm for as much as £12, with what looks like a premium of an ounce of gold for the lease, 'but the men who took it were ruined'. So they had been at Pettaugh (440b), and the rent had had to be reduced from £3 15*s*. to £2 5*s*., less than the values given for *tunc* and *post*. From both the manor of Combs (291) and its fifty free men rents far in excess of previous values had been demanded, and while from the manor 'it could hardly be rendered', the free men 'could not suffer it without ruin'. One hundred shillings of the £20 rent of Assington (416), worth £10 in 1066 and

£12 later, could not be paid.[1] Kembrook (343) had been and was said still to be worth £6, but the men of the Hundred gave its value as 48*s*. only.

As elsewhere in England, we find the royal manors farmed by the king's officials at prices far above their former levels. Quite often a *gersuma* was being asked for the lease: £1 at Thurlow (286), £2 at Mendlesham (285b), an ounce of gold at Cretingham (406b). Improvement in the receipts was sometimes obtained by demanding the sum previously exacted in counted coin (*ad numerum*) in weighed or blanched silver (*ad pensum, librae blancae*), which must have made a substantial difference to the proceeds.[2]

One of the classic passages of DB is that concerning East Bergholt (287). Though of the 210 pre-Conquest sokemen only 119 remained in 1086, this decline in itself might make no difference to the value of the manor, to which Bentley and Shotley had been added, for though the free men who belonged in Bergholt are said to have paid the reeve 4*d*. a year and 'rendered soke as the law enjoined' they may have had few or even no labour services to perform. But when Roger Bigot became sheriff he instructed his officers (*ministri*) to cause them to pay £15 (the previous due, it seems, should have been only about £2), which they had not paid in 1066, and Robert Malet, on attaining the sheriffdom, increased this to £20, a charge maintained by Roger when he again took over the office. However, we are told that in 1086, under Ælfric 'Wanz', Roger's reeve, the same customary due was rendered as in the time of King Edward. Probably the debtors simply could not find such a sum, and Roger had to take what he could get. This has to be reconciled with the information that when Robert Malet was in power the manors paid £60 by weight and £8 in counted coin *de gersuma*, against £9 when Earl Gyrth had them. Roger's reeve said the sum was the same when his master supervised it, but Roger said that it was 40*s*. and a mark of gold more, and though the reeve was supposed to pay £60 by

[1] For similar instances, see Stanningfield (291), Drinkstone (381b), Ringsett (393b), Thorpe (409).

[2] e.g. at Blythburgh (282). At Bosham in Sussex (16a2) £65 of unassayed weighed coin was found to be the equivalent of only £50 of coins from which the dross had been expelled.

weight, he said that the revenue of the manor did not enable him to do so.

But sometimes we find also heavy falls in value, also unexplained. Barham, where the teams had declined from 11 to 7, and the recorded villeins and slaves from 30 to 26, had dropped from £12 to £5; Barton Mills (435b) from £8 to £6 and then to 30*s*. Here there was only one team as against four in 1066, while the recorded population had fallen by 37%. Local tragedies, engendered by war or pestilence or crop failure, may sometimes have caused many such declines in value.

A high proportion of the sums given are in round figures. But not infrequently we find very odd amounts, and these are most readily explained by suggesting that they represent the total of rents paid by a number of persons possessing holdings of varying size and prosperity. Boynton (395) was worth 11*s*. 5*d*., Poslingworth (413b) £1 0*s*. 11*d*., Stonham Aspall (375b) £2 0*s*. 4*d*. Some of the fluctuations in values certainly look as if they had been caused by the incorporation of additional tenants or the loss, for whatever cause, of some holdings and the addition or subtraction of their rents. The value of Kirkham (395) had improved from £1 to £1 3*s*. 2*d*.; of Akenham (422b) from 16*s*. to 19*s*. 4*d*.: this looks like a rent of twelve *orae* of 16*d*. being swollen by one of two *orae* of 20*d*. At Charfield (406b) one *ora* of 16*d*. had gone from the former value of 24*s*.

The probability that the actual rents required or received are often given when the text reads *valet* is enhanced by the very large number of occasions on which there seems to be direct relationship between the quantities of pence and of acres recorded. While this is often so for the glebe-lands of churches, it is frequent also for the holdings of free men and sokemen. Suggestions of acres valued at from 1*d*. to 6*d*. are common, and it is noticeable that frequently the number of acres, and hence the *valet*, are not round numbers. At Mildenhall (392) and Bures (435b), for example, holdings of 60 acres are valued at 5*s*., or 1*d*. per acre. Horham church (438) possessed 22 acres and was worth 22*d*., a holding at Bromeswell (324b) of 16 acres was valued at 1*s*. 4*d*., and two acres at Sharpstone (285) at 2*d*. Coddenham church (338), with 12½ acres, is valued at 2*d*. per acre, or 2*s*. 1*d*. An Ely sokeman (Glemsford, 382) had 8 acres and in the IE (H, p. 155) his land was valued at 1*s.*, or 1½*d.* per acre. Acres valued at 2*d.* are extremely common; e.g. 24 at 4*s.*, 20 at 3*s.* 4*d.*, 7 at 1*s.* 2*d.*, 1½ at 3*d.*, half an acre at 1*d.*[1] Twenty acres at Rede (401) were each valued at 3*d.*, 1½ at Mellis (371) at 4*d.*, and 16 at Gillingham (322) at 5*d.* Perhaps these variations reflect the potentialities of the holdings.

The *ora,* as is to be expected in an area where Danish influence had been considerable, figures prominently in the values and rents. Fifty acres at Cornard (360) were worth six *orae*; the church at Marlesford (281b), two. Amounts which seem to reflect either the *ora* of 16*d.* or that of 20*d.* commonly occur. Two holdings at Hawkedon (396b, 397) were worth 6*s.* 8*d.* and 13*s.* 4*d.* (but note that together these make £1); one at Thelnetham (327b) was valued at 5*s.* 4*d.* and one at Burstall (373) at 8*s.* 4*d.* Such sums are extremely frequent in Wangford Hundred, which probably had many Scandinavian settlers; we find 2*s.* 8*d.*, 6*s.* 8*d.*, 10*s.* 8*d.*, 11*s.* 8*d.*

The above examples are mostly taken from the Suffolk text. But the Norfolk Domesday can furnish instances of all the types of entry mentioned. The account of the royal land again contains frequent mention of a *gersuma*, of blanched and of counted or weighed coin, and of heavy increases in rents.[2] A 'farm of six nights' was rendered by Necton and its components (235), commuted for £60 by weight, and references to the *firma* asked and received are frequent.[3] Sculthorpe (168) had been worth £6 *tunc et post*, and was worth £10 in 1086, though it was *ad firmam* for £15, 'but it could not pay it'. Stanford (238b) was worth £10 but was rendering £15 (*valet, sed reddit*), Merton (252) had been worth £5 in 1066 and later £6, but it had rendered £8. The increased rent of Rainham (231b) could be raised only *cum magna pene*.[4]

Norfolk, too, displays the enormous increases seen elsewhere. Fakenham (111) is said to have risen in value from £8 to £43; Great Massingham (109b) from £2 to £10 although many of

[1] Layham (445b), Thorney (409b), Cotton (391), Olden (383), Creeting (446).

[2] e.g. Halvergate (128), Mileham (136b), Horningtoft (120b), Saham Toney (110).

[3] e.g. Hunstanton (135b) and Swanton Morley (226b), which had been worth £8, and in 1086 £12, but Ralf of Beaufoy had 'given it to farm' for £25.

[4] See also Runton (184b), Aldborough (185), and Starston (186).

its sokemen had been appropriated by local magnates; Wymondham (137b), which had suffered severely in 1075 and lost many sokemen, from £20 to £60; Southmere (109b) from £7 first to £20 and then to £30.[1]

If we take the figures for the royal manors in Norfolk, we find that they are said to have appreciated in value from about £466 to almost £1,000, a rise of 114%. This seems almost incredible, and rather suggests that in many instances the pre-Conquest figures for those component holdings, or for land added to the manor since the Conquest, were not included. It is difficult to make out just which holdings were valued in Earsham, but on the lowest count there were concerned 182 free men and sokemen with 10½ carucates. If their rents were not included in the 1066 value of £11 of Earsham (138b), the difference between this and the £40 of 1086 does not seem so great, and we are told that the £40 includes 'all those things that belong', which must cover the tenants' rents and dues. Some portion of the increase is surely explained by the statements that some sokemen had been added to the manor by Roger Bigot, and that the Brockdish free men used to render 40*s*. to Stigand in 1066, but in 1086 paid £16 by tale, Richard Pugnant having included them in Earsham's rents (*adcensavit*, 139b). But this unfortunately does not permit us to estimate the 1086 value of Earsham itself.

In addition to the use of *reddit* rather than *valet*, rent is indicated by the use of *census*. Holdings are said to be *in censu* of their parent manor (e.g. Martham, 113b). The free men at components of manors, e.g. of Shottisham (124), had not been *ad censum*, but we are told that Robert Blond, perhaps when he was sheriff, subjected them to payment of rent (*adcensavit*).[2] Robert Blond held Filby (278) *ad censum*.

Acres appearing to be rated at from 1*d*. to 6*d*. are frequent, especially where the glebe-land of churches is concerned. Of

[1] It is, I suppose, a possibility that the many holdings included in the manor of Fakenham were included in the 1086 valuation but not in that of 1066. Somerton (146b) had been worth £5; in 1086 it was worth £9 'with the sokemen who are in the Hundred'. Is the apparent increase, or some of it, represented by the value of the West Flegg Hundred-soke?

[2] Other royal officials are said to have done this, e.g. at Redenhall (125b) and Somerton (138).

the 116 Norfolk churches for which a value is given, 44 seem to be valued at 1*d.* per acre, and several at 2*d.* But for 144 Norfolk churches no value is given: in several of the *breves* we are told that 'all the churches are valued with the manors' whose headquarters they served.[1]

The *ora* is specifically recorded in a few entries, each of which mentions rents of two *orae* or 32*d.*, though the amount of land varies considerably. At Stody (112) the sokeman who paid this rent had only 2½ acres, but four Shottisham free men (185b) 60 acres, and by 1086 their value had risen to 10*s.* A Morston free man (128) is said to be 'worth' this sum. The *ora*, though not so called, is apparent elsewhere also. 3½ sokemen with 12½ acres at Newton (112) were worth 16*d.*; 2*s.* 8*d.* and 5*s.* 4*d.* appear at Moulton (113b) and at Caston (110b).[2]

Gersuma is sometimes contrasted with *consuetudo*, which here seems to cover the whole value; at Fersfield (130, 130b) there had been £7 6*s.* 8*d.* between the two, increased to £12 6*s.* 8*d.*, of which sum the free men contribute £5 6*s.* 7*d.* (? *recte* 8*d.*).[3] Customary dues are contrasted also with honey-renders. Saham Toncy (110), worth £12 in 1066, had furnished 'half a day's honey' and customary dues of honey: this had been commuted for £20 by weight; Foulsham (114), worth £13 earlier, had rendered 'thirteen quarts of honey with the custom', and the honey-render had been commuted for a payment of £11 10*s.* blanch, with a value of £23 by weight.

Food-farms rarely appear in DB, except for the *firma noctis* of royal manors. But the account of Bury St Edmunds (372) mentions thirteen reeves 'in the shadow of the abbey', and Lennard rightly connects them with the system of food-farms organised in thirteen monthly periods we find described a little later in time.[4] Toli the sheriff had held Broome (211b)

[1] See, e.g., fols. 116 (*Terra Regis*), 159b (William of Warenne), 208 (Hermer de Ferrières), 234b (Rainald fitzIvo).

[2] The berewick of Holt at Hempstead went up in value from 5*s.* 4*d.* to £1 3*s.* 4*d.* Some of these sums, e.g. 6*s.* 8*d.*, may represent proper fractions of the £ rather than *orae*.

[3] See also Halvergate (128b); 40*s.* *de consuetudine ad numerum* and 20*s.* *de gersuma*. *Census* is also contrasted with *consuetudo*: *inter censum et consuetudinem* (Fersfield, 130b).

[4] Lennard: *Rural Eng.*, p. 121, and see Douglas: 'Fragments of an Anglo-Saxon Survey from Bury St Edmunds' (*EHR*, xliii, 1928, pp. 128–43).

from St Edmund in return for a farm of two days. Ely Abbey operated a system under which the demesne manors were organised to furnish provisions for a 51-month (?*recte* 52) cycle.[1] St Paul's in London also adopted a system based on months, weeks, and days, and this may not be entirely post-Inquest.[2] The Kentish estates of the archbishop and monks of Canterbury and of the bishop of Rochester, according to the *Domesday Monachorum*, were similarly organised for fortnightly supplies.

Exotic material in connection with values is infrequent. The value of the pasture at West Hall (221b), perhaps a rent to be paid for using it, was included in the value of the manor, and the fact that the value of the villeins' land at South Acre was 'in the rent of the Hundred' is mentioned. Values are sometimes given *exceptis liberis* (Elveden, 358b; Santon Downham, 359), and the mark of silver appears at Thorington (412b).

EVALUATION OF THE STATEMENTS

To deduce how to estimate the justness of a *valet* from the Domesday evidence is frankly impossible, nor are comparisons between apparently similarly equipped manors necessarily trustworthy. All the statistical factors mentioned in DB would presumably affect the value, but how can we determine the relative importance of four plough-oxen or 30 acres of woodland or the presence of two saltmakers? We have seen that changes in the number of teams, or of recorded inhabitants, seem to have no obvious bearing on changes in value *tunc et post et modo*. A decline in the amount of woodland, intermittently and irregularly recorded, might imply less swine-pasture, more actual or potential arable, or even its unrecorded transference to another manor.[3] Some of the Essex woodland is indeed said to be wasted (e.g. Fanton, 14; Bowers Gifford, 86), and whether this was done to sell timber or to clear the ground for agriculture we do not know, nor at what point in time this was

[1] Blake, pp. 152–3; H, pp. 168–73; see also Lennard: *Rural Eng.*, p. 131.

[2] Lennard: *Rural Eng.*, pp. 119–21.

[3] At *Brictriceshaga* (433b) wood which formerly could pasture 16 swine could in 1086 feed only 3; the holding is said to be *in Cretingham*, which manor may have taken over some of the rights in the woodland.

done and whether the manors concerned had in consequence become more productive. Where woodland had been transferred from one manor to another, one entry might record its loss, but the other give no indication that the quantity mentioned included an addition. When we are told that at Pitsea (98), where there was half a hide of wood, 30 acres of woodland had been added, the value of one manor may have been slightly increased, but the total amount of woodland in the county has not changed. When Hamo the steward took 200 acres of marsh and 80 acres of arable into his hands from Peldon (94b), this seems to account for a fall in the value of the manor from £6 to £5, for the value of what had been taken away was £1, but we do not know to which holding of Hamo's they were added.[1] The passages which mention the loss of woodland are comparatively few, and represent holdings in all parts of the area.[2]

Changes, often considerable, in the number of demesne livestock, cannot tell us a great deal either. The manor may have become more pastoral or less agricultural, there may have been acute mortality among the beasts, or a proportion may have been sold off because a smaller number of villagers made it impossible adequately to care for them. The villagers' own livestock may often have been of no profit to the lord, but there are instances in which we are told of rents demanded from them for pasture. Sometimes we are told that when a manor was granted to its new owner, he received no livestock with it. There were no demesne beasts at Eynesworth (38) when the manor was received; in 1086 there were 32 swine, 52 sheep, 2 *animalia*, and 3 hives of bees. At Maplestead (84) no stock had been taken over on transference of the holding, but in 1086 there were 2 cows, 14 swine, and 57 sheep. If things go well, an appreciable amount of livestock can be bred over fifteen years from small beginnings. But at Black Notley (84) the rouncey and two cows which had apparently been all the demesne stock had gone by 1086. It would be easy to think of many other factors which would help to determine the rateable value of a holding.

[1] Wigborough (55b) was his only manor in Winstree Hundred, in which Peldon lay, but its value had not changed; perhaps what he took from Peldon compensated for the half-hide and the hide of woodland taken away by others from the manor.

[2] For the relevant entries, see H. C. Darby: *The Domesday Geography of England*, i, pp. 128, 181, 236.

What is plainly apparent is that manorial values, and the rents actually charged, had on the whole increased both since 1066 and the time when manors had been transferred, and on the whole had increased appreciably. The improvement in them, it seems, is comparatively rarely attributable to an increase in capital equipment, and we have no evidence to suggest that estates were being managed more efficiently than formerly.[1] We are then compelled to conclude that the new masters of English land were setting higher rentable values on their properties, and demanding increased rents from their tenants and villagers, for the sub-tenancies and thegnlands often show marked increases in value. Whether increased labour services were demanded from the villagers is problematical; the conservatism of Anglo-Saxon England, backed by custom and tradition, may often have made them difficult to exact.[2] But if, as we shall see is highly probable (p. 188), many free men had become villeins or bordars, villeins reduced in status, and the lord freed from the obligation of maintaining much of the previous servile population, the services received may in fact consequently have increased. These, and increases in individual rents, would help to push the peasantry further down the social scale.

[1] One classic entry (222ai) implies that Aldwinckle was *not* being run properly.

[2] H. R. Loyn has said (*Anglo-Saxon England and the Norman Conquest*, p. 328) that 'increased imposition of labour service appears to have been enforced in some areas; normally, however, it was probably by a clearer and more accurate definition of service that the newcomers made their demands more onerous'.

CHAPTER XIII

The Economic and Social Effects of the Conquest

Domesday Book for the eastern counties, the one section of the record where we are given information for King Edward's day, for unspecified moments after the Conquest, and for 1086, regarding items additional to manorial values, first invites the student of economic and social history to make what he can of this, and then, all too frequently, induces in him a sense of frustration. He finds comparative figures available in only a limited number of entries; very rarely, in any entry, is he given the details for all the items of information; and often he is left to guess whether the quantity furnished for one of his three dates applies to the others also, or at least to one of them. Statistics and deductions, then, have to be presented with reservations, and at times it is found that there is insufficient material to make detailed geographical analysis profitable.

In common with the record of the other circuits, very little information about the lesser peasantry, the villagers, is provided. We can be confident that we are not being given the full tale of manorial attributes such as saltpans and fisheries, and we are told virtually nothing of the livestock where these were not associated with the lord's demesne. Intermittently we receive a strong hint that the number of plough-teams available is less than it had been or might be, and that the arable is not being cultivated to its full capacity. The first and last of these aspects must be briefly considered before the fuller information regarding plough-teams and population and valuations is examined.

THE HOLDINGS OF VILLEINS AND BORDARS

We are told, in a somewhat surprisingly large number of entries, of either the physical amount of land or the geld-liability of certain villeins and bordars. The former would appear to be the more probable interpretation. There are more than thirty instances of its occurrence in both Norfolk and Suffolk, but far fewer in Essex. Sometimes it is the individual's land which is noted, sometimes that of a small group of either or both villeins and bordars. Twice villeins are named; each has the above-average holding of 20 acres.[1] At *Estolleia* near Latchingdon in Essex (3), a royal manor, there was a villein who had a virgate, and another with half a virgate. A villein had a 15-acre holding at Shelfhanger (130), and he had two bordars to help him with his half-team, 'wood for five swine', and 2 acres of meadow. In Norfolk one at Corpusty (225) had 40 acres; so had an Essex villein at Fanton (17b). But these are somewhat exceptional quantities, as are the two carucates held by two villeins at Easton Bavants in Suffolk (282), and a villein's half-carucate at Acre (120), for we find a number who possessed 10 acres, and many had less. In view of the smallness of the holdings of many free men and sokemen, this confirms the suggestion that many a villein must have been as prosperous, or even more well-to-do, than a number of those who enjoyed a higher social status.

A bordar we find with as little as half an acre (*Thicchebrom*, 327b). But we find also four bordars who had half a carucate between them (Shadingfield, 288b), and at Roudham (344) one with 10 acres. Twice in Essex we find bordars who 'hold no land' (Brightlingsea, 6; Leigh, 75), and from their situation and the fact that those at Leigh are said to be *super aquam* Round deduced that they were engaged in maritime activities.[2]

In one entry 'free villeins', *liberi villani*, are mentioned (Barford, 145). The extent of their holding is not mentioned, but we may think that their manorial services, if any, were limited to occasional boon days. We also hear that of the four pre-Conquest bordars at Burlingham (199b) one was *libera* [*sic*]. Sometimes we are informed where the service of the villeins lies; one living in Banningham (234b) who had 16 acres paid a rent of 5*s*. in the manor of Cawston.[3] A Thrandeston villein

[1] Wulfric at Uggeshall, Osketel at Chediston (444b).
[2] *VCH: Essex*, i, p. 434, n. 8.
[3] See also Ellough (335b), Brome (354b), Cotton (370b), Hemley (431b).

is very unexpectedly said to hold 24 acres of the demesne of Eye (321).

POSSIBILITY OF THE EMPLOYMENT OF MORE TEAMS

One of the most curious features of vol. ii is the frequent reference to the possibility of the employment of more teams than were available in 1086. It is, however, a feature by no means confined to vol. ii.[1] Its appearance is highly irregular, and is confined neither to certain Hundreds nor to a small selection of fiefs. It is found twenty-seven times for Essex and on twenty-six occasions in the Suffolk text, but in over one hundred Norfolk entries. Since it occurs also in the IE, the information must have been furnished for the original returns.[2] The relevant entries are concerned with both demesne and the villagers' teams. For some reason the non-adjacent Hundreds of Launditch and Guiltcross account for 40% of the Norfolk instances, while there are none in about one-third of the Hundreds in that shire.

The formulae employed are highly variable. Often we are told that *n* teams could be 'restored' (*possunt restaurari*). Other phrases are *possunt fieri*, *possunt esse*; once *refieri* is used (Staverton, 325). Very occasionally a little more detail is provided. At Thorney (281b) there had been a single demesne team *tunc et post*, though in 1086 there was none, but in King Edward's day there could have been two. Again, here seven sokemen had 'always' had half a team, but in King Edward's time there had been 'one team between four of them'. At *Eilesforda* (25b) the half-team which could be employed there in 1086 was available when Odo of Bayeux received the holding; nothing is said about 1066. Once we are told that the diminution of villagers' teams from sixty to twenty-four was 'made by Ralf before he paid forfeit', an obvious reference to his treatment of Wymondham (137b) during his rebellion.

The logical deduction would seem to be that in these holdings there was arable land additional to that which was actually being tilled, and the use of 'restored' certainly suggests that

[1] It is found also in the east midland and west midland circuits.

[2] See, e.g., H, pp. 133–4.

teams had been cultivating it in King Edward's day. Indeed, we may here be given what in vol. i would be the number of ploughlands, but the irregularity of appearance of the information does not imply that where it is not given there were necessarily as many teams as there were ploughlands.

Normally the number of teams said to be available and which could be employed is equal to the number said to have been on the holding in 1066. But there are exceptions. At Thaxted (38b) eight demesne teams had fallen in number to seven, and thirty-four teams of the villagers to eighteen, but only sixteen are said to be replaceable. At South Benfleet (43) three demesne teams had been reduced to one, but only one could be 'restored'. A few times we are not told how many teams there had been earlier, but the number which could be used is given, e.g. at Cowbridge (81b). Several times the total would exceed that of the previous teams. There had been two demesne teams at Roding (61b) in 1066, and there were two in 1086, but a team could be 'restored'.[1] At Fanton (14) there was both in 1066 and 1086 a demesne team, while the villagers' teams had fallen from four to one. But we are told that two more in demesne were possible.[2] Clavering (46b) presents an odd state of affairs. There had been four demesne teams in 1066 and when the manor changed hands, and five in 1086, together with twenty-five villagers' teams in both 1066 and 1086. Yet we are told that one team could be 'restored'.[3]

The above examples are all drawn from Essex. But parallels can be found in the other shires; e.g. at Shotley (287), Bridge in Dunwich (331), and Wrentham (399).[4] Norfolk provides a score of instances in which adding the number of teams said to be employable to those said to be operating would give more than there had been in 1066, and nine where full restoration would not be effected. In three entries where it is said that the

[1] No villagers' teams are, however, recorded, and perhaps a 1066 quantity was omitted.

[2] Similar discrepancies are recorded for Thorrington (25b), Great Wakering and Canewdon (44), High Easter (60), and Shellow Bowells (61). There is always the possibility that the composition of the manors had been enlarged.

[3] Possibly the manor had really been a team short in 1066.

[4] See also Stradbroke (328b); twelve villagers' teams *tunc et post*, five *modo*, yet twelve, it is said, could be 'restored'. This must mean 'restored to twelve'.

holding is waste, or that there is 'nothing there', we are told there could now be teams at work.[1]

The phrases used are sometimes found referring to other things than teams; e.g. at Chadwell (23) there had been a fishery, which was not there in 1086, 'but it could be made'.

We could with reason expect to find that a diminution in the number of teams would be accompanied by a decrease of population in the holding. But, as Round pointed out, often we do not: indeed, in some instances the number of inhabitants has actually risen, e.g. at Benfleet (1b) or Buxton (222). At Blythburgh (282) there was land for five teams in demesne, but Roger Bigot received only three oxen when he took over the manor, and in 1086 there were still only three.[2] But the population had remained constant.

ESSEX

The Essex text does not give us as much statistical information as we should like to have for the moments described as *tunc* or *post* or *quando recepit*. The items for which the information is most frequently given are plough-teams, population, values, and livestock. From each of these something can perhaps be learnt.

Plough-teams

For plough-teams figures for *tunc* occur in 126 entries, giving us 155 opportunities of comparing quantities, 60% of which are concerned with demesne oxen. For nine of the twenty-two Hundreds we have no figures, and the majority of the examples come from the north of the shire. Forty-four of the quantities show no change from those of 1066, and many of the others represent no alteration in the total teams employed on a holding. But we cannot confidently assume that the use of *semper* invariably implies no alteration in the number of teams at either of the relevant dates. We are, for example, told that there were 'always' two demesne and four villagers' teams at Higham, (78b), but equally it is noted that when it was received the

[1] Holkham, Quarles, and Egmere (113)

[2] This looks like a rare East Anglian reference to ploughlands.

new owner found 'only one ox and one acre sown'. Losses recorded 'in the time of all the sheriffs', 'when Sweyn and Bainard were sheriffs' (Hatfield Broad Oak, 2; Witham, 1b), since neither was sheriff in 1086, cannot be ascribed to any definite date.[1] If we did place this interpretation on *semper*, we should have to argue that there were 'afterwards' only a little over a hundred fewer teams than the 4,483¾ in 1066 for which we have comparative figures, and this, in the light of the evidence which follows, seems improbable. 682½ teams declining to 548⅛, from the comparable figures, a 20% fall, seems far more likely.

Fortunately, however, we have figures for 1066 and for 1086 for over 90% of the recorded Essex teams. Apparently during the interval there had been an appreciable fall in their number, a fall of some 14½%.[2] The decline is by no means spread evenly over the county. It is strikingly high in Tendring Hundred (36½%), and fairly high in most of the other coastal Hundreds, very small in two metropolitan Hundreds (Becontree and Waltham) and in the Hundreds controlled by Sweyn (Rochford and Clavering), and in Uttlesford. Though the Hundreds display no consistency of proportion, the drop is greater for the villagers' teams (19%) than for those of the demesnes (12%); though the proportion of demesne to villagers' teams changed very little between 1066 and 1086.

Possible reasons for the decline must inevitably be speculative. One could be a limited shift from an agricultural to a pastoral economy. As only the quantities of demesne livestock are recorded, and these on the whole display no comparable increase, this is no more than a possibility. Another is a more economic basis of cultivation under new and sterner masters, reducing capital investment. A third is general or local animal mortality, either from losses similar to those quoted above, which may have been due to disease, or from involuntary slaughter to feed troops or what seems to be a substantially increased population (see p. 190). Many of the coastal

[1] These phrases suggest to me the sheriff at the time of the Inquest, Peter de Valognes, stressing that this loss to his royal master did not occur during *his* tenure of the office.

[2] The figures are: 1066, 4,483¾ teams; 1086, 3,835¼: these, of course, are for only the entries which give us comparative figures.

Hundreds show considerable falls which might be attributed to the royal order of 1085 to devastate the seaboard to deprive a potential invasion of sustenance, or to similar measures adopted in 1069–71 when Scandinavian raiders were attacking most of eastern England. A map of percentage decline by holdings unfortunately does not suggest the track of either pestilence or war, though taken in conjunction with the comparative figures for population changes and alterations in values it does rather give the impression that there had been activity of a kind unfavourable to local economy along and in the neighbourhood of the London–Colchester and coastal road. Certainly the results amply demonstrate that they cannot be attributed to the policy of the individual landowner.

Demesne livestock

The 301 Essex entries, giving 987 comparable quantities, enable us to compare the livestock on the demesnes at some unknown date and in 1086, and fortunately their figures represent, for almost every category, over half the total beasts concerned. Moreover, the proportion of arbitrary round numbers in them is not high, and only 136 record no change, of which as many as 59 are concerned with rounceys. In the calculations which follow, the basis has been that if an entry mentions a category for 1086, but not for the earlier date, the figures have been ignored; equally if an entry gives figures for *tunc*, and adds *modo similiter*, or uses *semper*, these too have been ignored. We are never given figures for all the three dates as we sometimes are for plough-teams and population.[1]

	No. of examples	10??	1086	% rise	% of 1086 DB total
Sheep	257	20,061	25,763	22	60
Swine	239	6,590	7,360	11¾	56
Animalia	228	1,945	2,199	13	55
Goats	43	1,400	1,166	–16¾	31
Rounceys	184	397	451	13½	57

[1] e.g. for Dunmow (36b): 'then 10 swine and 30 sheep, now 9 beasts, 80 sheep, 12 goats', only the sheep have been counted. It is highly improbable that there were, e.g., 318 sheep and 172 swine at Writtle (5) at both dates, as the text suggests.

Except for goats, we find a modest increase such as we might expect, highest for sheep. This might suggest a post-Conquest development of sheep-farming which could also account in part for the general decline in the number of plough-teams. Equally an appreciable increase in the number of packhorses might suggest an extension of trade, and be caused in part by the general increase in livestock enhancing the need for the carriage of wool and hides.

But there is no consistency about the figures; both rises and falls in quantities are often immense, and some numbers unexpectedly small. Six sheep at Wormingford (66) had become 200, 15 at Dunmow (69) 104, yet of 260 at Goldhanger (88) there were only 50 in 1086. At Debden (73b) the swine had fallen in number from 250 to 110, and at Sandon (54) from 100 to 14, while at Lammarsh (74b) they had risen from 11 to 54 and at Stow Maries (63) from 5 to 70.

The principal falls in the number of livestock seem to be along the line of the London–Colchester coast road, which fits in happily with the results displayed by plough-team and population figures. The fact that several entries report that no stock was present when the new owner took possession may suggest post-Conquest troubles.[1]

Population

Most writers have commented on the large increase between 1066 and 1086 in the number of bordars in Essex, and the decline in the number of villeins and serfs.[2] Again we have comparative figures for over 90% of the relevant recorded population. Where we have these figures, the bordars have increased by 64%, while the slaves are less by 30% and the villeins by about 5½%. For the combination of these classes the appreciation is 14¾%. Before the Conquest villeins had

[1] All the stock had gone in 1086 from Birch (32b), Patching (67), and Notley (80). There had been no stock when the manors were received at Asheldham (46), Foulton (48), Salcot (65), Purleigh (64b), Yeldham (81), and Maplestead (84) – all but one in the coastal Hundreds.

[2] e.g. Maitland: *DBB*, p. 363. In *VCH: Essex*, i, pp. 359–63, Round, however, pointed out that the process of the change was by no means uniform.

accounted for about 39% of the lesser peasantry, bordars for $37\frac{1}{2}$%. By 1086 villeins had dropped to 32%, and slaves from $23\frac{1}{2}$% to 16%, so that the proportion of bordars had risen to 52%.

Again there is no consistency of change. The increase is highest (20%) in the western Hundreds, but falls to about $3\frac{3}{4}$% in those bordering the coast. This in some respects brigades well with the fall in teams; where these have declined sharply, the increase in population is small. Nor is there consistency for any particular category. For each quite frequent instances can be found of both gains and losses. Some of these are striking and at first sight would seem to be quite incomprehensible unless there had been considerable changes in the composition of manors (which certainly happened in Devon and Somerset) in the score of years following the Conquest. But the Essex Domesday rarely mentions substantial additions to or ablations from manors in these instances. We do, however, find examples such as the following. In the manors of East and West Ham (64 *bis*) the number of teams had increased from 19 to 36, and of the recorded inhabitants from 107 to 187, while the values had risen, after falling from £26 to £19, to £42. Yet at Thaxted (38b), where the 25 teams were fewer by 17 than in 1066, the population had declined by only three, and yet the value of the manor had doubled. There are plenty of entries where the total recorded population had remained constant, but the composition had changed, e.g. Weston in Foxearth (88), where five bordars had become ten and nine slaves four, or Terling (72), where instead of 11 villeins and five slaves we find in 1086 five villeins, 11 bordars, and no slaves.

Several interpretations suggest themselves. There may have been an increase in the birth or the survival rate at an appropriate interval earlier. The advent of so many foreigners and mercenaries, who would not in the early stages of the Conquest be accompanied by women, may imply an enhanced marriage-rate, or at least association-rate, the effects of which, in terms of able-bodied peasants, would be displayed by the time of the Inquest. As may have happened in Yorkshire, and quite possibly elsewhere (e.g. Cornwall), men may have been deliberately moved from unrewarding to potentially more prosperous settlements.[1] Possibly quite large numbers of free men and sokemen lost their independence and were reduced to the status of villeins and bordars, while villeins sank to the level of bordars. Unfortunately there are not many entries which show us fewer free men or sokemen on a holding in 1086 than there had been in 1066; for the most part we are left to guess whether those recorded as existing in the latter year, or their children, were still on the holdings concerned. At Steeple (4b), however, there had been four free men in 1066: 'now they are not there'. But at 'the other Navestock' (13), where there had been seven free men in 1066, there were in 1086 'in this land' twelve 'men'. The high rate of increase in the western Hundreds might have been caused by an increased demand from London for agricultural produce; it might even be that in the east Colchester townsmen had been compelled to become agriculturalists to an increased degree.

It is obvious that many a villein, facing increased rents, may well have been reduced to the position of a bordar.[2] It is equally probable that in an area where Church and monarch were not really large landholders, and demesnes apparently not extensive, Norman efficiency may have converted many a slave to the category of bordar and provided him with a small holding rather than be entirely responsible for his maintenance. The slave was a total liability when old or sick.

The statistics for slaves produce a problem. When, as we often are, we are told that there were 'then as now' *x* villeins and *y* bordars, but 'then' *z* slaves, does this imply that in 1086 there were no slaves? In view of the high number of occasions in which slaves had totally disappeared, it has been assumed in such instances that there were none in 1086. For we are told that at Occold (410b) there were 'then' two slaves, and nothing is said about slaves in 1086; however, the IE (H, p. 153) says 'now, none'.

What does need explanation is why the large increase should

[1] T. A. M. Bishop: 'The Norman Settlement of Yorkshire', in *Studies in Medieval History presented to Frederick Maurice Powicke* (R. W. Hunt, W. A. Pantin, and R. W. Southern, eds.), pp. 1–14.

[2] We must remember that the clerks' differentiation between villeins and bordars may not have been scrupulous, and it would suit those making returns to treat many as bordars rather than as villeins.

come primarily among the bordars. If it was indeed due to the depression of the free men, one would expect to find them sinking no lower than villein status. But it seems as if the holdings of these small peasant proprietors were frequently divorced from the nucleated village from which the manor took its name (p. 56), and those who supplied the information may have thought of them as somehow distinct from the 'villager', and classed them as bordars.

Many Domesday scholars have commented on the apparent disappearance in many areas of the free peasantry, including Cambridgeshire, where the number of sokemen seems to have fallen during the reign by something like 75%.[1] No doubt some of these had been reduced to the status of a villein or even lower: at Benfleet in Essex (1b) we read of a free man who had held half a hide, but by 1086 'had been made one of the villeins'. Of Abberton (46b) it is said, 'then one free man, now one bordar', but that does not necessarily mean that it was the free man who had become a bordar. But where, as at Chignal (58b), there had been three free men and were now three villeins, it does look as if we have an instance of slipping down the social scale. In Essex we do indeed occasionally hear of sokemen who were fewer in 1086 than in 1066, but the decline is quite small, and in some instances, where on the royal manors they had merely been appropriated by rival powerful landowners, may really be only apparent.[2]

It does not, indeed, look as though in Essex sokemen or free men had generally been reduced to the level of bordars. In just over fifty entries we can compare pre- and post-Conquest figures, and while the free men have fallen in number only from 127 to 121, the sokemen have in fact increased from 291 by three.[3] There can be no doubt of the survival of these, or of their heirs, for they are recorded by such expressions as *tenent*, *manentes*, *modo adhuc tenent*, *adjacent semper*, *habens*, *remanentes*, *in hanc terram sunt*.[4]

[1] e.g. Maitland: *DBB*, p. 63.

[2] e.g. at Lawford (6), Copford (10b), and Grays Thurrock (90).

[3] These represent about 12½% and 43% respectively of those recorded for 1066. But we must remember that in addition many persons named are styled 'free men'. Named sokemen are rare, but we have, e.g., Ælfric at Radwinter (78) and Godemann at Berden (47).

[4] e.g. fols. 83b, 47, 29b, 101, 81, 90b, 34, 58.

But probably there had been some decrease, for a variety of reasons, in their numbers; of the four there had been at *Vluuinescherham* (4b) it is said, *modo non sunt*. At a Purleigh holding (27b) two men had dwelt (*homines . . . manserunt*): the only recorded inhabitant in 1086 is a priest; yet the value had risen from 16*s*. 8*d*. to 22*s*. Perhaps Eadgifu, the former holder, had a family who still worked there.

In 1066, apart from those named, there had been in Essex nearly a thousand free men and nearly 700 sokemen. Doubtless, as many commentators have thought, some of these were men who were recorded more than once. In any case, we cannot separate the two terms. In many Essex Hundreds we hear of no sokemen, or of only very few, and it may be that in these they either were not recorded or were treated as free men.[1] We may suspect that some of those who continued to live in England after 1066 or 1071 sank lower in the social scale, but we can prove virtually nothing.

But there must *be* a reason for an increase in the Essex villager population of over 1,500 recorded persons, especially when East Anglia displays the same tendency. We can hardly altogether account for it by assuming a general depression in the social scale of small free farmers. Indeed, if some of these are indeed recorded more than once, we have not sufficient numbers for 1066, even assuming a surplus of births over deaths, to produce the 1086 quantities of DB. Did those lesser thegns and free men have unrecorded families and household dependants, the latter unnecessary under the new régime, who in 1086 were counted among the bordars?

Values

What the figures have to tell us of a fall in the number of teams and an increase in the quantity of villagers and slaves is to a limited extent confirmed by the figures for values. For both 1066 and the moments recorded as *post* or *quando recepit* we have information for about 35% of the 1066 values, and this shows

[1] e.g. Thurstaple, Dengie, Rochford, Chelmsford. They are most numerous in Lexden, Tendring, and Hinckford (in the last they contribute about 45% of the total recorded). It is thus possibly significant that they are chiefly to be found where the East Saxon joins the East Anglian land.

only a small total decline, of about $2\frac{3}{4}\%$. It looks, then, as if Essex, a shire largely outside the troubles of 1066–71, did not suffer as other counties undoubtedly did. Between 1066 and 1086 values appreciated by 17%.[1]

Again the rise is smallest in the coastal Hundreds, only $4\frac{1}{2}\%$, and if we omitted Sweyn's Rochford Hundred, would actually show a $1\frac{1}{4}\%$ decline. No fewer than eight Hundreds, largely in the northern half of the shire, show appreciations within the limited range $35–39\frac{1}{2}\%$. The highest figures come from the western Hundreds, especially from Waltham and Becontree, where there had also been a small decline in teams but a large increase in population. Only Ongar of the Hundreds near London produces a figure below the average. Again, this might be due to the influence of London and her increasing demands, or to a desire to hold or rent property conveniently close to the capital.

EAST ANGLIA

All the difficulties and uncertainties about changes in the number of plough-teams and the numbers and categories of the villagers and slaves which were encountered for Essex confront us in East Anglia, and in an intensified and often disconcerting fashion. This is of course in part the result of the peculiar construction of this portion of Domesday Book. But the number of entries in which we have no comparative figures, or from which we can be reasonably confident that information is missing, is unpleasantly large. Nevertheless, study of the analysed statistics suggests that a reasonably accurate picture of changes in the twenty years following the Conquest can be obtained. Fortunately the scope is considerable; in Suffolk we are dealing with nearly 2,500 recorded holdings distributed over more than 600 villages, and in Norfolk with nearly 2,800 holdings and close on 800 villages.

[1] In this and the following calculations I have omitted the royal manors, where many increases in value seem to be entirely arbitrary (p. 167). Even so, they would bring the figure only up to 18%. Where other manors are said to be valued at one sum but in fact paid a higher one, I have throughout used the lower figure.

SUFFOLK

One of the difficulties in deducing post-Conquest changes is the infrequency of information for the period between 1066 and 1086. On less than 200 occasions are we given a definite figure for demesne teams, and in only about fifty instances the villagers' teams. We are rather better off when it comes to population statistics, but have far fewer figures than we should like to possess. Instead of information regarding *tunc et post et modo*, we are all too frequently told that there have 'always', *semper*, been so many teams or inhabitants. In a Hundred selected at random (Stow), out of fifty-nine instances where no change in numbers is recorded, *semper* is used for forty-nine of these. It does seem improbable that in so many holdings no changes occurred at any one of these dates. Any calculation of alteration of quantities in the years immediately following the Conquest must then be given with appreciable reservation. In consequence of the overwhelming number of instances of the use of *semper*, the figures at our disposal would suggest only slight diminution of teams and increase of population during this period.

To compare changes in East Anglia on the basis of the Hundred is unwise. Where a Hundred includes a number of large complex manors, especially royal manors or the demesne possessions of the bishop or St Edmund or St Audrey, we shall get a picture very different from that presented by Hundreds where the bulk of the holdings are small and had been held by the individual small free man or by groups of free men. It is necessary to look at the results of statistical analysis in terms of larger units.

Plough-teams

From the 2,500 holdings or thereabouts we have 1,932 figures for *tunc*, 2,223 for *modo*, counting demesne and villagers' teams separately, but only 237 for *post* as opposed to *semper*, which is a quantity insufficient for reasonable deductions to be made. The risk of always interpreting *semper* literally is shown by entries such as that for Whatfield (440), *semper valuit vi solidos, modo xx.*[1]

[1] Here, I suppose, *semper* might imply *tunc et post.*

In the Hundred of Stow, for example, 118 teams *tunc* had become 89½ *post*, a decline of 24%. But if we include the entries which say *semper*, the fall is from 159¼ to 130¾, or only 18%. It is possible, though, that the former figure is the one more likely to furnish an idea of the facts.

For the average decline in the number of teams, where we have comparable figures, is 20½%. But there are also a quantity of instances where we are told of teams existing in 1066 but no 1086 figure is given, and many more where the reverse occurs. If we take all these into the reckoning, the fall is only 14½%. The objection here is that for such entries teams said to have been working in 1066 may not have altogether disappeared, while it is obvious that there may in 1066 have been more teams than are recorded for 1086. We can only say that the number of teams at the Inquest was probably less than 25% lower than that of 1066, but not much more than 15% less. The fall is heavy in the eastern Hundreds, and this might be caused either by the fact that these contain the largest number of the holdings of small free men or to deliberate wasting in 1085.

The fall in demesne teams is on the whole less than that for villagers' teams, especially in the western Hundreds, where St Edmund's demesne manors were numerous. The decline is at its lowest in the western and northern Hundreds, and in the south and east more than twice as heavy as the average fall, with the south showing a drop of 38%. These are areas in which the holdings of once independent free men, and small manors, predominate. The chances here of a loss of plough-oxen after the Conquest, from seizure or from financial stringency, or from incorporation in a larger manor, necessitating the employment of fewer beasts, would be high.

There are occasional instances where we find more teams in 1086 than in 1066, but the reason might well be an extension of the arable, an enlargement of a manor, or a transfer of the oxen of small proprietors to the lord. Some of the big falls in numbers might be due to mortality, to a shift from arable to stock-farming, or even to manorialisation or urbanisation. For at Eye (319b), the Malet headquarters, with its new castle and market, 23 teams became 11, the dozen slaves were all gone (there would be less need of them with fewer demesne teams), and villeins were only about half as numerous as they had been, while bordars increased only from nine to 16.[1] Two-and-a-half teams at Weybread (329b) had been reduced to a single ox; the seven teams of 35 Akenham free men (422b) to half a team; the ten at *Grenewic* (347) to four, and while the number of villagers here remained unchanged, the value fell from £2 to 10*s*. In 1086 there were no teams at Bardestone in Mendlesham (425b) where there had been eight; six bordars became four, and the value fell by 40%. The ten teams of the Stratford St Mary villagers (402) were reduced to five, but since five 'could be restored', this can hardly be because of a conversion of arable to pasture. Forty-six teams at Thorney in Stowmarket (281b) in 1066 had become only 19 by 1086, though the only change in the population was the disappearance of all six slaves, while rents increased from £15 to £40, a possible instance of redeployment of the land. *Eruestuna* (409) had possessed three teams in 1066; now, it is said, 'the men have scarcely one'.

The fall in teams varies not only locally, but with the fief also. On the lands of Sweyn of Essex it is 31½%, with the decline in villagers' teams three times that of the demesne oxen. A similar fall is to be seen for Geoffrey de Manneville's fief, where the teams of the free men are less than half what they had been, and those of the villagers have decreased for more than those of the demesne or of the sub-tenants. On the Ely lands the fall, as we might expect in view of her vicissitudes, is substantial: 17% on the demesne land, 26% on that of the villagers, and 43½% on that of the sub-tenants, averaging 28½%.

But with the estates of St Edmund all is changed. The demesne teams have increased by 3%, and those of the villagers and the free men and sokemen have fallen by only 4½% and 6½% respectively; the majority of the entries record that the number of teams had remained unchanged: *semper* II *carucae*. The abbey, indeed, possessed 14% of all the Suffolk teams, and the figures suggest that here at least there was no major change from arable to stock-farming.

[1] The Clare teams (389b), where Richard fitzGilbert made his local headquarters, fell first from 76 to 65 and then to 54, yet while the villagers were after 1066 diminished from 70 by five, they had increased by ten by 1086.

Population

In 1086 472 of the holdings contained some villeins, 1,099 holdings bordars, and only 326 slaves, which shows how many free men and sokemen had none but their families and neighbours to help them. Where comparative figures are available, these represent 77% of the total villager population for 1086, and there is very little difference between the total for 1066 and that for 1086. Here we have the same problem as that which affected teams; large numbers recorded for 1086, especially of bordars, where we have no 1066 quantity. A limited number of the bordars probably represent enfranchised slaves, or villeins and free men who had suffered a loss of status. Again we not infrequently find quantities for 1066 but not for 1086, and vice versa, and the objection adduced for teams to reliance on these is of equal weight. The bulk of such quantities relates to 1086, and if we strike a balance we have to include, besides the figures where comparison is possible, over 150 villeins, but nearly 1,600 bordars. The entries hardly affect the figure for slaves at all.

But the inclusion of these men for whom no comparative figures are given raises a fresh difficulty. While some of these bordars are no doubt former villeins or slaves who have been counted in the 1066 figures, we do not know how many were, and it is incredible that there should always have been no persons of any category in 1066 where we have only a 1086 figure. A Chevington sokeman (357) had always possessed a team, and in 1086 he had two bordars to help him. Are we to suppose that the effect of the Conquest was to enable him to obtain extra help with his land? A free man at Risby (356b) is not said to have any villagers in 1066; in 1086 he had four bordars and a slave. If all these had been added to his equipment since the Conquest, would the value of his estate have remained at 10*s*. throughout? Such instances could be multiplied indefinitely. Thus the *total* figures now to be given for East Anglia have to be viewed with suspicion, and the apparent rise in village population may not have been nearly as great as they suggest. But they are none the less not completely useless, and it is suggestive that their use shows us villeins and slaves decreasing and bordars increasing in very much the same proportions for all three counties. The only disharmony, intelligible in a more manorialised area, is the greater fall in Essex slaves, with a consequent smaller increase in bordars.

Using all the available figures, villeins represent 29½% of the total, bordars 62%, and slaves only 8½%; in 1066 villeins had represented 38% and slaves 13%.[1] The totals show an increase from 1066 in these three categories of 22½%. The four areas chosen for consideration of the teams are not, however, suitable for studying population changes. In the extreme western Hundreds and in the Sandlings region in the east the appreciations are well below the average, 9¼% and 16%. So is the rise in the eastern portion of mid-Suffolk, 10¾%. But in the remainder of the county it is 40%, and is particularly marked in the St Edmunds Hundreds. Unfortunately, a further reservation has to be made. In certain eastern Hundreds, population statistics are infrequent, for the district is one in which small proprietors are numerous. In some of these, e.g. Colneis, Claydon, Wilford, and Plomesgate, the slaves recorded total only from two to eight, and represent only 1¼% of the unfree population. Some may have been omitted; still, a low figure for slaves is here to be expected, for the area abounds in the holdings of small free men who could not afford them.

Though the increase is so considerable, there are plenty of large holdings on which the population has declined. Some of these instances are perfectly intelligible; the 12 bordars at Dunwich (311b) had become two, and here the sea had carried away one of the two carucates. It is not in every holding that we find an increase in the number of bordars; they had fallen from 25 to ten at Long Melford (359), where the quantity of villeins and slaves remained unaltered, and from 32 to 23 at Stoke by Nayland (401), where the villeins were reduced from 25 to 15 and slaves from eight to six. Sometimes we find an increase in the number of villeins, e.g. at Woodhall (382b), from two to seven. Sometimes decline in one or more

[1] All figures are based on the Domesday county, thus they are not comparable with those of the *Domesday Geography of England.* In any case, no two people would ever produce identical figures; several entries can be variously interpreted, and there could be disagreement as to which entries duplicate each other. I have ignored, among certain other figures for boroughs, the bordars at Bury St Edmunds, for whom we have no comparative figure.

categories is virtually compensated by an increase in others. Melton (387) had included 18 villeins and two slaves; the slaves were gone, and the villeins only half their former number. But the bordars had increased from six to 13, while at Earl Soham (294) the eight bordars had become 21 and at Playford (314b) the eight villeins had been halved and the six slaves reduced to one.

A frequent sharp increase in bordars is often well marked. Their numbers rose from ten to 30 at Clare (389b), from 21 to 55 at Assington (416), from five to 22 at East Bergholt (287), and from one to 16 at Hoo (388). Some of these might well be due to their incorporation in a manor to which they were not attached in 1066.

We do indeed find every variety of alteration in the categories, and some of the shifts are extraordinary. Badingham (328b) always had 26 bordars (and no slaves), but the villeins increased from four to 21, though ten demesne teams and seven villagers' teams had each become five, and the value had fallen from £10 to £5. We find, too, plenty of holdings where free men had none but their families and neighbours to help them; the three free men at Thurston (317, 400b) had no teams and were the sole inhabitants.

Of the holdings of villeins and bordars we receive occasional glimpses. Twice at Raydon (411, 411b) we read of a villein with 30 acres; in the solitary entry for *Litelcros* (318) there are alone seven villeins with 40 acres, a team, and three acres of meadow, worth 10*s*. A Hemley bordar (431) is said to have 5 acres. But in those passages where villeins seem to be singled out for mention, we might be quite wrong in thinking on that account that they were markedly superior to their fellows. Often they seem to be recorded because they occupy a detached portion of a manor, or perhaps have been transferred to some manor. A villein apparently named Osketel had 20 acres and a half-team at Chediston (444b), but he is 'in the value of Easton'.[1] The Gedgrave villeins and bordars (294) are 'in the value of Carlton', and those of Easton Bavants (282) 'added to the manor of Blythburgh'.

[1] For other apparently named villeins, see Uggeshall (444b) and Boulge (425), but the latter entry may mean that he was Wulfric's villein, not called Wulfric.

Once we turn from the villagers to the quasi-peasant proprietors of small estates we are faced with yet another difficulty. How are we to estimate the number of free men and sokemen living within the shire in 1086, and so arrive at an approximate density of population? Often there is no clarity whatever as to whether those said to have held estates in 1066 were still in existence in 1086.

Ballard queried the figure, 7,460, for Suffolk free men given by Sir Henry Ellis.[1] His objection rested on the supposition that many free men must have been counted more than once, and that in, e.g., the Hundred of Colneis the 315 free men named could be reduced to 122, assuming that the repetition of a name in various entries implied the individual, not several different persons. While I do not altogether agree with the figures Ballard gives, his argument seems to be a sound one.[2]

Neither Dodwell nor Darby has agreed with Ballard's conclusions.[3] The former considered that he had insufficiently taken into account the fact that some personal names were very common, and that the number of free men and sokemen who held more than one tenement was small. This is open to doubt; certainly many quite minor named free men had several scattered holdings. When we find a 'Leofstan of Falkenham' (314b) and a Leofstan holding at Falkenham (340b, 341), we may legitimately here see the individual. Maitland suggested that 'there is reason to think that some of the free men and sokemen . . . get counted twice or thrice over because they hold land under several different lords', and Maitland's opinions should never be lightly dismissed.[4]

[1] A. Ballard: *The Domesday Inquest*, p. 144; Sir H. Ellis: *A General Introduction to Domesday Book*, ii, pp. 488–90. The figure is for the Domesday county, while for the modern county Darby (*The Domesday Geography of England*, i, p. 379) has given 7,666.

[2] Ballard may have included, e.g. Northmann (339b), Guthmund (406), and Beorhtmær (423b), who were all influential persons and not of the status of the minor *liber homo* (the last-named 'held many lands'). Again 'Lurc' (406b) and Burric (342) may stand for Leofric (six occurrences) and Burgric (340), each recorded elsewhere also; Wihtric (314b, 340) might be the Wihtric whose name is variously spelt (339b, 342b), and Edwin (385b) and 'Edwin the Carlwood smith' (314b) the same person.

[3] B. Dodwell: 'The Free Peasantry of East Anglia in Domesday' (*Trans. Norf. & Norwich Arch. Soc.*, xxvii, p. 157); *Dom. Geog.*, i, p. 170.

[4] *DBB*, p. 20.

To estimate the number of free men or sokemen of 1086 is indeed impossible, for many may inadvertently be counted more than once. The formulae of DB are of little use here. Sometimes we can be certain of the presence of free men in 1086: at Earl Stonham (294b) five hold (*tenent*) 12 acres of Earl Alan's demesne; phrases such as *isti sunt liberi homines* (339b), *habent xxx liberi homines* (446b), and mention that they have been *additi*, *adjuncti*, to a manor, demonstrate their survival. The common formula is *in ⁊ n liberi homines*, implying current occupation, whereas for the named thegns and greater free men we find *tenuit*, and a newcomer in possession.[1]

Here and there we find increases in the numbers of free men and sokemen. Where there had been a free man and his wife, in 1086 there were four free men (Grundisburgh, 300). A free man had held a small estate at Sutton (319): 'now there dwell there his three sons'. At Walpole (292b) seven free men had become 17, but there may here have been an extension of the estate as it was in 1066; at Burgh (406b) there were three *homines* where there had been a single free man.[2] At Hadleigh (372b) a free man and a sokeman had each held 60 acres (which does not suggest serious inequality of wealth); in 1086 there were three free men and three sokemen on these holdings.

One simple instance will show how far we might be from the truth. If we use only the comparative figures for Thingoe Hundred, the villager population increased by less than 3½%. But if we include those for whom no 1066 figure is given, the increase is ten times as much. Moreover, we are taking no account of the 128 free men and sokemen of 1066, some of whom might be represented in our 1086 figures already.

Values

In considering values we are faced in intensified form with the problems encountered in studying changes in the number of

[1] There are numerous errors: *ten.* often has to be extended as *tenuit*, and we have *tenet Ælfric camp* (Cornard, 448) where Richard fitzGilbert has succeeded him, following Wihtgar his *antecessor*. At Elveden (303) Ælfsige had held T.R.E., but *post* Ingelric, and *modo*, accordingly, Earl Eustace.

[2] For other examples, see Fincham (250b), Bungay (288), Chediston (293).

plough-teams and population, especially as the character of the holding is so dominant a factor. The general increase cannot be related to the character of the area: the Lackford Hundred holdings have risen by 40%, but those in Risbridge by 26% and in Blackbourn and Bradmere by less than 15%. Where we have comparative figures, the Ely holdings have appreciated by 30%, but the bishop's by only a little over 1%, and there is no indication why Hoxne (379) should have declined so substantially in value unless it was because of the damage caused to it by the Malet development of Eye. We do not know why a Brockley sokeman's holding (390b), where throughout he had a plough-team and a little meadow, should have doubled in value, and the Ingham manor of a former thegn (348) lost 75% of its worth, or what caused a Stokerland holding (324) to be valued at three times the pre-Conquest sum, or Witnesham (427b) to have quadrupled its valuation.

Demesne livestock

We shall see when we come to examine Norfolk that little can be learned from the figures for East Anglia available. Potential deduction is vitiated by the fact that of 128 comparative quantities for *Terra Regis* only 15 record any change in quantities. On the vast demesnes of St Edmund, in over 200 instances of livestock, only 29 give comparative figures, and only seven of these record any alteration in numbers. To take the matter further is useless.

NORFOLK

The Norfolk figures raise doubts even more freely than do those for Suffolk. Of the 1086 villager population 85% are recorded in entries which enable us to compare figures with those of 1066, but the number for which we have no comparative figure is unfortunately very large. What does seem strange is that, using the comparative figures, bordars are more numerous by less than 200 (less than 3%), whereas in Suffolk, with a population of only 65% that of Norfolk, they had increased by nearly 600 (nearly 13½%), and thus are less adequately represented in Norfolk than we could wish.

Plough-teams

Demesne teams are noted for 1066 in 1,857 of the entries, and for 1086 in 2,119.[1] But for the period variously described as *post* or *quando recepit* we have only 275 quantities, and, as in Essex, thus cannot set much value on a comparison with 1066. For the villagers' teams the quantities are *tunc* 645, *post* 245, *modo* 672. Throughout the proportion of totals of demesne to villagers' teams is found to be very close to 2 : 1.

The teams for 1066 which can be compared with figures *post* total 1,579. The *post* figure is only 1,185½, and a decline of about 25% for the period seems a highly probable figure. When we compare the *tunc* and *modo* figures we seem also to be on reasonably firm ground; 5,319⅜ at the Conquest, 4,767⅜ at the Inquest.[2] A 10½% fall seems reasonable. From *tunc* to *post* demesne teams decreased more than did those of the villagers (27–21½%); from *tunc* to *modo* the reverse is true (5½–18½%). This again seems reasonable.

Mapped, the results show a general, and, on the whole, even rate of fall over the whole county. The two areas well below the average are the Fenland with the Breckland, and the Broads, and these are perhaps the districts in which we should expect to find it impossible thoroughly to manorialise the holdings, to introduce an economy demanding fewer teams, or to extend demesnes. The other four regions of vol. i of the *Domesday Geography* show only 3% difference between their extremes. Yet we might have expected the marshland to carry greater numbers of sheep, and so, in all probability, far fewer teams, in 1086 than in 1066.

What is interesting is that a map of percentage decline in the number of teams displays marked lines of frequent and heavy falls radiating from Norwich. The most obvious one is in the neighbourhood of the road to Eye, and continues southwards through Suffolk towards both Clare and Sudbury. Another is in the direction of Ipswich, and the trend of one less well

[1] The teams on the holdings of free men and sokemen, unless said to be 'of the men', have been treated as demesne teams. Often it is specifically said that they are *in dominio*. *Semper*, fortunately, is only rarely used in the Norfolk text.

[2] All figures are based on the Domesday county, thus they cannot be compared with those of the *Domesday Geography of England*.

marked towards Cambridge. Here we may be seeing the still effective results of the rebellion of 1075. For two of the barons who confronted Earl Ralf in the royal interest were Robert Malet and Richard fitzGilbert, and Eye and Clare were the centres of their local power. Either Ralf's retreating forces or the king's champions' levies (these last might well concentrate at Eye) may have slaughtered considerable quantities of oxen to provide themselves with sustenance, while Ralf's men may have been active in devastating the countryside to deny his opponents provisions.

There are visible also certain other potential factors. The weakness of the Cambridge–Norwich line may be due to the fact that much of the country through which it passes was not rich in plough-teams. The fact that the symbols are less concentrated and less noticeable near Clare and Sudbury than farther north might be because forces leaving their bases may not immediately have need to live off the country. There is again a marked concentration north of Norwich, and lesser signs east thereof, as though the city had been invested – as we know it was.

Of devastation in the coastal areas to fulfil the royal order to deny an invader provender in 1085 there is small sign. It is doubtful whether most of the Norfolk coast offered opportunity for anything but small-scale landings, though it had been raided by Tostig in 1066. There are, however, some quite heavy falls in the north of the county, near the coast.

The falls in the quantity of teams outnumber the increases roughly in the proportion of four to one. Increases might be accounted for in several ways – extension of the cultivated area, concentration of teams on the large manors rather than in the smaller holdings (and the headquarters of large manors are commonly to be found where the soil is agriculturally most rewarding), a purchase or confiscation of oxen by the rich and powerful from those unable, from recently induced poverty or social and economic insecurity, to retain theirs. We can find plenty of instances in which demesne teams have increased but those of the villagers are fewer; e.g. Grensvill (217), $1\frac{1}{2}$ demesne teams increasing to two, but two villagers' teams declining to a half-team: the total of teams often remains unaltered. On a

Gayton holding (222), the teams increased from a half-team to two full teams. On the royal manor of Foulsham (114) two demesne teams had become three, and 18 of the villagers 20.[1] Moreover, there were 33 villeins where there had been 30, and 44 bordars where formerly there were 38, and the value of the manor increased from £4 by 50%. Though the demesne teams at Sporle (119b) rose from one to four, those of the villagers fell from ten to three; 32 villeins became 20, and two slaves six, while three bordars appear as against none recorded for 1066. But we are more apt to find situations such as that at Banham (168):

	demesne	villagers'
tunc	4	5
post	0	0
modo	2	3

with a 10% decline in the value of the holding.

Population

Using only those entries which give comparative quantities, we obtain the improbable result that between the Conquest and the Inquest the villager population fell by about 5%. We must accordingly make use of all our figures; we have to add only 211 to the 1066 comparable quantities, but 2,475 to those for 1086, 1,988 of whom were bordars.

Villeins were fewer in 1086 than in 1066 by only 3½%, slaves by 22%. Bordars increased in number by 28%; the increase for all classes is only 8¼%. By 1086 slaves represented 6¾% of the total against 9½% in 1066; bordars increased from 54½% to 62¾%, and villeins declined from 36% to 30½%. The comparatively small change in the proportion of slaves is probably accounted for by the fact that the slave element in East Anglia was constantly a comparatively slight one. Some no doubt had passed into the bordar class.

The increase, like the fall in teams, is spread fairly evenly over the whole county. It is at its lowest in the west midland and the north-eastern areas, but is probably of no real significance because of differences in the character of the holdings; e.g.

[1] Quantities did not change *tunc* to *post*.

between those of the western Bury estates and those of the mass of small free men in the south and east.

We find the same sort of population shift as was produced by the Essex details. At Mundford (213b) 14 villeins became ten and four slaves two, but the bordars increased from four to eight. Newton by Castle Acre (120) had eight villeins and seven bordars in 1066; by 1086 the villeins had decreased by six but there were four more bordars, while the number of slaves remained static at four. The eight villeins at Bodney (237) in 1066 were reduced to four *post*; none is recorded for 1086, but there were then seven bordars, a category unrecorded for *tunc* or *post*, while the six slaves became three. A striking instance is Kerdiston (157). Thirty villeins became 16, and while no bordars are recorded for 1066, there were 14 in 1086, the number by which that of the villeins had fallen.

Some of the appreciations and the reverse are considerable. The bordars at Shouldham (250b) rose from two to 12, though the only other change was a villein additional to the 14 of 1066. At Methwold (136) villeins fell from 28 to 18, bordars rose from four to 13, and the 24 slaves did not change in number. Yet though at Wymondham (137b) the men's teams declined from 60 to 24, we are told that there was no change in the total or distribution of the 118 recorded inhabitants, and the value of the manor trebled. Redenhall (125) lost two-thirds of its 30 villeins, but there were six bordars at both dates, though the slaves fell from four to one. Hardly any change in the total population of the Hempstead lay holding (248b) is shown, yet the figures are:

	tunc	*modo*
villeins	54	34
bordars	41	66
slaves	7	0

From a quite considerable number of holdings the slaves of 1066 or later have altogether disappeared. Proportionately they have fallen less than they did in Essex, while there is nothing like the enormous rise in the number and element of bordars to be found in that county. The situation was perhaps more stable in Norfolk than in Essex, and might in part be due to its appreciably unmanorialised condition.

While it is to be presumed that some free men and sokemen were constrained to become villeins or bordars, there is no real suggestion of a large drop in their numbers. There are indeed passages in which their diminution is recorded, e.g. at Swannington (147b) there were 'then' eight sokemen, 'afterwards' and 'now' five. But such passages are often counterbalanced, e.g. at Hockering (227b) there were 'then' three sokemen, 'now' seven, while at Welburne (166) the free men had doubled in number and in 1086 amounted to a score.[1] Some entries are at first sight deceptive. The number of sokemen at Wymondham (137b) had apparently dropped from 87 to 18, but the missing men had been appropriated by four barons, and the total number is unchanged, as it was at Bintree (269b): 'then as now ten sokemen'.

Demesne livestock

1,739 Norfolk passages affecting 535 holdings record the presence of the five main categories of demesne livestock – sheep, swine, goats, rounceys, and *animalia* and cows. Occasionally we are given the quantities *tunc et post et modo*.[2] But on nearly 500 occasions no comparative figure is provided; we have only that described as *tunc*, *post*, *quando recepit*. Moreover, of the 1,245 passages by means of which figures can be compared, only 531 record alteration of quantity. Indeed, only eleven of those under *Terra Regis* show a change of figure, and since this section provides over 200 of the material passages, and quantities here are naturally high, the whole picture is thus affected. Also, few changes are recorded on the lands of the bishop and of Bury and of Ely. The result is that we can put no trust in a comparison for either the shire or the Hundreds. For it is highly unlikely that there were throughout exactly 1,300 sheep at West Walton (213), or 440 at Snettisham (142), or 381 at Ormesby (115b). It is all the more irritating because some changes in quantity are precise; e.g. a fall in the number of sheep at North Creake (179)

[1] For other falls in quantities, see, e.g., Hudeston (249), Saxlingham (217), Sisland (131), Seething (140); for increases, Barnham Broom (166) and Kimberley (121). Some of the changes (perhaps at Kimberley, where there were 'then' 30 acres of land, 'now' 40) might be due to alterations in the extents of estates.

[2] e.g. Stiffkey (233), Newton by Castle Acre (244b), Barney (258).

from 320 to 264, and from 41 to nine swine at Bodney (237). Also, we have comparative figures for about three-quarters of the sheep and swine.

Fluctuations, often spectacular, do indeed occur. Several times we are told that 'now there is nothing'.[1] The 180 sheep at Fulmodeston (168b) had altogether disappeared, the 180 at Flitcham (173) had been reduced to a solitary specimen, the 200 at Frettenham (243) to a couple. But at Hempnall and Hudeston (248b, 249) five had become 186 and one 190 respectively. There were no swine at Wighton (112b) when the manor was received, but at the Inquest a score, while at Barton Bendish (250b) 60 had become 15. Often one might think that livestock had been transferred by their owner from one manor to a neighbouring one, or so the dissected figures suggest. For example, 24 and 240 sheep at Thorpland and Stow Bardolph (206) became 80 and 160 respectively.

It is perhaps surprising that we find on the whole so small an increase in the numbers of demesne livestock. Where figures can be compared, we have:

	pre-1086	1086
Sheep	33,167	35,194
Swine	6,398	6,297
Goats	1,788	1,642
Animalia and cows	1,544	1,634
Rounceys	557	517
	43,454	45,284

But the character of the figures and their distribution makes it impossible even to outline the local changes. Sheep seem to have increased principally in the northern coastland and in south Norfolk; no material increase is discernible in the areas in which the map on p. 145 of the *Domesday Geography* shows them to have been most numerous. They seem to have declined appreciably in the Hundreds immediately north of Norwich. Swine were more plentiful in 1086 than earlier only in the Loam region and mid-Norfolk, but declined in the south.

The obvious difficulties of dealing with such figures have been

[1] Crostwick (243b), Shouldham Thorpe (250b), Dersingham (256).

pointed out by Darby, and we can never be sure of our interpretation of the formulae.[1] Does 'now 36 goats' imply that there were none in the manor earlier? Surely, where 534 beasts of various kinds are recorded for 1086, there were some in the manor earlier also, though none is mentioned?[2] The 30 swine and a like number of sheep which Godric found on taking over Newton by Castle Acre (120) can hardly all have gone by 1086. 'Then nothing, now two rounceys, now four *animalia* and 30 swine and 250 sheep' (Barsham, 168) can be variously punctuated and interpreted.

The livestock are often said to be 'on the demesne' or 'in the hall', but there seems to be one exception to the rule that those mentioned were the lord's. For Igborough (242) had been held by four free men, who at the Inquest were Walter Giffard's, and they had possessed four swine and 100 sheep.

The wealth of statistical detail of this draft of Domesday Book promises so much and so far seems to yield so little, and to pose as many problems as it solves. It is, however, possible that a rigorous classification of its figures according to the type of holding and its situation and ownership might furnish profitable information.

Consider, for example, the Norfolk Hundred of Clavering, in which there were 100 separately noted holdings, with one in duplicate, six of which were components of manors in other Hundreds. Fourteen, including those styled manors or berewicks, were substantial estates, where neither teams nor population changed much, save for a 40% decline in the number of slaves. These alone included villeins in their composition, and their value had risen by over 150%. Eighteen are said to have been held by 113 sokemen, whose holdings ranged from a single acre worth 2*d.* to 1½ carucates shared by five men, and averaging 10 acres. On only six of these holdings were there no teams; the teams had not greatly changed in number, and they average 1½ oxen per man. On three holdings owned by individuals there were two or three bordars apiece, but only two more had any bordars. We know little of their values,

[1] *Dom. Geog.*, i, p. 143.
[2] Whissonsett (178b); Thornham (191).

though that of a St Edmund's sokeman was worth 10*s*., for these are included in the entire manorial values. The remainder had been held by 279 mostly anonymous free men, some of whom, unless they possessed several holdings, were very minor persons; two at Hales (212b) had a solitary acre worth only 4*d*., while holdings of less than 10 acres are common. There are no individual estates of more than 60 acres, and only about a dozen where one man had 30. One-quarter of the teams seem to have gone, and less than 2½ oxen per head of the population is the average. Eighty bordars were distributed over 18 of the holdings. The occasional larger holding was worth as much as £2, but there were many of just a few shillings. Over the Hundred teams had declined by 15½%, the villeins, bordars, and slaves by 3½%.

After all these somewhat dreary statistics, perhaps one small comforting thought may remain. We should perhaps expect Norfolk to be even less manorialised than Suffolk, and thus to display less change than the two other eastern counties. So the general result would suggest; teams declined in both Essex and Suffolk by roughly the same amount, but by a lower figure in Norfolk. It is in Norfolk, too, that the apparent increase in population is at its lowest.

APPENDIX A

Persons named as antecessores

Over fifty persons are named in vol. ii of DB as being the *antecessores* of those holding in chief in 1086; a few of these came to England at or after the Conquest, but no indication is given of whom these had succeeded. There are also a great many passages in which this word is used but no person is named; this suggests that witnesses and clerks knew perfectly well who a baron's legitimate *antecessor* was. But in the *breves* for a number of prominent men the term is never employed, though often the text makes it perfectly clear to whose lands a man had succeeded. Obviously Sweyn had inherited most of the fief of his father Robert fitzWymarc, and Earl Alan many of the lands of the fair or rich Edith: the *VCH* chapters give a considerable amount of information about succession. Those who *are* named are:

	antecessores
Aitard de Vals	Alfred, Wulfric
Alan, Earl	Cola
Aubrey de Ver	Wulfwine
Brian of Brittany	Wulfnoth
Drogo de Beuvrières	Rada
Eudes fitzHerbert	Ælfric 'camp', Lisois de Moustières†
Eudes *filius* Spirewic	Henfrid, Wulfric
Eustace, Earl	Ingelric
Geoffrey de Manneville	Ansger the marshal, Halfdan
Godric *dapifer*	Edwin
Hamo *dapifer*	Thorbiorn
Hermer de Ferrières	Thorkill
Hugh de Houdain	Ælfwine
Hugh de Montfort	Bondig, Godric, Guthmund
Peter de Valognes	Anant
Ralf Baignard	Thored
Ralf de Beaufoy	Eudes *filius* Clamahoc,† Osmund
Ralf de Limésy	Edgar, Northmann
Ralf Peverel	Saxi, Siward of Maldon

† Not pre-Conquest figures.

	antecessores
Ralf de Savigny	Saxi
Ralf de Tosny	Manno
Raymond Gerold	Roger of Poitou†
Richard fitzGilbert	Finnr, Wihtgar
Robert Blond	Aki
Robert Gernons	Ælfric
Robert Malet	Ælfhere, Edric of Laxfield, Godwine son of Ælfhere, Leofric, Ulf, Wulfmær
Robert Malet's mother	Leofric
Robert of Mortain	Brian of Brittany†
Roger Bigot	Æthelwine of Thetford, Brune, the Ipswich reeve, Leofric Hobbesune, Leofwine, Vigulfr, Wulfsige
Roger of Poitou	Ælfleda, Wulfmær
St Edmund	Wulfric
Sweyn of Essex	Godric
Tihel de Helléan	Leofstan
Walter the deacon	Theodoric his brother
Walter Giffard	Bodin
Wihenoc	Herman
William d'Auberville	Godric of Ringshall
William of Warenne	Ulfketel

† Not pre-Conquest figures.

Such a list is obviously highly unsatisfactory. Though the word *antecessor* is not in the following used in DB, it is plain that Earl Ælfgar's lands had been bestowed on Queen Matilda, and that those of a thegn named Friebern had gone to Geoffrey de Manneville. Ralf Peverel had Ketel also as his predecessor, and Hermer de Ferrières Bondig the marshal, while Walter the deacon, some of whose estates had been given to him by Queen Edith, inherited those of Leofwine of Bacton.[1] William of Warenne acquired the lands of his brother-in-law Frederick, who himself had inherited these from a certain Thorkill ('Toka'), and also of an Ælfgifu. Only the text of DB for all the shires concerned can give us the complete picture.

[1] Round (*VCH: Essex*, i, p. 351) pointed out that Leofwine is also styled 'Harold's free man' and 'a thegn of King Edward', and is described also as *cilt* or noble. On succeeding pages Round dealt further with the English predecessors of Essex tenants-in-chief.

APPENDIX B

Some Possessors of Sokeright

The great majority of entries attribute sokeright to 'the king', 'the king and the earl', Earl Ralf, the local bishop, and the major ecclesiastical foundations, or say that soke was 'in the Hundred' or a named manor or vill. These are far too numerous to list; the following are the remaining instances in the East Anglian text (those in Essex were given on p. 140). Many entries say nothing whatever about sokeright. The majority which do relate to manors.

SUFFOLK

Pre-Conquest

	fol.	
Ælfgar, Earl	289b	12 Badmondsfield free men
	373b	3 Eleigh free men
	402	Pannington?[1]
Ælfgifu	323	Rishangles, Thorndon ('under Stigand')
	373b	3 Brandeston free men
Ælfric of Wenham	425	Brantham, 'under Harold'
	429	Cranley (shared equally with the king)
	430b	Belstead
Æthelgyth	413b	25 Kedington free men (*antecessor* of Ralf Baignard)
Æthelmær, Bishop	379b	Chickering
	380	Elmham, Flixton
	380b	3 Flixton free men
Æthelwine (? of Thetford)	355	Lavenham
Æthelwold, Harold's free man	448	Cavendish
Ansger the marshal	411	Holton St Mary, Raydon

[1] The text reads *Robt. soc. Algarus de Sueno*. The manor had been held by Robert fitzWymarc (if *tenet* should have been *tenuit*), but Sweyn had a tenant named Robert, who perhaps had the soke of a manor held of Sweyn by an Ælfgar.

Pre-Conquest	*fol.*	
antecessor of Earl Hugh (? Æthelmær)	302b	Framlingham
	384, 440b	half the soke of Pettaugh
antecessor of Richard fitzGilbert (? Wihtgar)	397b	Kersey
Auti	425b	over the demesne of Wenham
Burgheard	285b	Mendlesham; soke of free men and villeins at Cotton (disputed)
Edith 'the fair'	285	Many free men in Bosmere Hundred; 5 free men in Blakenham
	295	Wenham, Bournethall
	295b	Bentley, Woolverstone, Pannington, Wherstead, Kirton
	296	Wenham
	431	Gusford (this may be another Edith)
Edith, Queen	426	Swilland
Edric of Laxfield	319b	Eye
	328b	Badingham
	329	8 Hoxne sokemen
Fridebern	411b	part of 9 acres at Stutton
Godemann	351	Willisham
Godwine	414	Wixoe (possibly not the Godwine named below)
	442	2 named sokemen at Little Bealings
Godwine son of Æthelsige	304	Edwardstone, Chilton
	306	Belstead, Brantham
Guthmund	408b	Haughley; 'over the demesne of the hall only'.
	410b	Occold (presumably given him by his brother Wulfric when abbot of Ely)
Harold, Earl[1]	289b	Bergholt, Bramford, Brantham
	312b	Free man at Peasenhall
	319	Eye; of Svartrikr, a free man
	360b	Free man at Onehouse
	419b	A Brantham free man
	423	Higham, in Bergholt
Leofwine *croc*	350	over hall and bordars of Buxhall

[1] Uncertain whether these were in his private capacity, or as king or former earl.

Pre-Conquest	*fol.*		
Northmann, *antecessor* of Ralf of Limésy	349b	15 acres at Boxted	probably the same Northmann
Northmann fitzTancred	350	a Preston free man	
Rada, *antecessor* of Drogo de Beuvrières	432	Sotherton	
Ramsey Abbey	378b	Lawshall	
	419b	*Manesfort*	
Robert fitzWymarc	395b	Freston, and some free men in Risbridge Hundred; a number of manors recorded in his son Sweyn's *breve*; 41 Ipswich burgesses.[1]	
Siward of Maldon	416	Acton, Assington and its free men; free men at Acton, the Waldingfields, and Manton	
Skalpi	419b	Churchford, Stutton, 'under Harold'	
Stanwin	313	2 Peasenhall free men	
Sweyn *vicecomes*	402	41 Ipswich burgesses	
Thorthr, *antecessor* of Roger Bigot	414	30 Reydon free men	
Uhtræd	428b	Newton ,'under Harold'	
Ulf	429b	Syleham	
Wihtgar	349b	5 Boxted free men	
	350	Free man at Preston	
	352	Half the soke of Barsham	
	391	Many entries to fol. 397	
Wulfgifu	321b	5 Wyverstone free men; Stoke Ash	
	323	Rishangles, Thorndon, 'of Stigand'	
	323b	Braiseworth, 'of Stigand'	
Wulfmær, a thegn	350	Waldingfield, ? 'under Harold'	
Wulfric, *antecessor* of the abbot of St Edmunds	372b	Free man at Topesfield	
Wulfwine, *antecessor* of Aubrey de Ver	322	Cypping, a free man, at Gislingham	
	323b	Half the soke at Mellis	
	418b	Waldingfield, Burgate	

[1] Presumably his sokeright passed to his son Sweyn.

Between 1066 and 1086

	fol.	
Eudes fitzHerbert	403	6 sokemen at Lakenheath and Brandon, rightly Ely's
Poitou, Roger of	350	Free man at Preston

At the Inquest

Alan, Earl	293	2 Chediston free men
	293b	Kettleburgh and components
	294b	Coddenham, Westerfield free men
	355b	Holton, except Osbert's land
	399	Free man at Wrentham
Baignard, Ralf	413b	2 Poslingford free men
Bigot, Roger	310b	Free man at Kelsale
	330b	35 Kelsale free men
	333b	Thorpe
Godric *dapifer*	355b	Blyford
Holy Trinity, Canterbury	373	Monks Eleigh
	416b	One of the 1½ carucates at Loose had been 'of their soke'
Hugh, Earl	298b	Half the soke at *Manuuic*, Thorpe, and Ashfield (also fols. 305b, 306)
Malet, Robert	314b	Playford
	315	*Necchemara*, Kesgrave
	316	Snape
	317	Hollesley, 'of the king'
	331	3 acres in Dunwich belonging to Bridge
	333b	Knoddishall
		2 acres of Dunwich belonging to Thorpe
	334	Free man at Knoddishall
Northmann	331	Peasenhall, and of 2 free men there
	333	Yoxford
	338b	Saxmundham
	349b	15 acres in Boxted
	428	Cavendish
Ranulf *frater Ilgeris*	425	Waldingfield
St Mary, Grestain	291	Onehouse
Sweyn *vicecomes*		presumably soke earlier his father's

NORFOLK

Pre-Conquest	fol.	
Æthelmær, Bishop	194b	Beighton, over bordars and those owing foldsoke, bought from Earl Ælfgar
antecessores Frederici	165b	Scarning
antecessor of Ralf de Tosny	244	Free man at Oxborough
Edric of Laxfield	180	9 free men at Stalham, shared equally with the king and the earl
Edric, a free man of Stigand's	217	Saxlingham Thorpe
Harold, Earl	116	32 Norwich burgesses
	161	Massingham
	190b	3 free men at Beechamwell
Osmund	167b	Free man at Bradenham
Withri	179b	Hanworth, Alby, Aldborough, Thurgarton, Calthorpe
Between 1066 and 1086		
Dol, Walter de	152	Shropham, by gift of Earl Ralf; the soke rightly lay in the king's manor of Old Buckenham
Moustières, Lisois de	239b	Free men in Rockland and three other places; the soke rightly lay in the king's manor of Old Buckenham
Poitou, Roger of	243b	Spixworth; had been Stigand's
Raymond Gerold, then Roger of Poitou	139b	Some land in Earsham Hundred
At the Inquest		
Alan, Earl	147	20 sokemen at Weston; the soke rightly lay in the king's manor of Foulsham, but Earl Ralf had possessed it
	205	16 free men at Hethersett
Baignard, Ralf	248b	Hempnall and Boyland
Bigot, Roger	173b	Great Massingham; had been Stigand's

At the Inquest	*fol.*	
d'Écouis, William	223b	Salthouse
	225	Weston; the soke rightly lay in the king's manor of Foulsham
de Ferrières, Hermer	206	17 free men at Stow Bardolph; shared with St Benet, Ramsey
fitzAubrey, Humfrey	262b	Billingford; the soke rightly lay in the king's manor of Foulsham
fitzHerbert, Eudes	239b	He had retained the sokeright appropriated by his predecessor Lisois (above), and had that (fol. 240) of Postwick and Catton
fitzIvo, Rainald	230	10 free men at Barton Bendish
Giffard, Walter	240b	Bintree; soke also rightly lay in Foulsham
	241	Free men at Guist, Swannington, Ringland, Attlebridge, and Felthorpe; soke rightly lay in Foulsham
de Noyers, William	121	4 free men at Weasenham; the soke had been Stigand's, but in 1086 was in the king's manor of Mileham, of which William had the custody
Ralf, the bishop's man	197b	detained the soke of 2 Great Cressingham free men
Tofig	264b	18 sokemen at Holkham

It is obvious that the above, even when instances where the soke is said to be possessed by one of those authorities listed at the beginning of the Appendix are taken into account, gives us only a partial picture of the possession of sokeright.

Bibliography

GENERAL

BALLARD, A. *The Domesday Boroughs*, Oxford, 1904.
—— *The Domesday Inquest*, London, 1906.
BARLOW, F. *The Feudal Kingdom of England 1042–1216*, London, 1955.
—— *William I and the Norman Conquest*, London, 1965.
DARBY, H. C. (ed.) *Historical Geography of England*, Cambridge, 1936.
—— *The Domesday Geography of England*, vol. i, Cambridge, 1952.
DOUGLAS, D. C. *The Social Structure of Medieval East Anglia*, Oxford, 1927.
—— *Feudal Documents from the Abbey of Bury St Edmunds*, London, 1932.
ELLIS, SIR H. *A General Introduction to Domesday Book*, London, 1816.
FINN, R. WELLDON *The Domesday Inquest and the Making of Domesday Book*, London, 1961.
—— *An Introduction to Domesday Book*, London, 1963.
FREEMAN, E. A. *History of the Norman Conquest*, vols. iv and v, Oxford, 1871 and 1876.
GALBRAITH, V. H. *Studies in the Public Records*, Oxford, 1948.
—— *The Making of Domesday Book*, Oxford, 1961.
LENNARD, R. *Rural England: 1086–1135*, Oxford, 1959.
LOYN, H. R. *Anglo-Saxon England and the Norman Conquest*, London, 1962.
—— *The Norman Conquest*, London, 1965.
MAITLAND, F. W. *Domesday Book and Beyond*, Cambridge, 1897.
MATTHEW, D. J. A. *The Norman Conquest*, London, 1966.
(PUBLIC RECORD OFFICE). *Domesday Re-Bound*, London, 1954.
ROUND, J. H. *Feudal England*, London, 1895.
STENTON, SIR F. M. *Anglo-Saxon England*, Oxford, 1942.
VINOGRADOFF, SIR P. *English Society in the Eleventh Century*, Oxford, 1908.

VICTORIA COUNTY HISTORIES

ESSEX (ed. J. H. Round), vol. i, pp. 427–578, London, 1903.
NORFOLK (ed. C. Johnson), vol. ii, pp. 38–203, London, 1906.
SUFFOLK (ed. Miss B. A. Lees), vol. i, pp. 357–416, London, 1911.

TEXTS AND EDITIONS

BLAKE, E. O. (ed.) *Liber Eliensis*, Camden Soc. Pubns., 3rd ser., xcii, 1962.

DAVIS, H. W. C. (ed.) *Regesta Regum Anglo-Normannorum: 1066–1154*, Oxford, 1913.

DAVIS, R. H. C. (ed.) *The Kalendar of Abbot Samson*, Camden Soc. Pubns., 3rd ser., lxxxiv, 1954.

HAMILTON, N. E. S. A. (ed.) *Inquisitio Comitatus Cantabrigiensis . . . subjicitur Inquisitio Eliensis*, London, 1886.

HART, C. (ed.) *The Early Charters of Eastern England*, Leicester, 1966.

ROBERTSON, A. J. (ed.) *Anglo-Saxon Charters*, Cambridge, 1939.

WHITELOCK, D., DOUGLAS, D. C., AND TUCKER, J. I. (eds.) *The Anglo-Saxon Chronicle*, London, 1961.

SPECIALISED ASPECTS

Chapter I

RITCHIE, J. *The Normans in England before the Norman Conquest*, Exeter, 1948.

STENTON, SIR F. M. English Families and the Norman Conquest, *Trans. Roy. Hist. Soc.*, 4th ser., xxvi, 1944, pp. 1–12.

Chapter II

DAVIS, R. H. C. The Norman Conquest, *History*, li, 1966, pp. 279–86.

MORRIS, W. A. *The Medieval English Sheriff to 1300*, Manchester, 1927.

Chapter III

DOUGLAS, D. C. The Norman Conquest and English Feudalism, *Econ. Hist. Rev.*, ix, 1939, pp. 128–41.

Chapter IV

BARLOW, F. Domesday Book: A Letter of Lanfranc, *EHR*, lxxviii, 1963, pp. 284–9.

GALBRAITH, V. H. Notes on the career of Samson, bishop of Worcester, *EHR*, lxxxii, 1967, pp. 86–101.

Chapter V

SAWYER, P. H. The 'Original Returns' and 'Domesday Book', *EHR*, lxx, 1955, pp. 177–97.

Chapter VI

GALBRAITH, V. H. The Making of Domesday Book, *EHR*, lvii, 1942, pp. 161–77.

Chapter VII

FINN, R. WELLDON The *Inquisitio Eliensis* Re-considered, *EHR*, lxxv, 1960, pp. 385–409.

MILLER, E. The Ely Land Pleas in the Reign of William I, *EHR*, lxii, 1947, pp. 438–56.

—— *The Abbey and Bishopric of Ely*, Cambridge, 1953.

LE PATOUREL, J. H. Geoffrey, Bishop of Coutances, *EHR*, lix, 1944, pp. 129–40.

Chapter VIII

DAVIS, H. W. C. The Liberties of Bury St Edmunds, *EHR*, xxiv, 1909, pp. 417–31.

GALBRAITH, V. H. The East Anglian See and the Abbey of Bury St Edmunds, *EHR*, xl, 1925, pp. 222–8.

Chapter IX

DOUGLAS, D. C. Fragments of an Anglo-Saxon Survey from Bury St Edmunds, *EHR*, xliii, 1928, pp. 128–43.

LENNARD, R. The Origin of the Fiscal Carucate, *Econ. Hist. Rev.*, xiv, 1944–5, pp. 51–63.

TINGEY, J. C. Some Notes on the Domesday Assessment of Norfolk, *Norf. Arch.*, xxi, 1923, pp. 134–42.

Chapter X

DODWELL, B. The Free Peasantry of East Anglia in Domesday, *Trans. Norwich & Norfolk Arch. Soc.*, xxvii, 1939, pp. 145–57.

—— East Anglian Commendation, *EHR*, lxiii, 1948, pp. 289–306.

Chapter XI

AULT, W. O. *Private Jurisdiction in England* (Yale Historical Pubns., x), New Haven, 1923.

GOEBEL, J. *Felony and Misdemeanour*, New York, 1937.

HURNARD, N. D. The Anglo-Norman Franchises, *EHR*, lxiv, 1949, pp. 289–323, 433–60.

POLLOCK, SIR F., AND MAITLAND, F. W. *The History of English Law*, Cambridge, 1911.

ROBERTSON, A. J. *The Laws of the Kings of England from Edmund to Henry I*, Cambridge, 1925.

STEPHENSON, C. The *Firma Unius Noctis* and the Custom of the Hundred, *EHR*, xxxix, 1924, pp. 161–74.

—— Commendation and Related Problems in Domesday, *EHR*, lix, 1944, pp. 289–310.

Chapter XII

ASTON, T. H. The Origins of the Manor, *Trans. Roy. Hist. Soc.*, 5th ser., viii, 1958, pp. 59–83.

DEMAREST, E. B. The Hundred-Pennies, *EHR*, xxxiii, 1918, pp. 62–72.

—— *Consuetudo Regis* in Essex, Norfolk and Suffolk, *EHR*, xlii, 1927, pp. 161–79.

HOYT, R. S. The Farm of the Manor and Community of the Vill in Domesday Book, *Speculum*, xxx, 1955, pp. 483–506.

ROUND, J. H. The Domesday *Ora*, *EHR*, xxiii, 1908, pp. 77–9.

STENTON, SIR F. M. *Types of Manorial Structure in the Northern Danelaw*, Oxford, 1910.

Chapter XIII

LENNARD, R. The Destruction of Woodland in the Eastern Counties under William the Conqueror, *Econ. Hist. Rev.*, xv, 1945, pp. 36–43.

—— The Economic Position of the Domesday *Villani*, *Econ. Journ.*, lvi, 1946, pp. 244–64.

—— The Economic Position of the Bordars and Cottars of Domesday Book, *Econ. Journ.*, lxi, 1951, pp. 341–71.

—— The Economic Position of the Domesday Sokeman, *Econ. Journ.*, lvii, 1947, pp. 179–95.

SPECIALISED AND LOCAL ASPECTS

BULLOCK, J. H. (ed.) The Norfolk Portion of the Chartulary of the Priory of St Pancras of Lewes (Norfolk Record Society, xii, 1939).

DARBY, H. C. *The Medieval Fenland*, Cambridge, 1940.

DAVIS, R. H. C. East Anglia and the Danelaw, *Trans. Roy. Hist. Soc.*, 5th ser., v, 1955, pp. 23–39.

RAFTIS, J. A. *The Estates of Ramsey Abbey*, Toronto, 1957.

SAWYER, P. H. The Place-Names of Domesday Book, *Bull. John Rylands Lib.*, xxxviii, 1955, pp. 483–506.

—— The Density of the Danish Settlement in England, *Univ. Bgham. Hist. Jour.*, vi, no. 1, 1958, pp. 1–17.

STENTON, SIR F. M. St Benet of Holme and the Norman Conquest, *EHR*, xxxvii, 1922, pp. 225–35.

—— The Danes in England, *Proc. Brit. Acad.*, 13, 1927.

PLACE-NAMES

ALLISON, K. J. The Lost Villages of Norfolk, *Norf. Arch.*, xxxi, pt. 1, 1955, pp. 116–62.

ANDERSON (later ARNGART), O. S. *The English Hundred-Names*, Lund, 1934–9.

ARNOTT, W. G. *The Place-Names of the Deben Valley Parishes*, Ipswich, 1946.

EKWALL, E. *The Oxford Dictionary of English Place-Names* (4th edn.), Oxford, 1960.

REANEY, P. H. *The Place-Names of Essex*, Cambridge, 1935.

RYE, W. *A List of Norfolk Place-Names*, Norwich, 1923.

SKEAT, W. W. *The Place-Names of Suffolk*, Cambridge, 1913.

STENTON, SIR F. M. The Historical Bearing of Place-Name Studies: The Danish Settlement of Eastern England, *Trans. Roy. Hist. Soc.*, 4th ser., xxiv, 1942, pp. 1–24.

Index

Places and persons mentioned only incidentally in the text have not been indexed. A common name, e.g. Ælfric, may not refer to the individual. Persons have normally been indexed under the place-name by which they were known, e.g. Beaufoy, Ralf de.